The Presidential Election and Transition 1980–1981

Edited by Paul T. David and

David H. Everson

Published for Sangamon State University

Southern Illinois University Press

Carbondale and Edwardsville

Printed in the United States of America

Edited by Dan Seiters

Designed by Richard Hendel

Production supervised by John DeBacher

Library of Congress Cataloging in Publication Data
Main entry under title:

The Presidential election and transition, 1980-1981.

Includes bibliographical references and index.
Contents: The presidential nominating process in
1980/William Crotty—The 1980 Democratic primary in
Illinois/John S. Jackson III—The 1980 Republican
presidential primary in Illinois/James D. Nowlan—
[etc.]
1.   Presidents—United States—Election—1980—
Addresses, essays, lectures.   2.   Presidents—United
States—Transition periods—Addresses, essays, lectures.
3.   United States—Politics and government—1977-1981—
Addresses, essays, lectures.   I.   David, Paul Theodore,
1906–   II.   Everson, David H., 1941–
E875.P73 1983   324.973′0927   82-19145
ISBN 0-8093-1109-7

★ ★ ★

★ ★ ★

★ ★ ★

Contents

★ ★ ★

★ ★ ★

★ ★ ★

Tables

★ ★ ★

★ ★ ★

★ ★ ★

Preface

Sangamon State University, founded in 1969, is the public affairs university for the state of Illinois. In pursuit of its mission the university has established four public affairs research centers, publishes a public affairs magazine, *Illinois Issues,* and operates a public radio station, WSSR. This book exemplifies Sangamon State University's commitment to public affairs research in the nation and Illinois.

In the early spring of 1979, Alex B. Lacy, Jr., president of Sangamon State University, asked Professor David Everson of the political studies program to coordinate the university's public affairs examination of the 1980 presidential election. Everson agreed to undertake the project, which would emphasize the ability to reach the public provided by WSSR and *Illinois Issues.* As part of the preliminary activity, a lecture was given by Professor Leon Epstein of the University of Wisconsin, Madison, in April 1979. His lecture, which looked forward to the 1980 presidential nominations and elections, was broadcast by WSSR.

Shortly afterward, however, Everson accepted the directorship of the Illinois Legislative Studies Center of Sangamon State University. It was impossible for him to carry on both sets of activities. In the fall of 1979, therefore, a search was conducted for a replacement to direct the project. The university was fortunate enough to obtain the services of Paul T. David, Professor Emeritus, University of Virginia, and the author of numerous works on national nominating conventions and presidential elections. He arrived at Sangamon State University in late February of 1980. With the addition of Professor David, the idea to produce a book on the election was inevitable, given his past experience. The book would focus on both the national level and the state of Illinois, which serves as a microcosm of the nation's politics.

To bring in several noted scholars of various aspects of presidential elections, a lecture series was scheduled during the 1980–81 academic year. All were broadcast by WSSR. After the lectures were delivered, they were then revised for publication by the authors. Twelve lectures constitute the chapters of this book, coedited by Professors David and Everson.

The first chapter, "The Presidential Nominating Process," is by William J.

Crotty, professor of political science at Northwestern University and the author of many works on political reform and American politics. Crotty describes the nominating campaigns in both parties and discusses the impact of past reforms on the process and the likelihood of future changes. The second chapter, by John Jackson, professor of political science at Southern Illinois University, Carbondale, examines "The 1980 Democratic Primary in Illinois." (Jackson was a delegate to the 1980 Democratic convention.) Jackson contends that the Illinois Primary, given its new importance in the nomination process, "had a lot to do with helping to shape the events which came after it." Jackson also deals with Illinois' role in the Democratic convention. On the Republican side, James Nowlan, director of the public administration program, (and a former state representative and candidate for lieutenant governor) of the University of Illinois, Urbana-Champaign, describes "The Republican Nominating Campaign in Illinois" from the perspective of both a political scientist and practitioner. A major conclusion of Nowlan's paper is that "what preceded Illinois [in the nomination campaign] was more important . . . than what transpired within the state itself." The final chapter devoted exclusively to the nominating process is Paul David's "The National Conventions." Professor David examines both parties' conventions and discusses the functions of the conventions as performed in 1980. He concludes that although in terms of the nominations, the conventions "often meet merely to ratify a previous decision . . . the other functions of the conventions remain important."

The next chapter, written by David Everson, describes "The Presidential Campaign of 1980." Everson contends that the campaign is significant in policy terms and argues that "the 1980 . . . campaign represented as wide a variety and clarity of choices as we have seen in American politics in many years." Chapter six, written by Lois Moreland, professor of political science at Spelman College, Atlanta, Georgia, and author of *White Racism and the Law,* explores the role of "Minorities in the Politics of 1980" and examines the participation of minorities in the primaries, the conventions, and the general election. Herbert E. Alexander, director of the Citizen's Research Foundation and professor of political science at the University of Southern California, acknowledged to be the nation's foremost authority on campaign finance, describes the role of money in the 1980 campaigns. Among the topics he considers are the effects of expenditure limits, finance in the general election—including the John Anderson candidacy—and the use of "Presidential PACs," or political action committees created by interested groups to raise and spend money for political activities including, but not limited to, campaign contributors. (Presidential PACs are organized in behalf of potential presidential candidates prior to their official candidacy, thus enabling them to "campaign" without having to worry about the spending limits applied to announced candidates who accept federal matching funds.)

The next chapter, by Robert D. McClure, professor of political science at The Maxwell School of Syracuse University, explores the "Media Influence in Presidential Politics." Professor McClure's thesis is that the "mass media is the primary . . . link between candidates and voters." Moreover, he argues that the media are ill-suited for the task: "Mass media elections not only result in a less well-informed, more volatile, and disorganized electorate, but also lead to a more cynical and alienated electorate."

Chapters nine and ten examine the outcome of the election, first in the nation, then in Illinois. Paul David focuses on the national election and finds that the election was "clearly a rejection of President Jimmy Carter" and that "the Reagan mandate should be read mainly as an opportunity." Peter Colby, director of the master's program in public policy administration, State University of New York, Binghamton, and Paul Green, professor of public service, Governor's State University, discuss "Illinois and the Presidential Election of 1980." They claim that "the 1980 presidential election in Illinois should lift the hearts of the Republican party." In chapter eleven Laurin Henry, professor of political science and dean of the school of community services, Virginia Commonwealth University, and author of *Presidential Transitions*, reviews the 1980–1981 transition from Carter to Reagan.

In the final chapter, Professor James Ceaser, associate professor of government at the University of Virginia, analyzes the effects of the election on "American Parties in the Eighties" by considering whether they are "declining or resurging." Ceaser argues that the determinist thesis that party decline is irreversible is self-defeating: "Advocates of stronger parties accordingly owe it to themselves to make the effort at change."

These twelve chapters cover virtually every aspect of the 1980 election from a variety of perspectives. They also provide a close-up view of the election in one representative state, Illinois.

Many staff members of the Illinois Legislative Studies Center helped to put this volume together. Joan Parker, Research Associate in the Center, helped to plan and execute the lectures. Jackie Wright typed many of the lectures and the final manuscript. Rita Harmony played a major role in getting the final manuscript in shape. Without their efforts, this project would not have been possible.

Springfield, Illinois
September 1982

David H. Everson

Chapter 1 The Presidential Nominating Process in 1980

William Crotty

Running for president is like hitting your head against the wall. It feels so good when you stop, or so said Congressman Philip Crane, a conservative candidate for the Republican party's nomination in 1980.[1] The process is tedious, "a severe test of your stamina, your digestion, and your marriage," said Morris Udall, a candidate for the Democratic party's nomination in 1976.[2] Maybe so. Nonetheless, many are willing to try. Senator Edward Kennedy of Massachusetts and Governor Edmund ("Jerry") Brown of California were even willing to challenge an incumbent president, Jimmy Carter, for the Democratic party's nomination. At least six were willing to make a serious bid for the Republican party's nomination.

The process is long. It begins informally at least a year before the national conventions and eight months before the first delegates are selected. It weaves its way through the endless primaries and caucuses before coming to a conclusion with the national conventions. In the interim, much can happen, as 1980 certainly proved. This prenomination year was marked by

—perhaps the longest campaign in history
—the most primaries ever
—a great deal of volatility in voter attitudes and support patterns
—a greater media presence in the process than ever
—and, perhaps most importantly, the greatest public disillusionment
  with the results in recent memory.

The prenomination battles gave rise to another phenomenon, the fielding of a third party, or independent, campaign in an effort to offer voters another alternative and to take advantage of the public disillusionment with the two major party candidates.

To begin with, and for the record, President Carter and Governor Reagan won early, easily and often in their quest for their party's presidential nominations, amassing most of the delegate votes cast at their respective national conventions. Both easily captured their party's presidential nominations.

The Democrats

For the Democrats, Senator Kennedy, Carter's chief opponent, won only eight primaries:

—Massachusetts (77 of 111 delegate votes) his home state and neighboring Vermont (7 of 12 delegate votes) on March 4

—New York and Connecticut on March 25 (New York, 151 of 282 delegate votes and Connecticut 28 of 54 delegate votes), much needed and unexpected boosts to his flagging presidential campaign

—and he did very well in the superbowl primaries on June 3. He won in California (166 of 306 delegate votes), New Jersey (68 of 113), Rhode Island (17 of 23), South Dakota (10 of 19), and he split the delegates in New Mexico, (10,10). Unfortunately for Kennedy, the nomination was well out of reach by superbowl Tuesday.

In between his infrequent victories, Kennedy managed to lose key tests, including the first two delegate selection contests. He lost the first-in-the-nation Iowa caucuses on January 21 (31 percent to Carter's 59 percent), a loss that threw his campaign into a tailspin from which it never recovered, and he lost the New Hampshire primary on February 26 (9 of 19 delegate votes). Both losses were highly publicized.

Kennedy was also defeated by Carter in key industrial states that were critical to the big city, New Deal, labor and ethnic-oriented coalition he hoped to fashion to wrest the nomination from Carter. He lost Illinois on March 18 in a crushing defeat, capturing only 16 of 179 delegate votes (a loss possibly having more to do with his association, at least in the Chicago area, with the Byrne administration, than with the appeal, or lack of it, of his own campaign).

—he lost a close race in Pennsylvania on April 22, 90 of 185 delegate votes, the first contest after his surprise victories in New York and Connecticut.

—he lost in Michigan on May 12, despite having the support of the UAW and its president, Douglas Fraser, another major defeat in a state hard-hit by unemployment and inflation.

—and he lost Ohio on June 3 (72 of 161 delegate votes).

Kennedy did poorly in the major southern states, losing Florida decisively on March 11 (24 of 99). He lost equally decisively in the complicated Texas caucus procedures on May 3, 38 of 146. He did poorly in the other caucus states, winning outright in few.

Nonetheless, Kennedy carried his fight to the Democratic National Convention, challenging Carter on a rule adopted by the Democrats that bound a delegate to vote for the candidate he had pledged to support in his home state. The rule was a new departure for the party. Kennedy wanted to loosen the Carter forces' control over their own delegates in order to take advantage of the Democrats' continued dissatisfaction with the Carter administration's leadership and policies and the president's continued low standing in the polls. Kennedy hoped to demonstrate his own strength early in the convention. It was a desperate gamble.

The point of attack for the Kennedy forces and others who favored an "open convention" was to argue that conditions had changed since the delegates had been selected; that Carter, in effect, was unelectable; that the rule went against party tradition and the party's charter; and that the delegates could be reduced under the provision to "robots." "For the first time in 150 years," Edward Bennett Williams, a Washington lawyer and the leader of the Committee for an Open Convention, told the convention, "delegates to the national convention are being asked to deliver their final freedom of choice, and to vote themselves into bondage to a candidate."[3]

The Carter forces contended that support for the new rule was simply "fair play"; that the only reason the rule had become an issue since its proposal by the Winograd Commission two years earlier was the realization by Carter's opponents that he had a lock on the nomination. Should you allow a "fifth ball, a fourth out or a tenth inning?" asked Atlanta Mayor Maynard Jackson in presenting the Carter administration's position.[4]

The controversy had little to do with fairness, Democratic party tradition, or the proper role of the delegate within the convention. It was a power struggle for the nomination between the two finalists, and it was perceived as such by the delegates and the media.[5]

The anti-Carter strategy failed. Kennedy lost decisively, 1,936.4 to 1,390.6. Carter was able to hold 98 percent of his delegates in the showdown. With that, Kennedy finally withdrew from the contest, one that had been over long before.

The senator did receive some measure of satisfaction from an emotional speech that he delivered on the convention's second night. The speech was intended as a statement in support for adding several minority planks on economic issues to the party's platform. It went well beyond this, however. Kennedy opened by declaring he had not come to "argue for a candidacy, but to affirm a cause."[6] He congratulated the president on his victory (although he did not endorse him), and he called for unity in the general election. But he did not concentrate on either attacking or supporting Carter. He chided Reagan for, among other things, quoting Franklin Roosevelt in his acceptance speech at the Republican National Convention, calling for the redistribution of wealth "in the wrong direction," and for attacking (in previous campaigns) unemployment insurance as "a prepaid vacation for the unemployed." Kennedy spoke forcibly on traditional liberal issues ("The commitment I seek is . . . to old values that will never wear out."), for expanded job programs, national health insurance and federal aid to restore worn-out cities. "The ideal of fairness will never wear out." Kennedy concluded: "For all those whose cares have been our concern, the work goes on, the cause endures, the hope still lives and the dream shall never die."[7]

The convention delegates gave him a tumultuous 40 minute ovation. Even the president's mother, Miss Lillian, rose to applaud the senator's remarks and the president spoke of the address as "one of the greatest speeches I have ever heard."[8]

Miss Lillian, perhaps too honest for her son's own good, later told Walter Cronkite in a television interview that, having heard the speech, she didn't know how Kennedy had ever lost the nomination. She had a point. If Kennedy had articulated the rationale and policy focus of his campaign and his reasons for opposing an incumbent Democratic president early in the campaign as clearly and forcibly as he did before the convention, he might well have unseated an unpopular president with a weak hold on his party's coalition. Kennedy had his opportunities: in November when he announced his candidacy; after the Iowa defeat in his Georgetown University address; or after the crushing defeat in Illinois or the surprise victories in New York and Connecticut. That he was never able to capitalize on these opportunities; that he never was able to give his campaign the focus and direction that it needed; that he never communicated to Democrats the fervor and commitment he expressed that night mark his candidacy's failure. To many, he was a candidate seeking the presidency to satisfy private, or family, ambitions, and with little to offer voters beyond a flawed personal history (and one that the Carter campaign took full advantage of).

Kennedy's speech was the highlight of either party's convention. In its afterglow, he and his supporters won major platform concessions that they felt somewhat vindicated their long campaign.

Carter won the nomination decisively, with 2,123 (64 percent) delegate votes out of a total of 3,331, 457 more than needed for the nomination. Governor Edmund ("Jerry") Brown of California, Carter's only other opponent in the prenomination phase, won no primaries or caucuses and had withdrawn from the race early. He received only one vote in the convention balloting. Kennedy received 1,150.5, despite his withdrawal.

The Republicans

The magnitude of Ronald Reagan's victory was enormous, even more decisive than Carter's. The former California governor easily vanquished all of his opponents. Reagan won an outstanding 97 percent of the national convention's delegate votes. George Bush, his only opponent to show any electoral strength, received only 13, even less than John Anderson's 37. For all of their trouble, Philip Crane, Howard Baker, Robert Dole, John Connally, and the others (Larry Pressler, Lowell Weicker, Harold Stassen, Benjamin Fernandez, etc.) were not even represented in the convention balloting.

When the Republican nomination campaign began, it was the field against Ronald Reagan. The only question was: could Reagan be denied the nomination after his strong showing against incumbent President Gerald Ford in 1976?

The Republican contenders seemed formidable: Senator Howard Baker, of Ervin Committee fame, and Senator Robert Dole, former Republican National Chairman. Baker had served as the minority leader of the senate and Dole as the vice-presidential candidate under Ford in 1976. John Connally, a forceful and eloquent speaker, had access to lavish campaign funds (Connally was the only candidate in either party to bypass federal funding for his race). Connally had extensive administrative experience under both Republican and Democratic presidents. He had served as governor of Texas and at one point (after the resignation of Spiro Agnew), Richard Nixon had wanted to appoint him vice president. Nixon was widely quoted as believing that Connally was the most able person in his administration.

From this group, however, George Bush emerged as the only one to contest Reagan with any success. Bush, an oil drilling company executive from Texas, also had impressive credentials. He had served as envoy to China once diplomatic relations had been established, as chairman of the Republican National Committee, director of the CIA, ambassador to the United Nations and a two-term congressman from Texas. Bush had a conservative voting record while in the Congress and an issue base close to Reagan's. (The AFL–CIO's Committee on Political Education (COPE) had given him a "0" rating in 2 of his 4 years in the Congress; Americans for Democratic Action (ADA) had given him an average score of only 7 on a scale of 100; both are, of course, liberal organizations). But Bush attempted to mobilize the moderate Republican vote in opposition to Reagan's conservatism. He spent almost two years on the campaign trail, depending primarily on hard individual effort in organizing the early caucus and primary states at the grassroots level and he enjoyed some early successes.

He won an unexpected victory in November of 1979 in a straw poll at the Maine state convention, a result that, while not binding, served to publicize his campaign and attract the media attention he needed. The victory came at the direct expense of Senator Howard Baker, the expected victor, who arrived from Washington with a convoy of reporters expecting to claim his due and successfully launch his 1980 presidential bid.

Bush went on from there to another unexpected, and significant, victory in the Iowa caucus, the first of the delegate selection tests. Bush had visited Iowa two dozen times in the preceding months, moving one son into permanent residence in the state for the duration of the campaign, and laboriously building his precinct-level organization. Even then, he needed some luck to win. Reagan, from neighboring Illinois, had been a radio announcer in Iowa; however, in line with his early campaign strategy of remaining aloof from the field, and not provoking controversy, Reagan declined to debate his opponents in Iowa. It was a fatal mistake. His popularity among Iowa Republicans plummeted and Bush won a narrow, and totally unexpected victory. With it, he received national media exposure and he began to gain on Reagan in the national polls. "Big Mo" (momentum), as Bush called it, was working in his favor.

Not for long though. Reagan reversed his campaign strategy, returning to the folksy, direct approach that had served him so well in prior campaigns. He invested heavily in time, energy and resources in New Hampshire. He even managed to reverse his stand on debating, appearing at a debate sponsored by the Nashua *Telegram* and scheduled between himself and Bush, angry that the other contenders, whom he had in tow (Dole, Baker, Anderson and Crane), had been excluded. He demanded that they be allowed to debate. Bush supported the newspaper sponsoring the debate in restricting the field to two. Anderson, Baker, Dole and Crane returned to an adjoining room and bitterly attacked Bush. Reagan managed to appear as the apostle of Republican unity and openness. He crushed Bush in the New Hampshire vote and was never seriously threatened again in the prenomination race.

Bush did manage to win occasional, and scattered, victories. Unfortunately for him, he came in third in the Illinois primary March 18th, behind Reagan and Anderson, a blow to his prestige. As Reagan's campaign funds became low—his heavy investments in the early tests had nearly exhausted them—the Bush campaign, which had managed their funds better, picked up. Bush began to put more into the media and the results showed. He won the Pennsylvania primary on April 22 and ran Reagan a close race in Texas May 3.

But Reagan's delegate strength and his popular support were too strong to overcome. On May 20, Bush won possibly his most impressive race since Iowa when, with the strong support of Michigan governor William Milliken, he won that state's primary. The victory was hollow. That same day a number of media accounts reported that Reagan now had enough votes to claim the nomination. Six days later (May 26), Bush, saying "You gotta know when to fold 'em," withdrew from the race.[9]

His efforts were not totally in vain. After a flirtation with Gerald Ford as a possibility for the vice-presidential nomination, Reagan chose Bush to be his running mate, uniting the front-runner and his only opponent of any consequence in the prenomination season on the Republican ticket.

The Reagan Prenomination Campaign

The story of the Republican nomination fight was thus Reagan's consistent, and remarkable showings, and the strength of his candidacy. He won twenty-eight of the thirty-four Republican primaries and most all of the sixteen caucuses. Without doubt, he was the overwhelming choice of the Republicans who took part in their party's caucuses and primaries. Nonetheless, Reagan did make a few mistakes— some consider these the hallmark of his campaigns—and he did have a few difficult moments.

Iowa was one. Reagan's first campaign director, John Sears, had Reagan run a national campaign and ignore his Republican opponents. He directed Reagan's attention to attacking the Carter administration's record and appeared to assume that the Republican nomination was Reagan's for the asking. In line with this approach, Reagan did little personal campaigning, depending on television instead, and, as noted, avoided the debates there. Many Iowa Republicans felt he was avoiding them also.

With his loss in Iowa, Reagan fired Sears (on the day of the New Hampshire primary) and reshuffled his campaign staff. He returned to the in-person campaigning that he did so well and even showed himself the master of television debating. The changes served him well during the remaining primaries.

Reagan did tell an ethnic joke in New Hampshire that was widely reported, and for which he apologized, but otherwise managed to keep his campaign free of the blunders that later characterized his early general election drive.

Reagan, under John Sears' direction, spent heavily in the fall preceding the 1980 election year and in the early caucus and primary states on national television and on in-state advertising. His speech announcing his candidacy on November 13 was carried on ninety-eight independent television stations, covering 70 percent of the nation's population. It cost $400,000. As a consequence, it became clear early that Reagan might expend his limit of $14.7 million federal and other funds well before the end of the prenomination season. He came close, of course, but his one remaining opponent (Bush) was unable to capitalize extensively on the Reagan campaign's financial shortcomings. There was talk at one point that the Reagan campaign had not enough funds left to even organize their convention forces and to pay for their national convention expenses. The fear proved unfounded, but it does suggest how limited the funding had become.

What could have been Reagan's biggest potential problem never quite materialized. Former President Gerald Ford was conceded to be the candidate with the greatest possibility of denying the nomination to Reagan. Ford, however, took himself out of the race early. On October 19, 1979, he announced that, barring "unforeseen circumstances," he would not be an active candidate for his party's nomination.[10] The decision appeared to give Reagan a clear track. When the other Republican contenders began to fail, however, Ford let it be known in March of 1980 that he was actively reconsidering his stand. After several days of rumors and deliberations with Republican notables, he announced that he would not enter the race. It is unlikely that—with no organization, no established funding, campaign apparatus or a developed media campaign—he could have done much at that time to deny Reagan the nomination.

Ford was to appear once more in the Reagan campaign. The biggest story to emerge from the Republican Convention was the effort of the Republicans to field a "dream ticket" of Reagan for president and Ford for vice-president. If he had accepted, Ford would have been the first president to subsequently run for vice president. Republican polls reportedly had shown that Ford was the one Republican who could strengthen the ticket for the general election campaign. With this in mind, Reagan met with Ford on the convention's second day and asked him to think over the possibility of joining the ticket. No firm offer was made. The two met the next day to continue their discussions. Coincidentally with their meeting, "friends" of the two met over the two-day period to iron out the specifics of the arrangement. The negotiators included former Secretary of State Henry Kissinger and former chairman of the Council of Economic Advisors, Alan Greenspan, on behalf of Ford and Edwin Meese and William Casey, Reagan's campaign directors, and his pollster Richard Wirthlin, on behalf of Reagan.

The chief stumbling block appeared to be Ford's insistence on an agreement giving him a responsible role in the Reagan White House. Ford made his position clear in television interviews with Walter Cronkite of CBS and Barbara Walters of ABC. He told Cronkite that "I would not go to Washington and be a figurehead vice president. If I go to Washington I have to be there in the belief that I would play a meaningful role."[11] He did not make his specific demands clear, but he reiterated to Walters that, to be acceptable, his job had to be "nonceremonial, constructive and responsive" and that he was more interested in the "substance than the glamour" of the position. He acknowledged that his definition of the vice presidency would require a "far different structure" of the position than it had previously had.[12] For some, it seemed to mean that Ford was bargaining for some type of co-presidency with Reagan. It was later revealed, in the aftermath of the collapse of the negotiations, that Ford wanted to be insured a position similar to that of White House chief of staff with responsibility for the Office of Management and Budget, the National Security Council, the Council of Economic Advisors and the domestic policy staff.

Reagan refused to accept the conditions and terminated the discussions between the Ford and Reagan aides. In an unusual move meant to quell the growing delegate enthusiasm for, and media attention given to, a Ford vice-presidential candidacy, Reagan appeared before the convention at 12:15 a.m. on the morning of its final day to announce the choice of Bush to be his running mate.

The Ford controversy was not only the biggest story to emerge from the Republican National Convention, it was one of the more unusual ideas to come out of the campaign year.[13]

Some Observations on the Nominating Process

The nominating *process* itself, in 1980, was chaotic. Change from 1968, or the "old party system," has been profound. This, in itself, is not bad. What is troublesome is the *constant* change in party rules and state statutes governing the nominations, especially in the Democratic party. Every four years, in effect, we are getting a new nominating system. After each election a new party commission is formed to review the rules and recommend changes.[14] The result is that whatever party or candidate faction, for the Democrats, that controls the commission introduces the rules that it thinks reflects the political realities of the period. At times, these are little more than projected changes intended to help candidacies favored by the majority of the commission members. Whatever their genesis, or value, the rules are then *required* of the states. The 1980 election year was as good an example of this as any election year.

There was no significant dissatisfaction with the 1976 nominating rules. Some party members still fought reform in any form and others wanted to extend the reform initiatives by making proportional representation universal. Neither of these groups figured prominently in the drive for the creation of another body to assess presidential selection processes. Rather, the initiative came from elsewhere.

A commission had been established by then Democratic National Chairman, Robert Strauss, in 1975 to contend with the proliferation of primaries and to explore ways to limit their influence in choosing presidential nominees (primaries were believed to weaken the party's control over its nominating processes). The commission, named the Winograd Commission after its chairman, was the first reform body not mandated by a national convention.

This was rectified by the 1976 national convention, which endorsed its existence and, with the backing of the Carter forces, expanded its mandate to encompass a review of all aspects of the presidential selection process. Its job was to fashion a new set of rules for 1980.

Jimmy Carter, once president, controlled the appointments to the expanded commission. As a result, the commission was weighted two to one with administration supporters. It included, among others, a White House representative, Tim Kraft, later one of Carter's 1980 campaign managers, and another aide to Hamilton Jordan. They introduced a package of rules that, although controversial, were adopted by the commission, and eventually enacted in major part by the Democratic party. These included:

a. limiting the nominating season to a three-month period between early March and early June, which would help an incumbent and work against those without the money, organization, and name recognition that can be gained in a six-month nominating season. The rules, while arcane to most observers, do have profound consequences. They can result in, and contribute to, serious political infighting among factions within the party and among the supporters of the probable presidential candidates. (For example, once the new rule was enacted, the Democratic National Committee—under control of the Carter White House—exempted from the provision limiting the nominating season to three months both Iowa and New Hampshire, states in which Carter had done well in 1976 and in which he had organized early and expected to do well again in 1980. Technically, it was agreed that because the states had Republican legislatures and/or Republican governors they could be exempted from the provision. On the other hand, Massachusetts was pressured to move its March 4 primary back, preferably to late April. When the home state of Kennedy resisted, it was threatened with expulsion from the national convention, although the Credentials Review Commission of the DNC eventually relented.)

b. The Winograd Commission also attempted to move qualifying dates for candidates back to a period ninety days before a state's primary or caucus, to prevent late entries and to raise the floor, or base vote received in a primary to 25 percent (later 15 percent, 20 percent and 25 percent) before a candidate received any national convention delegate votes. Again, a well-known candidate should do well with the higher floor. (This provision was later changed to a formula based on the total number of delegate positions divided by the number of candidates for delegate seats in a district, with a minimum percentage of the vote needed to qualify for any position.)

c. One of the rules the Winograd Commission introduced was the binding delegate rule. Although little noticed at the time, it was to prove important in the convention's deliberations. This represented a new departure for the party.

The 1980 rule redefinitions are symptomatic of one problem facing nominating processes. The system is in constant turmoil. It does not inspire respect or confidence.

The Dominance of the Primaries

A second point relating to the process is the rise in number and significance of primaries. They have increased significantly (see table 1–1).

Approximately one-third of the delegates to the national conventions were selected through primaries in 1968. Many of these were uncommitted, in effect (as in Illinois) simply following the lead of party bosses who controlled the pre-reform system. Today, 75 percent of the delegates in both parties are chosen through primaries. For better or worse, primaries play a far more significant role in presidential nomination now than ever before. The danger is that primaries will completely replace the state party convention and caucus process.

Minority Group Representation

Along with the rise in the influence of primaries has been the increase in minority group representation within the system and specifically within the Democratic party's processes. This was one of the objectives of the reform movement, and it appears to have borne fruit (see table 1–2). There have been especially impressive gains in both parties by women. Blacks have increased their representation in the Democratic party's conventions, although not Republican conventions. "Youth" also has increased its representativeness, although this is the least cohesive and politically the least significant of the groups examined.

Table 1.1

The Increasing Number of Primaries

Year	Democrat	Republican
1968	17	16
1972	23	22
1976	30	29
1980	33	34

SOURCE: Democratic and Republican National Committees

Table 1.2

Minority Group Representation Within the Parties
(in Percentages)

National Convention	Blacks	Women	Youth (under 30)
Democrats			
1968	7	13	4
1972	15	40	22
1976	11	33	15
1980	14	49	11
Republicans			
1968	2	17	1
1972	3	35	7
1976	3	31	7
1980	3	29	7

SOURCE: Democratic and Republican National Committees

Participation in the Process

Along with increased minority group representation and the spread of primaries, has come a dramatic increase in the number of people participating in the nominating system. Participation had increased between two and three times the levels of 1968 by 1980. The increase has been in both parties and in both caucus/ convention and primary systems (table 1–3).

A major goal of reform was to open up the process to get more people to participate. The reforms have succeeded in this regard. From 1968 to 1972 participation jumped 10 million, and it has been increasing since. It may be that people are participating more and enjoying it less—but they are participating.

Presenting Party and Elected Officials in the Process

As people in general are participating more, the role of professional politicians in the process—at least in the Democratic party—appears to be on the decline. The differences between the "old party system" and the new ones are substantial (table 1–4).

The Winograd Commission instituted an "add-on" rule in 1980, stipulating that an extra 10 percent be added on to each delegation to be composed of party

Table 1.3

Participation in the Nomination Process, 1968–1980

	Democrat Type of System	
Year	Primary	Caucus
1968	8,247,000(n = 17)	219,000(n = 34)
1972	16,715,000(n = 23)	771,000(n = 28)
1976	18,884,000(n = 31)	639,000(n = 20)
1980	17,580,000(n = 33)	539,000(n = 18)

	Republican Type of System	
Year	Primary	Caucus
1968	4,571,000(n = 16)	105,000(n = 35)
1972	5,887,000(n = 22)	256,000(n = 29)
1976	9,724,000(n = 30)	546,000(n = 21)
1980	13,301,000(n = 35)	370,000(n = 16)

	Totals by Party and by Year		
Year	Democrats	Republicans	Grand Total Participating
1968	8.4 million	4.7 million	13.1 million
1972	17.5 million	6.1 million	23.6 million
1976	19.5 million	10.3 million	29.8 million
1980	18.1 million	13.7 million	31.8 million

SOURCE: Democratic and Republican National Committees

professionals. The idea was, that these professionals would bring seasoned judgment to national convention deliberations; that they would be unswayed by the passions and candidates of the moment; and that they would add a corrective balance to the decision of the grassroots activists. Judging by the 1980 convention, at least, this has not happened, because the "add-on" delegates were required to be as committed to their candidates as the activists who voted in the primary. They exercised no more, or any less, independent judgment while at the convention. Thus a question arises. One might ask the value of the "add-ons," given the experience in 1980. More probably, they were reserved for local- and state-level officials whose political loyalty and support the candidates could rely on.

Table 1.4

Delegates to Democratic National Conventions

	Old Party System (1956–1968)	New Party System (1972–1976)	1980 National Convention
Percentage of Democratic Senators	75	27	14
Percentage of U.S. Repre-sentatives	41	15	14
Percentage of Governors	82	64	74

SOURCE: Democratic National Committee

This was not quite the intent of those who championed such a rules modification.

Media Influence

The new party system has seen a collapse in party control over its own nominating process. This much is clear. Candidates run with their own organizations and are subsidized by federal funds. The party—beyond specifying the rules—has little role in, or control over, the process.

The new power center is the media—and especially television. Candidates pay for air time and exposure. Success is being *perceived* as a winner in Iowa or New Hampshire. It means money, volunteers, an increased poll standing, and, as with George Bush, a cover picture on *Newsweek* or *Time*. Once these are achieved, a candidate has become a serious contender. The media determine this; they define—throughout the primaries—the winners and losers. The delegate count follows the media success of the candidate. Television has become the most powerful instrument in the prenomination phase (and probably postnomination phase also).[15]

Changing National Conventions

Along with the shift in the role of the parties, the decline in their power over nominations, and the rise in significance of the media, has been the change in status of the national convention. Under the old party system, the national convention was the single most important event in the nominating struggle and in the life and management of a political party. This is no longer true. National conventions now ratify decisions made in the state primaries and caucuses. Their most important function has been usurped collectively by the state-level outcomes.

Conventions are still important in framing a platform (as the Democrats showed); determining the rules for party management in the period between elections; choosing an acceptable vice-presidential candidate (as the Republicans showed); unifying the party (as both national conventions demonstrated); and launching the fall general election campaign. Is this enough? Probably not. It is unlikely that television will continue to cover national conventions, gavel to gavel, as they have in the past, but did not in 1980. If so, their importance is likely to continue to decline. The downward turn in convention stature parallels the decline in party fortunes and may well help to accelerate it in future years.

A Longer Process

Finally, in relation to the nominating process itself, is the time element; it gets longer and longer. Candidates declare earlier and earlier. Jimmy Carter never stopped running for renomination. In 1977 he began setting in place the nominating rules for 1980. His "town meetings" and the hiring of television and media consultants kept his name constantly before the public. A year before the first of the primaries he had begun building his organization within the states and had begun periodic visits to the states (especially New Hampshire and Iowa) by himself, his family, campaign officials, and members of his administration. It may be that the Carter administration's continuing concern with reelection hurt its concentration on policy and administrative matters and lessened its ability to govern effectively.

Among Republicans, also, it is fair to say that Ronald Reagan never stopped running. After losing a close race to Gerald Ford in 1976, Reagan returned to his California home to initiate a syndicated radio commentary and a syndicated newspaper column giving his views on public affairs. He used his excess campaign funds to start a PAC (political action committee) to fund conservative candidates and causes. His organization was in place a year before the conventions and he began his active campaign with the announcement of his candidacy in November of 1979.

The same is true for the less visible candidates (perhaps even more so). Congressman Philip Crane announced on August 2, 1978, 27 months before the 1980 general election. He campaigned in 44 states, gave 2,500 speeches and spent $5 million. In return, he established a debt of $200,000, won three national convention delegates, and was the target of slanderous attacks in two publications. William Loeb and the Manchester, New Hampshire, *Union Leader* accused him of heavy drinking and sexual misbehavior and *Stern,* a German magazine, accused his wife of sexual misconduct (having sexual relations with "all members of Congress").[16] She is suing for $9 million (he may yet come out ahead).

On the Democratic side, the Kennedy campaign, in effect, began with the formation of draft Kennedy committees in twenty-six states in the spring and early summer of 1979. By early summer, also, a national draft Kennedy organization was created to complement the state units. The Americans for Democratic Action endorsed Kennedy for president in June of 1979 and liberal and conservative senators and congressmen (Henry Jackson and Geoge McGovern, for example) urged him, publicly and privately, to run for the good of the party. Pressure was placed on Kennedy to indicate his intentions by Labor Day. He announced in early September that his family no longer objected to his candidacy and that he would actively consider running. This was taken by his supporters as tantamount to an announcement of candidacy, which it was. On November 7, Kennedy made it formal.

It is noteworthy that the first contest between Kennedy and Carter took place in Florida in the Fall of 1979, before the election year had even begun. No delegates were at stake; it was purely a media event, but it was considered important to demonstrate the relative strength of the two candidates.

The Carter Administration poured people, money, federal jobs and appointments into the state. They out-organized and out-maneuvered the Kennedy camp and they won a nonbinding straw poll at the state convention—the results were duly reported by the media.

While early, the event was significant. It reemphasized the fact that Carter was a fierce campaigner and that he knew how to use the powers of incumbency. It also served as a preview of what was to come. The Kennedy forces never did get organized; settle on a theme for the campaign; or even begin to effectively challenge the president. The race would be over, for all practical purposes, by March.

There is another point. Not only does the fight begin early, but it ends early also. Carter's victories in Iowa and New Hampshire effectively minimized any chance Kennedy had for the nomination. Although he played out the string, it would have taken a drastic turnabout for him to be able to claim the nomination.

Bush won a close vote in Iowa. By New Hampshire, Reagan had corrected his campaign problems and won convincingly. From there on he, as did Carter, won one major victory after another. There were occasional lapses in both campaigns, but not of consequence (a "dip in the road" as Robert Strauss, Carter's campaign manager would call it). The delegates piled up for both men. The only interest in the Republican campaign was the timing of withdrawal announcements by the other contenders: Dole dropped out in February; Baker days before the Illinois March primary; Connally in March after his failure in the South Carolina primary; Crane in March; Anderson in late April (to form an independent candidacy); and Bush, the last of the challengers, in late May. The nomination races were basically decided by late February. One reason the races seem so long is that they formally begin as early as two years before the first delegates are chosen and they end, for all practical purposes, in the late winter of the election year. Yet the primaries, caucuses, and media attention continue until June. The process appears to go on forever.

The Advantages of Incumbency

For the Democrats, 1980 provided another lesson in the advantages of incumbency. It is difficult to challenge an incumbent president for your party's nomination. This is a basic lesson and it was relearned in 1980.

Throughout the prenomination campaign, President Carter was able to set the agenda for media and public discussion; command television time and media exposure at will; woo state and local party leaders with all manner of federal grants and job opportunities; send administration and national party officials into key states to work on his behalf; and even, through his control of the national Democratic party, write, and then interpret and enforce, the rules for delegate selection in 1980. These are enormous advantages.

Even then, Carter had help. Unexpected developments can help, or hurt, an incumbent. In 1980, they very much worked to the president's advantage during the decisive early phases of the prenomination campaign.

Unexpected Events

On November 4, 1979, Iranian militants took control of the American Embassy in Teheran, in the process taking hostage fifty-three American diplomatic and military personnel. The takeover was in response to the admission of the Shah of Iran to the United States for medical treatment, a decision made by the administration. The militants threatened to put the Americans, or at least some of them, on trial for espionage and demanded the return of the deposed Shah to Iran for trial and restitution of the millions of dollars and treasures that the Shah and his family allegedly took from the country. The militants also demanded a formal acknowledgement of United States complicity in the Shah's crimes.

The American government refused to deport the Shah or to meet the other conditions specified and the battle was joined. The president took a daily personal interest in events, curtailed his campaigning and vowed not to leave the White House until the hostages had been freed. Presidential surrogates—the vice president, the first lady, cabinet members and campaign officials—would carry on the campaign from here on in. The president used the press of foreign business—the Iranian crisis and later the Russian invasion of Afghanistan—to withdraw from the scheduled debates in Iowa in January with Kennedy and Governor Jerry Brown of California. It may have been coincidental, but when Carter agreed to debate his rivals he was behind in the polls. When he changed his mind, he was on his way to being well ahead.

Kennedy Confronts the Issue

The political problems that the Iranian situation caused the Kennedy campaign were enormous. Overnight, the president had become the embodiment of the nation's unity in the face of crisis and of its resolve to free the hostages and to "stand up" to the Iranians. He was no longer simply a candidate for his party's presidential nomination. As an example of the transformation in perceptions that took place, a Harris poll taken in early November of 1979 immediately before the embassy takeover showed Kennedy leading Carter among Democrats and independents, 46 percent to 32 percent. The same poll repeated a month later (early December), gave Carter the lead 42 percent to 40 percent. The president was on his way.

Carter could stay in the White House, command national media attention and remain relatively immune to campaign attacks or confrontations, while his surrogates mercilessly pounded away at Kennedy. The Senator had no one to strike back at. Kennedy's repeated stress on economic issues—joblessness and inflation—seemed almost irrelevant in light of the national emergency.

The frustration showed. In a television appearance in San Francisco on December 2, Kennedy remarked that the Shah had "run one of the most violent regimes in the history of mankind."[17] The senator's comments were immediately pounced on by Carter supporters, surrogate campaigners, and some of the media as undermining the president's efforts to free the hostages. The reaction of Robert Strauss, one of Carter's campaign managers and a surrogate campaigner, to Kennedy's comments indicates how effectively the White House was able to use the issue to blunt criticisms directed against the president. Strauss, after decrying the senator's remarks as "ill-advised," went on to say that it was a mistake "to inject anything into a campaign that would endanger the lives of the American hostages over there."[18] Strauss concluded: "I really don't think Senator Kennedy understood the impact of those statements [on Iran]."[19]

At one point in the Iowa campaign it appeared that Vice President Mondale even questioned Senator Kennedy's patriotism for criticizing Carter administration policies. The incident was resolved amicably, but the problem of Iran and the tensions it created demonstrated the difficulty of dealing with such an issue effectively during a political campaign. The problem was never resolved by Kennedy or his advisors.

In February, when Kennedy complained that the administration was moving slowly on a proposal he had advanced for an international commission to look into the hostage situation, Carter retaliated in a nationally televised news conference: "The thrust of what he's said throughout the last few weeks is very damaging to our country."[20] Not Carter, but the country.

There was no evidence that Kennedy's remarks in any manner affected the Iranian situation. Nonetheless, Kennedy was made to appear as working against the United States and its best interests, and possibly the safe retrieval of the hostages. The situation presented Carter with a powerful tool and he used it repeatedly.

The president kept the focus on the Iranian crisis throughout the prenomination campaign, to his repeated advantage. On the weekend before the Wisconsin primary, Carter called the editors of the *New York Times* and the *Washington Post* to alert them to potentially favorable developments in the hostage situation. As the polls opened on the morning of the Wisconsin vote (April 1), Carter called a press conference to cite "positive developments" relating to the Iranian government's decision to take control of the hostages. As a consequence, the president said he would delay imposing further sanctions on Iran. An aura of optimism marked the televised conference. Nothing of consequence developed and the White House later acknowledged that they may have been a little premature in their anticipation. The day following the primary, families of the hostages complained that Carter was using the crisis to his own political advantage, but little else was heard. The effect, of course, was to marshall support in Wisconsin, and elsewhere, behind the president and away from Senator Kennedy.

Kennedy was not in a position to effectively challenge Carter on his handling of the Iranian situation nor on his conduct of foreign policy more generally. The administration's fierce reaction to the Russian invasion of Afghanistan, the grain embargo that followed and the Olympic boycott were never topics of sustained campaign debate or review. Alternately, Kennedy was not able to shift the focus of attention—at least until the national convention—to the economic issues he considered important and on which the Carter Administration was vulnerable.

A later, ill-advised military venture (April 24, 1980) into Iran to gain the release of the hostages (resulting in the death of eight American military personnel) or even later Carter's decision to leave the White House (declaring the Iranian crisis "manageable") to resume campaigning did little to hurt his campaign.

The "Perks" of Office

In a further use of his position, Carter was able to shower federal patronage—jobs, prestigious appointments, federal contracts and grants—on key officials in any state he decided was important to his renomination effort. His early actions along this line in Florida during the Fall of 1979 were indicative of what was to come. They left one Florida official wondering facetiously if the peninsula would sink into the ocean from the weight of the federal largesse.

When Mayor Jane Byrne, also in the Fall of 1979, first appeared to endorse Carter and then switched to Kennedy, the secretary of transportation warned that Chicago could no longer expect federal funds. The administration appeared good on its word.

Illinois was, nonetheless, vital to the president's reelection hopes. After the national conventions, when Mayor Byrne seemed to relent in her opposition to Carter, she began to receive weekly invitations to White House functions; grants were announced for federally sponsored housing, transportation, and "community development" projects; a military terminal at O'Hare Airport the city had wanted was traded for other city land, allowing for an expansion of the O'Hare facility; and a school desegregation battle that had been joined for two decades was quickly (if temporarily) resolved through a consent decree entered into by the city and the Justice Department. The city conceded little—unlike most consent decrees, this one is not specific—and civil-rights lawyers familiar with the case argued that the city gave up less than it had promised a year earlier in a related court case.[21] Whatever the merits of the resolution, Chicago became immediately eligible for federal educational grants to help in both the desegregation process and to subsidize the specifics of the working out of the agreement.

Lessons like this are not lost on practicing politicians. Few big city mayors or governors opposed Carter.

The Use of Surrogate Campaigners

The administration could also send in White House and Cabinet officials, the vice president, the first lady, and Democratic party officials to stump for the president's renomination. The strategy was effective. There were murmurings that the administration went too far, but the controversy did not spill over into the public domain until after the national convention. In September, 1980, Lloyd Cutler, the White House counsel, circulated a memo that followed FEC guidelines in strictly regulating the publicly paid campaigning of Cabinet and other top administration officials. Under the Cutler ruling there could be no politicking by administration officials on government business, unless the entire trip was paid for by the Carter campaign.

Carter campaign manager, Robert Strauss, angrily rejected the White House counsel's interpretation. Speaking to a gathering of Cabinet and administration officials, Strauss told them that they could use the president's name in connection with policies and, if asked any political questions, "you can damn sure answer them in favor of the president instead of pussyfooting around.''[22] Strauss pushed them to bring more administration resources into the president's reelection drive.

This is where the matter now stands. It is a grey area for all administrations. A failure to formally define the limits on the use of government officials—and the awarding of government contracts—during campaign periods leaves the matter unresolved. The problem received little attention in either the pre- or postnomination phases of the campaign.

All told, the possibility of events external to the campaign helping an incumbent, the resources available to an incumbent, the media exposure a president commands, and the control he exercises over a party and its processes, all make challenging an incumbent an extremely risky business, regardless of how unpopular he may be.

In relation to the 1980 campaign, it is possible that the Carter administration had exhausted the advantages of incumbency by the end of the primary season. The losses in the superbowl primaries might be one indication of this. By election day in November, the constant reminder in the media of the hostages' confinement and the Carter administrations's inability to deal effectively with the situation may have reinforced other feelings of frustration with administration policies and actions and contributed directly to Carter's defeat.[23]

The Tenor of the Campaign

For the Democrats, if was often a low-level prenomination campaign (especially at the state level). Attention was not centered upon Carter's stewardship in office or his economic policies. His campaign managed to make Kennedy the focus of attention in the state being contested and his media attack hammered away at Kennedy's integrity, character, and morality. The tone of the prenomination campaign elicited little comment or concern. Not surprisingly, much of this same tenor carried over into the early phases of general election campaign in the charges of racism, Klan support and war-mongering directed against Ronald Reagan.[24]

Voter Instability

The volatility of the voters in 1980 was unusual, and it may be indicative of an indecision and variability that will be with us for years to come. Unlike many previous election years, the polls were no longer safe calculations as to how the voters would go.[25] This was true throughout the primary season. In Iowa, in early January, Reagan had the support of 50 percent of the state's Republicans. His nearest challenger had only 14 percent. Going into the vote several weeks later,

Reagan still held a prohibitive 3–1 lead. Yet Bush upset Reagan in the Republican straw vote with 32 percent to Reagan's 29 percent (Baker 16 percent; Connally 9 percent; Crane 7 percent; Anderson 4 percent; Dole 2 percent; and 2 percent uncommitted).

The same phenomenon—a volatile vote—held true in New Hampshire. In the first New Hampshire poll taken in December of *1978* (another indication of how early this all begins), Reagan led Republicans with 36 percent of the vote; Bush had 2 percent. Going into the election year, Reagan was up to 50 percent, Bush had 8 percent. After Iowa, Bush's stock rose dramatically. He scored 45 percent among Republicans, beating Reagan who had dropped to 36 percent. After the New Hampshire debate, Bush started down and Reagan back up. The vote reflected the dramatic changes: Reagan 50 percent, Bush (now) 23 percent. (Baker 13; Anderson 10; Crane 2; Dole .4). Later New Hampshire polls show the trend continued. Reagan kept gaining in popularity (up to 58 percent) when the polls ended two days after the election and Bush kept falling (down to 14 percent). It was a volatile, unpredicatable electorate the candidates faced in the nominating battles (and Iowa and New Hampshire which were the most thoroughly polled indicate that).[26]

A Turned-off Electorate

Another factor the polls picked up was an electorate that was angry, frustrated and turned-off. This trend has been developing—and continues to develop—since the mid-1960s.[27] It continued in the primaries. The voters were disillusioned with everything—including the candidates they supported. Up to one-half in the *New York Times*/CBS polls indicated they either were unsure of whether they would support, or would not support, the candidate in the general election that they had supported in the primaries.

This helps to illustrate the deep sense of frustration evident in the electorate. It also indicates the general lack of enthusiasm for the candidates running, one reason that John Anderson withdrew on April 24th to actively explore a third party candidacy.

The frustration may feed something else. Party ties and party loyalties have weakened. Again this has been going on for approximately two decades. It is particularly severe among the young. (In 1976, 52 percent of the 18 to 20 year olds declared as independents; for the 60 and over group, the figure was only 22 percent). The American two-party system is in trouble. Nothing that happened in the prenominating elections of 1980 is likely to improve it much. In fact, if what we have said is close to correct, the events of January-August, 1980, have promoted a further deterioration in and disillusionment with the party system.

Discussion: More Reform?

Can anything be done? A number of people think so. At least they are trying. The Democratic and Republican parties have authorized commissions to review problems associated with presidential selection.

The Congress has been considering creation of a blue ribbon national panel to review presidential nominating procedures and to make recommendations.

Two committees of the Congress, one house and one senate, are considering fundamental changes in the system. Major private groups, such as the American Bar Association and several foundations, have announced their intention to analyze the problem and to recommend improvements. Presidential selection processes will not suffer from lack of attention over the coming years.

The Nature of the Reform Proposals

Some of the changes being considered include the adoption of a national primary, one massive election to be held on a specified date in late spring in which all delegates to the national conventions would be chosen. In effect, it would constitute one more general election; it would be expensive; the candidates would depend on the media to get their messages across; and it would further weaken the parties.

A second proposal would establish some type of regional primaries in which states would sign up—or be assigned by lottery—to hold primaries *only* on one of three to five dates (depending on the bill), three to four weeks apart, between March and early June. Some New England and southern states have experimented with a voluntary form of this type of approach, but any real regional set-up will come only through congressional or national party action.

A third proposal would set, as in the regional primary idea, four to five dates, approximately one month apart between March and early June in which a state would be assigned by lot to a day on which it could hold its primary or caucus. The distribution could be regional or it could be random. Drawings would be made between sixty and ninety days before the date of the caucus/primary, thus presumably limiting early-bird campaigns, but also confusing and complicating state election administration.

Another proposal would standardize and simplify all state requirements as to ballot access, petition and filing deadlines, the certification of delegates, and other such things so that the requirements in one state would be identical to those in another, thus taking much of the confusion out of the system, limiting the discretion of state legislatures and election officials and removing the more arbitrary aspects of the system.

Under some of these proposals, a federal nominating commission would be established to supervise the prenomination phase of the process. In effect, responsibilities would be taken out of the hands of state and national party officials.

Many political scientists and political commentators have advanced recommendations. Some favor a return to the "old party system" of 1968 and before—that is, a more closed system dominated by state and local party and elective officials and the representatives of the major interest groups in a party's coalition (the leadership of the AFL–CIO in the Democratic party, for example). This is not possible. The old system was found wanting and, for better or worse, it has been replaced. A return to the past is the most unlikely of the options before the parties.

Others believe that relatively minor adjustments will make present arrangements liveable. Some contend, for example, that the needed corrective is to assign up to 25 percent of the national convention delegations to elected and party officials. Based on the experience of 1980, this may not change things much unless they are free to decide how they will vote. Even then, the effects of such a change remain uncertain.

The ideas expressed by political scientist Everett Carll Ladd are fairly typical of the type of thought being given to the problem by a host of political scientists (although it is likely that few would agree on what constitutes the most desirable system). Ladd proposes the following:

—substantial federal subsidies to rebuild the national parties ($15 million to each political party).

—the creation of what Ladd calls a "mixed" system (although it is not mixed in the sense of a balance of caucus and primary methods of delegate selection). What Ladd is talking about is a "mix" between popular participation and elite party leadership. He would:

  a) reserve one-third of each delegation for national, state, and local party and elected officials who would not have to commit themselves to any presidential candidate unless they wanted to. Presumably this would add flexibility to the national conventions.

  b) a national primary, regulated by federal law, would be held on the third Tuesday in June in which both parties would select two-thirds of their delegates to the national conventions. The delegates would be committed to support the presidential contender on whose ticket they ran for at least one ballot at the convention.

  c) finally, the national conventions would be reduced in size to 1,000 to 1,200.[28]

Ladd's ideas would drastically change the system. I am not at all sure the results would be beneficial.

Finally, when the "President's Commission for a National Agenda for the Eighties" made its report in January of 1981, it addressed some of the problems implicit in presidential selection. The commission had been established by Jimmy Carter in the Fall of 1979 in line with his belief that a "malaise" gripped the American spirit. The commission was charged with identifying the problems the nation was likely to encounter in the coming decade and exploring some of the potential solutions.

The commission addressed the problem—as it related to political parties and the electoral process—as follows:

> We are particularly interested in strengthening the parties in the selection of presidential and congressional candidates. For the former, primary elections and the national media have tended to replace the decisions of party leaders, an event which has in turn worked to the disadvantage of candidates with experience in Washington and stature in the party, and in favor of candidates who run against Washington and are new to the national political scene. [This from a commission established by Jimmy Carter!] Working alliances along party lines between congressional party majorities and the White House have become steadily more difficult, while competition between the Hill and the president has become almost a tradition of government.[29]

To strengthen the parties and the electoral process, the commission recommended:

- —the public funding of congressional elections, with a portion of the funds to be routed through the national committees of the two parties to candidates of their choice;
- —limiting presidential primaries to four dates, grouped by time zone, and scheduled one month apart; and
- —reserving a portion of national delegate positions—from one-fifth to one-third—for elected and party officials.

The commission's ideas are neither new nor its recommendations comprehensive. What they do reflect is the national uneasiness with presidential selection practices and the vague hope that something will be done to improve them.

On the Likelihood of Change

Most of the proposals being put forward would require federal action. This, in itself, would be a new departure and, I believe, should be viewed with a certain amount of caution. A federal presence may open up all kinds of new, and unanticipated problems, and it introduces the government into a system where its impact has been minimal to date. A federal regulation could also cement both national parties into whatever forms are decided upon early. The system of the last decade may be too flexible. A federally-regulated system may be so finely tuned and legally defined as to defy relevant change. It is a prospect I would be slow to encourage.

The possibilities of change of some kind are good—although the results from whatever is enacted are not likely to quiet the dissatisfaction with presidential selection methods. Official—that is, congressional and presidential—interest in fundamental reform should cool. A president elected under a given system is not likely to push for a revamping of it. Both the president and the Congress are faced with devoting most of their energies to reordering national economic and social priorities and to dealing with an economy severely weakened by excessive inflation and unemployment. The chances are that they will have little time or desire to tackle questions relating to fundamental political reform.

Nongovernment groups—whether the American Bar Association, the League of Women Voters, or a research foundation—might generate publicity and a greater public awareness of the difficulties implicit in selecting a president, but they are less likely to directly stimulate significant change.

This leaves it to the parties. The Republicans have not been aggressive in seeking reform. The prospects are that the party's position will remain the same.

The Democrats have appointed a new reform commission, which will recommend further modifications in the nominating system. The commission's positive contributions are not likely to be great. In fact, its major contribution may be to reinforce the sense of a system in constant turmoil, primarily sensitive to short-run political concerns. It is unlikely to contribute much to the fundamental resolution of the difficulties plaguing presidential selection.

Conclusion

Change will come. That much is certain. The direction and consequences of the changes to be enacted are less clear. Whatever does emerge, however, should incorporate the strengths of the system now in place. These include an impressive increase in the number of people participating; the considerable number of choices among candidates offered to those who do participate; the distinctive policy alternatives available among the presidential contenders; and the amount of direct influence grassroots participants have been able to exert on the eventual choice of a presidential nominee. Reformers in the 1980s should build on the gains of the past.

Chapter 2 The 1980 Democratic Primary in Illinois

John S. Jackson III

The Illinois primary is a part of a larger political system and is moved by the same tides which move that larger political system. At the same time there are local adaptions to those national tides. Like all of American federalism, the Illinois primary is a complex interaction between national and state and local factors, all of which make for a subtle mixture of events, personalities, and outcomes.

The Illinois primary has changed dramatically since the 1968 prereform days. That year, Illinois sent a national convention delegation selected virtually without reference to the primary results, or national party rules, and without much intervention by the party-in-the-electorate. In 1968, party professionals at the state and county level were pretty much able to get what they wanted, (especially Mayor Richard Daley and such downstate leaders as Paul Powell, Mayor Alvin Fields, East St. Louis, and Representative Clyde Choate). The Democratic National Convention had as its backdrop the famous battle of Grant Park leading to the nomination of Hubert Humphrey and the subsequent narrow loss to Richard Nixon in the fall. Many people believed then that Humphrey lost the presidency during the stormy prenomination season and during the throes of the divisive Democratic National Convention of 1968. Certainly those were contributory, if not decisive factors, in the Humphrey and Democratic defeats of 1968.

The 1968 national convention was also one of the major stimulants of an extraordinary era of party reform within the Democratic party. This reform era has led subsequently through the McGovern-Fraser Commission, the Mikulski Commission, the Sanford Commission, the Democratic Mid-Term Conference, the Party Charter, the Winograd Commission, the Hunt Commission, and a whole intricate institutionalization of the rules of the game governing the selection of national convention delegates and the conduct of national conventions in particular and national party affairs in general. We went through the era of "quotas" for various demographic groups and this then gave way to "affirmative action." We developed detailed national party laws controlling the timing of the primaries, filing dates, and candidate-approval rights. All of this served to nationalize the procedure within the Democratic party to an extent unprecedented in previous American history. A review of all those national party law developments would be too extensive for the scope of this chapter; however, those developments constitute an important part of the context of this story.

Because of the new rules of the game, the 1980 Illinois primary was much more crucial than its predecessors, and it was a much different creature from those prereform primaries of 1968 or even 1972.[1] These new rules of the game plus the national, state, and local political parties formed the important parameters within which the 1980 Democratic primary was played out in Illinois. The Illinois primary, in turn, had a lot to do with helping to shape the events that came after it. Any national presidential campaign is a great confusing river of events, personalities, and places. Exploring in depth one of the major tributaries like the Illinois primary, in an intensive case study such as this, can better aid us in understanding the contours, moods, and behavior of the larger stream.

The Phases of the Primary Season

John Kessell in a recently published book, *Presidential Campaign Politics*, described the temporal pattern of the presidential contest. He notes that the chronological sequence sets "stern limits" on the candidates and their prospects. Kessel called the four nomination stages:

(1) Early Days–Time period: "The period between the midterm election and the initial selection of delegates." Major activities—the prospective candidates do early planning and organizing. Creation of the exploratory committees. Rudimentary staff assembled.

(2) Initial Contests–Time period: Iowa caucuses; New Hampshire primary—other early primaries and caucuses. Major Activities—the candidates and their staffs try to win or to do "better than expected" and create momentum.

(3) Mist Clearings–Time Period: approximately the midpoint of the primary season. Major Activities—Reduction of the field to usually two or three with realistic chance of victory. Struggle for delegates becomes crucial.

(4) The Convention–Time period: Usually July or August. Formal ratification of the decision which has emerged from primaries and caucuses. Beginning of the general election campaign.[2]

Kessell was dealing with the total national scene rather than one state primary; however, with some adjustments his emphasis on the chronological pattern and the imperatives of the calendar are also very relevant to the preprimary and primary campaign season in one state like Illinois. In this chapter, I will divide the Illinois primary season into three temporal phases:

(1) The Embryonic Stage–Time Period: November, 1978–Labor Day, 1979. Major Actors and Activities: Potential candidates position themselves; mass media, party activists, and public office-holders speculate about and handicap the potential runners.

(2) The Strategic Decisions Stage–Time period: Labor Day, 1979-Christmas, 1979. Major Actors and Activities: The candidates announce formally and form their campaigns within the state. The political elites choose up sides and announce their positions. Media coverage within the state intensifies.

(3) The Primary Campaign Proper–Time period: January 7, 1980-March 18, 1980. Major Actors and Activities: Candidates and their campaigns appeal to the public in an effort to win votes in the presidential popularity contest and to win the maximum number of national convention delegate positions as well as to create the image of momentum. The political party elites try to gain personal and political advantage. Media coverage within the state reaches its maximum intensity.

These divisions will provide the chronological and conceptual organization to this chapter. After the primary ends, an important new season begins. It includes the interim period between the primary and the national convention, and it ends, of course, in the climax of the convention itself. This new season will also be discussed briefly from the perspective of the impact of the primary, and how the new season, in turn, has an important impact on the general election campaign. One should always keep in mind that the whole primary and national convention periods are simply phases in the build up to the main event, the national election. However, they are crucial phases which go far in determining who the next president of the United States will be. The types of campaigns fought, the coalitions forged, and the positions adopted will even help determine what the president's subsequent policies will be, as we are clearly seeing in the early Reagan years. It is not only important for a candidate to *win* his party's nomination. Much also depends on *how* he wins, who he defeats, what positions are taken in the platform and public pronouncements, and how does it all look on television to the average voter who will render the final judgment. The stakes are extraordinary during the nominations season.

The Embryonic Stage

The embryonic stage of the primary season begins at approximately the point of the off-year elections two years before the presidential election. That would be November of 1978 for this particular campaign. By the end of the balloting, people are talking about what the off-year elections results mean for the party and president in power, what contenders are beginning to position themselves, and what their prospects are within their own party; and the polls are beginning to offer the presidential horserace to the American people. The 1980 nominations fight had a rather clear-cut beginning point for the Democrats. It began in December of 1978 in Memphis at the Democratic Mid-Term Conference. At that conference President Carter brought a bevy of Cabinet officers and top aides and tried to explain and defend administration policies. They also listened in glum silence to a lot of criticism and advice. Disgruntled liberals held a caucus in a pep-rally/ funeral atmosphere and talked openly about bolting the party or dumping the incumbent president. It was becoming apparent the party was confused and divided—in many ways reminiscent of the Lyndon Johnson era of 1966–68. Into this vortex stepped Senator Edward Kennedy with a rousing speech about the party's being true to its mission and not selling out to the Republicans. There was a lot of talk in the speech about "sailing against the prevailing winds" and the Democratic party tradition of help for the poor, minorities, and the oppressed people of the world. Most party activists who heard that speech and observed the maneuverings in Memphis concluded that the major battlelines were already being drawn for 1980. It was sixteen months until the Illinois Primary. It was twenty-three months before the general election.

Throughout the first eight months of 1979, President Carter's fortunes waxed and waned—but they mostly waned. Carter seemed to be struggling to put his administration and his presidency in order. In July, he retreated to Camp David for almost two weeks before descending to make his long-awaited "Crisis of Confidence" speech. In addition, he fired four Cabinet members and announced several new policy initiatives. Observers said he was trying to get his team into place for the upcoming campaign. Inflation continued to climb and Carter's standing in the popularity polls continued to decline. By Labor Day there was insistent talk about several Democratic alternatives to Carter—most notably Senator Kennedy who was, by then, actively encouraging the speculation. Governor Jerry Brown of California made no secret of his disdain for Carter and his desire for the presidency, although he continued to be viewed as something of an enigmatic darkhorse by the American public.

During the summer and in September and October of 1979 the polls had Kennedy far ahead of Carter in Democratic voters' favor for winning the Democratic nomination. Brown trailed both rather badly.[3] The national polls also showed Carter trailing former President Gerald Ford and virtually tied with Ronald Reagan. Kennedy led both Ford and Reagan by almost a two-to-one margin.[4] Political party leaders and prospective candidates alike watch these opinion polls and talk to their friends and other politicians, always trying to catch the mood and gain direction. They want to know as much as possible before irrevocable commitments are made. By Labor Day of 1979, major decisions were looming. Commitments had to be made. Campaign staffs had to be assembled. Media production and buys had to begin shortly. At that point, prospects looked grim for Carter; promising for Kennedy; and uncertain for Brown.

The Strategic Decisions Stage

The scene must shift now to the state and local level where the early straw polls will soon be taken, early state conventions will be examined under the mass media's unrelenting microscope, and the jockeying for positions will begin in earnest among those who would become the national convention delegates and the foot soldiers in the political warfare attendant upon the presidential primaries. Party leaders and activists up to this point could only observe and react to the events and decisions being made on the national stage. Now they must begin to make their own decisions. The embryonic stage set an important context within which the state and local political leaders must act as they make their own strategic decisions. In the strategic decisions stage, the process becomes very much a two or three-tiered action where each level must act and react.

It is true that some important decisions remain at the national level during this time. By the Fall of 1979, virtually everyone knew that Carter, Kennedy, and Brown were running for president, although their formal announcements had not been made as yet. Their campaign committees had been formed, the work was going forward on their behalf, and the contest was on. Indeed, Senator Kennedy did not formally announce until November 7, 1979; and Governor Brown quickly followed with his announcement on November 9, 1979. Carter delayed the obvious until a formal announcement on December 4, 1979. By then many important decisions had been made and crucial events had occurred. Perhaps the most important single event of the whole campaign season took place on Sunday, November 4, 1979. The Iranian hostage crisis began with the seizure of the American Embassy on that day. It was exactly one year before the general election.

One of the crucial variables in the strategic decisions stage is the public opinion polls. The party professionals read the articles taken from the opinion polls even more carefully then does the mass public, and they react to the polls as one of the many factors they must take into account in their own decision making. The party activists have their own agendas to attend to. While they may worry about such problems as "the national interest," and the best president, they want to establish their own personal and political vantage point.

Throughout the embryonic stage the national polls showed Carter to be in a vulnerable position. His presidential job-approval ratings were down and his results in trial heats with Senator Kennedy were disastrous for an incumbent President. For instance, an ABC-Louis Harris Poll taken in early September 1979, found that 56 percent of the public did not think Carter could win renomination and 70 percent did not think he could win reelection. A Gallup poll taken October 5–8 showed Carter's job-approval ratings at 29 percent approve, 58 percent disapprove, and 13 percent no opinion.[5] A CBS-*New York Times* poll of Democratic identifiers only published October 19, 1979, showed that 45 percent favored Kennedy and 25 percent favored Carter.[6] The results of a *Chicago Tribune* poll taken in early November, 1979, showed Kennedy leading Carter by a 43–34 percent margin (with 5 percent for Brown) in their prospects for the Illinois primary.[7] All of these results indicated that Carter's renomination and reelection possibilities were clearly in jeopardy at that point.

However, one of the major clichés about the 1980 election was that the polls and presumably the electorate were very volatile, and this cliché had a major element of accuracy to it. The Iranian crisis began on November 4, 1979. By mid-November, Carter's job-approval ratings and renomination prospects began to improve. For example, the Gallup poll taken November 16–19, 1979, showed Carter's job approval rating at 38 percent (up 9 percent) and his disapproval rating at 49 percent (down 9 percent) from the one taken October 5–8.[8] A *Time Magazine* poll conducted by Yankelovich, Skelly, and White between December 10–12, 1979, showed that Carter had a 53 to 33 percent lead over Kennedy among Democrats.[9] By mid-December the ABC-Louis Harris Survey was showing that Democratic voters by a 44–43 percent plurality were saying that Senator Kennedy had not lived up to their expectations. This result was compared with the 63 to 15 percent of the Democratic voters who were positive about Kennedy when he declared for the presidency six weeks earlier.[10] All of these results represented a remarkable turnabout of the relative fortunes of President Carter and Senator Kennedy during the short period of early November to Christmas of 1979.

During this most uncertain period of time the maneuvering and decision making among the party activists in Illinois were at their height. The political elites had to choose up sides, and they intensely disliked having to do so during a period of uncertainty. They wanted to go with a winner, if possible, because endorsing and working for a winner promised to yield personal advantage for them, perhaps establishing a future hold that could help the constituency. If they could not insure that they were going with the winner, they wanted to insure that they could minimize the personal and political damage they would suffer in the event of a loss.[11]

These are difficult odds to figure whether you happen to be the Mayor of Chicago or the Democratic chairman in some remote section of downstate. Politics is about decision making and the difficult decisions had to be made in September, October, and November of 1979.

The logic of the prenominations stage both nationally and in Illinois now compelled the party activists to make decisions which must come earlier than in the prereform era. For instance, nominating petitions for the presidential preference contest and for the national convention delegate slots had to be filed by January 7, 1980. However, the most important strategic decisions had to be made long before that in Illinois. By late November and early December of 1979, the major battle lines were drawn and the strengths/weaknesses of the candidate-armies were beginning to come more sharply into focus.

One has to understand the way the national/local nexus develops to really appreciate the federalization of the presidential nominations process. In October and November of 1979, President Carter's emissaries were especially active in Illinois. They were mostly young people out of limited political backgrounds of state and local races or perhaps the 1976 Carter-Mondale campaign. Some of the old-timers among them went as far back as the 1972 McGovern effort. Some had worked for the Democratic National Committee before going onto the Carter-Mondale payroll. These young political entrepreneurs criss-crossed Illinois all during October and November, working with and on the political party activists. They usually started with the county chairmen and the state legislators as the most important targets. From there they would fan out to the most prominent local office holders and party activists going all the way down to the grassroots precinct level. The message was always the same, "The President wants and needs your support; are you with us?" For the most important, there were hints of or down-right commitment to Carter-Mondale endorsement of that person for a delegate slot if the person wanted to run (and if they fit the demographic quotas). Prior to 1976, national candidates did not have the option of approving their potential delegates. Now they do, and this candidate approval provides an important re-source in their dealing with the local supporters. For others, there were other expressions of real or implied payoffs—a visit to a local fundraiser by an impor-tant Cabinet official; a promise of attention to some constituent's complaint; per-haps an invitation to a White House conference if the person's political stature warranted such enticement.

The party professionals in turn, danced a minuet around their own commit-ments. Mayor Jane Byrne used her clout to get President Carter to her Democratic fund-raiser in Chicago on October 16, 1979, where she practically endorsed him that evening. Two weeks later she then shocked the Carter-Mondale campaign, and all of political Illinois, by endorsing Senator Kennedy. Her well-publicized flip-flop on the matter was only the most prominent of many such episodes of political bargaining and maneuver. Some party professionals felt very strongly committed to either Carter or Kennedy from the first and refused to play coy. Others did not and were left with great room to maneuver. In marked contrast to the Republicans, statewide leaders and considerations were negligible. Among the Democrats, there was no recognized statewide leader active in this strategic period comparable to Governor Thompson or Senator Percy among the Republicans. Then Secretary of State and now United States Senator Alan Dixon announced his decision to remain neutral and worry about his own campaign. United States Senator Adlai Stevenson seemed to toy with the idea of running himself but then stayed neutral. As a result, the real action for the Democrats was at the county and the congressional district levels.

The point of all this is that the strategic decision-making phase is a time of conflict and bargaining. The national campaign organization has formidable resources at hand (particularly if it belongs to an incumbent president) which it can and does use. If it is the party of the governor, he can also have some considerable influence. The locals, on the other hand, are the people who are going to bring name identification and organization to the campaign for the delegate positions and the presidential popularity contest at the top of the ballot. At least in Illinois, the power of the local party is not to be ignored if one is a judicious politician— even though the organization has been beaten on occasion. National candidate organizations, however, take most of the initiative, do most of the organizing, and bring in most of the resources. The local parties then react and supplement the work of the candidate organizations.

Out of all the give-and-take, the delegate slates and the prominent endorsements were fashioned. By Christmas of 1979 it was almost all in place. The lists of delegates on both the Carter and Kennedy sides were made up. Most of the locally important politicos had endorsed someone; and the candidate petitions were being printed. On filing day, January 7, 1980, all the Carter, and most of the Kennedy slates, were ready for filing in Springfield. Curiously enough, Governor Brown never seemed to be much of a factor in Illinois. No party leader of any note in Illinois seemed able to take Brown seriously and his delegate slates were put together hastily by a motley collection of rank amateurs. So by the official date of the kick-off of the presidential primary race in Illinois, it had boiled down to a head-to-head confrontation between Senator Kennedy and President Carter. It was a confrontation neither man could afford to lose. It also turned out to be one that neither could win.

The Primary Campaign Stage

When the presidential candidates and their prospective delegates file their petitions in early January, the formal primary campaign season begins. By then, most of the political elites have chosen up sides—or have announced their decision to remain neutral (e.g. prospective Senator Alan Dixon and Senator Adlai Stevenson). At this point the focus of the campaign shifts drastically from the political elites to the mass public. Intense activity on the part of the campaigners is no longer directed at county chairmen, legislators, and precinct leaders, although they continue to receive some nervous attention as well. Instead, the get-out-the-vote and convince-the-voters stage has arrived. Toward that end phone banks are installed, voter registration lists are acquired, advertising time is bought, campaign sponsored public opinion polling begins, and all of the other paraphernalia of modern campaigning are rolled into place. The period from January 7 to March 18th is only about ten weeks duration. The Carter-Mondale campaign was ready for Illinois when the primary season formally opened, and intensive effort at the grassroots began in early January. By contrast, the Kennedy campaign seemed ill-prepared at the time. They apparently had relied on a ground-swell of spontaneous support and a rush of volunteers and money to materialize from the senator's announcement of his candidacy. When these did not materialize, the Kennedy campaign had to scramble for people and resources and the gap between the two campaigns which opened in November and December of 1979 was never closed in the winter campaign. For instance the data on spending patterns alone illustrate the large discrepancy between the Carter-Mondale and Kennedy campaigns (see table 2.1).

This gap meant that the Kennedy strategy had to be one of relying on major endorsement from prominent party leaders such as Mayor Jane Byrne in Chicago and Congressman Paul Simon in the 24th Congressional District at the extreme southernmost tip of Illinois. These endorsements were to be coupled with media coverage and an appeal directly to the people for popular support in the primary. The Kennedy organizational effort in Illinois was a pale shadow in comparison to the Carter-Mondale effort. Even the prominent politican endorsements contest was about a draw—with the Carter-Mondale forces picking up endorsements from two of the state's elected statewide office holders, State Comptroller Roland Burris and State Treasurer Jerome Cosentino. In fact outside Chicago the major party leaders and elected Dem-

Table 2.1

Spending on the Illinois Primary

	1979	1980
Carter-Mondale	$68,424	$1,047,003
Kennedy	48,520	218,327
Brown	0	16,005
Totals	$116,944	$1,281,335

Source: Federal Election Commission data supplied directly to the author.

ocratic office holders were content to stick with Carter—or at least remain neutral. This is indeed the pattern of behavior we would expect of the "professionals" when it comes to treatment of any incumbent and especially of an incumbent president.

There thus developed significant differences between the "presence" of the two campaigns in each of the congressional districts. The Carter-Mondale campaign had a paid staff person (and in some cases two) in each congressional district.[12] These staff people had some access to money and media resources from the national campaign, although they were also charged with the responsibility of raising as much support as possible locally.[13] They bought newspaper ads, were advised of the national media buys made out of Washington, and were provided bumper stickers, brochures and posters. In a number of key districts, coordinators were also given help in establishing phone banks directed by professionals (and manned by volunteers). The congressional district coordinators were also able to ask for (and in many cases receive) the scheduling of cabinet officials, celebrities, and other Carter-Mondale surrogate campaigners. While the president himself was staying in the White House to honor his self-imposed and highly publicized ban on campaigning during the Iranian hostage crisis,[14] there were a variety of Carter family members as well as occasionally the vice president available for forays into many of the congressional districts. For example, the 24th congressional district in remote southern Illinois played host to Rosalyn Carter, son Jack Carter, and Secretary of Energy Charles Duncan—all before the March primary. In addition, Senator Kennedy sent his brother-in-law, Sargent Shriver, to the same district on the occasion of Congressman Simon's endorsement of the senator for president. Although his trip later had to be cancelled, Kennedy was personally scheduled for a visit to the 24th district in February, but he did come to the district for a speech and tour in March. All of this attention was lavished on a rural district at the deepest southernmost end of Illinois where the largest city, Carbondale, has a population of 30,000 people! The Chicago area, of course, received even more attention, and other districts got their share. Later both President Carter as well as Vice President Mondale and Governor Reagan personally campaigned in the 24th district during late October 1980 in the waning days of the general election.

This intense national attention focused on Illinois in general and on a relatively obscure congressional district in particular illustrates vividly the degree to which our politics have become nationalized. The Illinois primary was only one hurdle in a long race, but it was a very significant hurdle. It came at the most opportune time, three weeks into the season, at a crucial juncture in that omnipresent quest for momentum.[15] It was also widely touted as a very legitimate test case on a big midwestern state where all the candidates had the opportunity to prove their appeal to a microcosm of American voters.

In 1968 and again in 1972 the Illinois primary was largely ignored by the national media and the major candidates.[16] By 1976, it was taken somewhat more seriously, and in 1980 it really came into its own as a major national test. The Illinois primary was a test most of the candidates could ill afford to fail. Kennedy, Bush, and Anderson probably had the most at stake in Illinois, as a win here could have rescued that elusive momentum all three so desperately needed. A loss here, coupled with any other subsequent bad news, would likely prove to be fatal. The frontrunners, Reagan and Carter, could probably survive a loss in Illinois, but the challengers definitely needed a victory.

As was pointed out above, beginning by mid-November and early December the polls had begun to take on a more optimistic look for President Carter. In January of 1980 Carter's comfortable lead over Kennedy and Brown continued to grow. The poll differences between Carter and Kennedy were even more pronounced in Illinois. A *Chicago Sun-Times* poll published February 3, 1980, showed Carter at 68 percent; Kennedy at 19 percent; and Brown at 3 percent among likely voters in the Illinois Democratic Primary.[17] By March 14–18, the weekend before the Primary, the *Chicago Tribune* poll had Carter at 56 percent and Kennedy at 23 percent.[18] In short, the Illinois polls were showing that the state was continuing to be a fairly good barometer of the national political trends. No one really expected any upsets in the Democratic primary and indeed much of the attention had shifted by then to the Republican primary where the polls were indicating a very close race between Reagan and Anderson.

On March 18, the Illinois primary produced major victories for the two eventual nominees. Ronald Reagan overcame his early shaky start in Iowa, built on his strong showing in New Hampshire, and overcame a possible small lead in the polls to defeat Illinois native son, John Anderson by a 48 percent to 37 percent margin. He swamped his future running mate, George Bush, who got only 11 percent of the vote. Neither candidate ever completely recovered from the loss to Reagan in Illinois.

On the Democratic side the results were decisive. Carter outdistanced Kennedy by a healthy 60 percent to 40 percent in the popular vote. More importantly, he clobbered Kennedy by 138 to 14 in committed delegate count. Carter won in all but one congressional district out of the state's twenty-four districts. Kennedy's campaign was so deflated it never was really taken seriously again until the last primary day in June, when he took five out of eight of the major state primaries. By then it was too late. With the pivotal help of Illinois, Carter had taken an insurmountable lead in his quest for the Democratic nomination.

Perhaps appropriately enough, the Carter-Mondale delegation from the State of Illinois became the single largest block of committed delegates in the President's camp at the August convention in New York. The Illinois Carter-Mondale delegates provided reliable and overwhelming numbers of votes in the direct clashes with the Kennedy forces. For instance, on the first and most crucial vote, i.e., the "open convention" or "loyal delegate" issue, Illinois furnished 153 votes for the Carter-Mondale position and only 26 for the Kennedy position–a likely loss of only 10 votes from the president's position.

In essence, each primary, each caucus is a building block in the structure of the nomination drive and the total edifice becomes the foundation for the general election campaign. The Carter-Mondale forces laid a careful foundation for the nomination victory in their efforts in Illinois and other early primary states. Even though that foundation was laid with care, it was still flawed by the deep divisions existing within the coalition that composes the Democratic party. In the years since Franklin Roosevelt glued together the New Deal coalition of minorities, union members, urban machines, conservative southerners, intellectuals, Catholics, and Jews who compose the backbone of the party, it has enjoyed majority, or near-majority status. That majority, which has been so adept at winning the congressional elections, has faced increasing difficulties winning the presidency. The basic fault lines within the Democratic party are one key to its difficulties. Unlike a congressman, the presidential candidate has to try to represent the entire spectrum of the party. In a party which is large and heterogeneous, this is difficult to do adequately. Representing and pleasing the party activists and the party identifiers is particularly important if one is to gain the nomination. Table 2.2 provides some data on the important characteristics of party activists who were chosen to be the national convention delegates from Illinois in 1980.

As table 2.2 indicates, the primary in Illinois, like most of the other primaries and caucuses, produced a national convention delegation which mirrored reasonably well the demographic composition of black/white, young/old, male/female, liberal/moderate/conservative Democrats who make up the Democratic party as a whole and especially the party activists. The biggest discrepancy was on the Carter-Kennedy preferences where the particular rules used allowed for winner-take-all at the congressional district level, and this worked to the advantage of Carter.

Since the nominations process worked so well, it produced a delegation profoundly divided between Carter and Kennedy forces. That division was even greater in other states and other delegations. Not surprisingly, then, when they got to New York the divisions ranged from difficult to impossible to reconcile. The unfolding nominating season and the events of the national convention set the stage on which Carter and Mondale had to play during the general election. The seeds of Carter's defeat were not only sown in the Illinois primary or in Memphis two years before, not just in Carter's four-

Table 2.2
*Demographic and Attitudinal Composition of the Illinois Democratic
Delegation Compared to all Democratic Identifiers and the National
Population (in Percentages)*

Delegates	Illinois	All Democratic Identifiers	National Population
Race			
Black	16[a]	19[c]	11[d]
White	84	81	88
	100[a]	100[c]	99[d]
Sex			
Male	49	44	52
Female	51	56	48
	100[b]	100[c]	100
Age			
Under 30	4	27	11
30 +	96	73	89
	100[b]	100[c]	100[e]
Ideology			
Liberal	21	21	19
Moderate	72	44	49
Conservative	7	26	31
	100[a]	91	99
Candidate Support			
Carter	90		
Kennedy	10		
Brown & Other	0		
	100		

[a]Data taken from official party sources
[b]Data taken from the author's survey of all national convention delegates
[c]Data assembled from seven CBS News/*New York Times* national surveys and reported in: Warren J. Mitofsky and Martin Plissner, "The Making of the Delegates, 1968–1980," *Public Opinion* (Oct./Nov., 1980) pp. 37–43.
[d]Data taken from U.S. Census
[e]Data taken from The Gallup Poll, Sept., 1980.

year record, although those were important enough; they go back to Lyndon Johnson's schizophrenic foreign versus domestic policy priorities, to Franklin Roosevelt's New Deal, and perhaps even to the Civil War. In the aftermath of the Illinois party, however, the nomination rather than the general election campaign was uppermost in the considerations of all the candidates and their staffs. After Illinois, Carter and Reagan were the clear favorites, and they left Illinois with the best positions in the presidential marathon. Carter and Reagan had collected by far the largest percentage of delegates. Both had that momentum and media attention necessary to pyramid resources and ultimately other victories. Both would stumble temporarily, but neither would be stopped after the Illinois primary.

Between Primary and Convention

After the national spotlight faded from Illinois, political activity receded to a much lower order of intensity for the local activities. In the February–April era, the major questions revolved around who would be the twenty-seven at-large delegates to be named in a state convention held in Springfield in April of 1980. Those delegates were carefully chosen to balance demographic and political considerations against the candidate preferences. At that convention, twenty-five Carter delegates and two Kennedy delegates were selected. The convention was supposed to be something of a victory rally with a good deal of obligatory rhetoric about anticipated Democratic victories; however, some of the talk had a sort of perfunctory quality to it.

Then in June, a statewide meeting of all the national convention delegates was held in Chicago. The major item of business was to select the leadership of the delegation. A carefully-crafted compromise was worked out by the Carter-Mondale forces whereby the two major contenders, State Treasurer Costentino, and State Comptroller Burris were both given cochair status along with State Senator Dawn Clark Netsch of Chicago and party activist Merele Franke of northwest Illinois. As a result of Cosentino's desire to go it alone as the only leader of the delegation, the compromise came apart in acrimonious competition before and heated debate during the delegate meeting. Cosentino, and other critics, denounced the slate as a "four-headed monster." The slate *was* an artful example of ticket balancing including one black male, one Italian male, and two female party leaders. Here, too, one can see that the Carter-Mondale forces prevailed in what was apparently again an intense conflict-laden atmosphere in Chicago. Although this victory was important, it, too, left scars and those wounds were to break open later during the general election.

A presidential candidate and his staff have to worry about a multilevel set of conflicts during the nomination process. They have to win the small and large battles leading to the nomination and get over that hurdle first. They have to be very careful about *how* they win, however, and *who* they defeat in the process. If it is a candidate representing a "cause" and a clear ideological persuasion where there are large levels of near-uninanity in the party, such as Reagan in 1980, then the former rivals can rally round the flag of the larger cause when they are defeated. This is apparently the source of the quiet convention held by the Republicans where the major excitement revolved around who would be the vice-presidential nominee. If it is a more centralist candidate or if the *man* himself becomes the issue, (e.g., Carter in 1980 or Barry Goldwater in 1964 or George McGovern in 1972), then it is perhaps more difficult to glue the coalition back together again. While the Carter-Mondale forces clearly carried the small battles during the interim state-level jockeying from March through July, it is now clear in retrospect that the Kennedy forces, the Anderson defectors, and even the skeptical American public were not being won over.

For the average delegate, the interim period between the Illinois primary and the national convention was an interesting time. It was an occasion to be the object of a rather phenomenal amount of lobbying and outright political pressure. The state convention was well orchestrated in advance so few contacts were made regarding that April meeting. The fight over the delegation leadership, however, brought out the Consentino and Burris forces in bitter confrontation. In the background stood the national Carter-Mondale campaign who were quietly, but firmly, pushing for their compromise joint leadership ticket. Almost all delegates got personal visits and phone calls from all three of these factions. By the time of the July meeting of the Illinois delegation in Chicago, a lot of arms had already been twisted. The state convention and the pressures leading up to it proved to be only a light workout for what was yet to come.

The level of lobbying grew in intensity as the August convention approached. At first, the delegates began to receive mailings from groups representing virtually every point on the political compass. Pro- and antinuclear groups, pro and anti-ERA, pro- and antiabortion, pro- and antisolar power, and a host of other interests were heard from—often several times. In addition, the Lyndon LaRouche campaign seemed to gain intensity in direct proportion to its diminishing prospects for success. The mail gave way to telegrams, which then, in turn, gave way to long distance phone calls. Most of the messages were insistent; some were downright abusive and threatening.

In addition the mass media were often in touch with the delegates. There was a variety of questionnaires and other inquiries received from national, state, and local media sources. Most delegates, especially those who were not legislators, were not accustomed to such attention and began to get the feeling of being a "celebrity-for-the-month." Phone calls and telegrams from CBS, NBC, ABC, the *New York Times* and the *Washington Post* can be heady stuff for anyone not accustomed to such attention.

All of this activity paled in comparison, however, to the pressure surrounding the "open convention" (or "committed delegate") conflict. This controversy is too extensive to review in detail here. Put simply, it was a technical question of whether to adopt proposed Rule F 3 (c) in the permanent rules of the convention.

This rule provided that delegates were bound to vote for the presidential candidate they were pledged to during the primary. If delegates "sought to violate" that pledge, they could be replaced by those who would be loyal to the pledge. In the case of Ilinois the Carter-Mondale campaign pointed out that a delegate signed an oath when filing for the primary stating that he or she supports Carter or Kennedy or Brown. In addition, that candidate's name appeared in parenthesis by the name of the prospective delegate. In essence, the people in the primary voted for the delegates, but also as a show of support for their presidential candidate. Some delegates were well-known and brought their own name recognition and clout to the ticket. Others were clearly elected by virtue of their association with the name of the presidential candidate whom they supported. Since those were the rules of the game adopted before the primary season started, the Carter forces argued that it was blatantly unfair to alter those rules at the end of the process. To do so would also potentially negate the expressed will of the voters in the Illinois primary, according to the Carter supporters.

The Kennedy forces (and others) wanted the rule eliminated so the delegates would be free to vote for whomever they chose. The Kennedy forces reasoned that there is a long delay between the Illinois primary in March and the national convention in August. In addition, times and circumstances change. Carter was very strong as a result of the Iranian crisis in mid-March, but that crisis was taking an increasing toll by mid-August. More importantly, the delegates should be "free to vote their consciences" and able "to vote for the best man" according to the Kennedy thesis. These delegates should be thinking, decision-making individuals and not "robots" said the advocates. The convention should be an "open" one where the decisions as who would be the nominee came out of national debate and compromise (also, perhaps a "compromise" candidate, e.g. Mondale or Muskie could be found). The national convention should be a decision-making arena rather than just the device to validate the primary results.

So the issue was joined. As the week of the convention neared, the debate grew fierce in the national media and among representatives of the contending candidates. The local manifestation of the debate was an intense amount of persuasion, education, and pressure focused on each individual delegate. Everyone from the national television networks, the *New York Times,* the Kennedy campaign, the Carter campaign, and local friends and neighbors got in on the act—either asking delegates how they would vote or telling them how they should vote, and why. Among the Illinois delegation, the Chicago delegates seemed to be subjected to the greatest pressures. The Chicago regular organization under the leadership of Mayor Jane Byrne reportedly exerted considerable pressure to gain votes for the Kennedy position. The Mayor and some of her lieutenants even flew to New York and took charge personally of some of the effort. Carter leaders on the other side were also offering their own inducements to keep their delegates in line.

In the end the major coalitions held in the open-convention fight. In a dramatic moment on Monday night the roll call was taken. The Carter forces voted in favor of rule F 3 (c) (and thus against the "open convention") by 1936 to 1391. This was almost exactly the same as the 60-40 percent delegate line-up the Carter and Kennedy forces had in the convention. As was pointed out above, the Illinois delegation voted overwhelmingly with Carter—losing only 10 votes as crossovers. These 10 votes presumably came from Chicago, but they represented a remarkable defeat for Mayor Byrne. The once proud and powerful Chicago machine demonstrated again that it could no longer deliver. Mayor Daley was gone indeed. The results of the Illinois primary plus the events in Madison Square Garden also demonstrated that no local bastions remain untouched by the larger national forces. Even though the Carter-oriented team had won this battle, it was one more step in losing the larger war. The rift in the convention was immediately apparent this first night, and it did not go away during that week or in the subsequent campaign.

The Convention

This brings the discussion to the convention arena itself. Madison Square Garden, New York City, in 1976 had been the scene of Jimmy Carter's greatest political victory up to that time. In August of 1980 it was to be the scene of one of his greatest political humiliations. It was also, unknown to him and his supporters at that time, symptomatic of the hard times to come.

As was indicated above, ceremony and debate over Rule F 3 (c) dominated the Sunday night and Monday meeting. During Tuesday and Wednesday the Carter-Mondale forces knew they had the votes to win the nomination itself. The rule F 3 (c) battle had settled that matter. The objectives then became two-fold. They had to get a platform which would not embarrass Carter by repudiating many of his past positions and policies. In addition, they needed to achieve at least the image of party unity. Those objectives were sought in the debates on the platform and in every movement, every word that emanated from the stage. The debate on the platform was long and hard but in the end the Carter-Mondale forces got a platform which they could largely live with. The president disavowed (in writing thanks to a new rule) three specific planks of the platform. Much of the rhetoric and some of the actions during that platform fight, however, clearly indicated the depths of the president's problems in such areas as jobs and the economy. The Republicans adopted their platform in one afternoon with only the merest hint of dissent about ERA and federal judges. The Democrats fought for two days and nights with the omnipresent television cameras carrying it all to the American public.

The Carter quest for the image of unity was finally lost irrevocably during the Kennedy speech of Tuesday night and Kennedy's actions on the podium on Thursday night. No matter how jaded, or Carter oriented, one could not help but be impressed with many delegates' emotional reaction to Kennedy's ringing declarations of the Old Time Religion for the Democratic party. Some said it was his finest speech ever. This author remembered another one very much like it was given in Memphis at the Mid-Term Conference two years earlier where this whole season began. It might also be worth noting that the quest for the 1984 nomination may well have begun on that Tuesday night in mid-August, 1980, in New York.

Thursday night, by contrast, was to have been Jimmy Carter's night. The long trail had ended for the second time. Kennedy, Brown, LaRouche, fatigue, cynicism, the liberals, the media, the odds, and a host of other adversaries had finally been beaten. It was all over once again. The roll call would be a formality. The speech would be a climax. The triumphant handshakes and victory signs with all the supporters and beaten rivals would be the successful conclusion. The victorious candidate could then rest a few days, get back to being president, and turn toward the greater threat of Ronald Reagan and the Republicans.

All the party professionals, the media and the interested public know the script. The wounds must be bound up, healed, or at least papered over so the general election campaign can be fought with one's own party under the tent. Unfortunately for Carter, someone forgot to give that script to Kennedy. One could hardly have staged an event better designed to do greater damage to an already damaged presidential image than the famous "handshaking" episode between Carter and Kennedy on Thursday. Carter practically chased Kennedy around the box. Kennedy's disdain was there for the world to see. The Democratic party was not united; it was divided as always. The unity was a facade—and it vanished in subsequent days. Carter's problem of "looking presidential" was exacerbated. It was the beginning of the presidential general election and the beginning of the end for Jimmy Carter. On November 4, 1980, Illinois, like the nation, voted overwhelmingly for Ronald Reagan to become the 40th president of the United States.

Chapter 3 The 1980 Republican Presidential Primary in Illinois: A Challenging Barrier

James D. Nowlan

The presidential election process has been described as "a marathon obstacle course that consumes time, money, and humans like some insatiable furnace," as a race in which "nearly all stick it out as long as money, physical endurance, and emotional stability last, and the dream of success is not overwhelmed by the reality of failure."[1] Each state's primary, caucus, or convention is a barrier along the course. The barrier presented by Illinois is higher, wider, and deeper than most.

This chapter will analyze the part Illinois played in this process in the 1980 running of the presidential sweepstakes. Such an analysis is best achieved by viewing Illinois as an integral part of a larger process, rather than as a distinctly separate, insulated arena of political activity. Indeed, as will doubtless become clear, the electoral outcome in the Illinois Republican presidential primary seems to have been affected much more by what preceded the Illinois primary than by what transpired within the state during the fleeting two weeks from the Massachusetts primary on March 4 to that in Illinois on March 18—two weeks during which the national spotlight focused briefly on the Prairie State.

In any major political contest, candidates and strategists sketch various prospective scenarios according to which their candidate can win, or may lose. The strategists attempt to shape winning scenarios. The longer the odds against a candidate—that is, the more limited the initial basic resources of people, money, skill, and time at the beginning of the contest—the fewer the winning scenarios imaginable.

The primaries are now crucial in presidential nominating politics. Since 1956 the winning candidates of both parties have amassed enough votes prior to each convention that there was little doubt about its outcome.[2] More than 70 percent of the delegates to the major party conventions are now selected through primaries.

The Illinois primary has become more important than most presidential primaries both because candidates and the press perceive it to be so, and for good demographic, sequential, and structural reasons:

1. Illinois is the first populous, heterogeneous state to be contested. Some scholars consider Illinois to be a kind of microcosm of the nation; it nearly always gives its electoral votes to the ultimate winner.
2. The ninety-two GOP delegates elected in 1980 were the first large bloc to be chosen.
3. Coming ninth in order of Republican primaries, Illinois is an expensive media-oriented state in which only those candidates with momentum or a continuing supply of money can compete.
4. Illinois is one of the few states where it is easy for independents and Democrats to cross over to the minority Republican party ballot. This is considered an important test of a Republican's appeal to those constituencies necessary for success in the general elections.

For these reasons, each Republican candidate in 1980 targeted Illinois in his plans. Illinois congressmen Philip Crane and John B. Anderson felt that "doing better than expected" in the New England primaries and coming in first, or certainly no less than second, in Illinois were essential to their long-shot scenarios. Senator Howard Baker called Illinois pivotal, "where the horses turn the corner after they've gotten out of the starting gate."[3] Bush hoped to defeat Reagan in Illinois in a major confrontation and to generate momentum for the remaining primaries. *Illinois Issues* reported that all candidates pointed to Illinois as the place where Reagan had to be stopped, if he had not been slowed down in earlier contests.[4] Since Reagan had greater total financial and people resources than other candidates, one state like Illinois was not so critical to his ultimate success; nevertheless, a solid win in Illinois could knock most or all of his competitors out of the race. As the *New York Times* put it: "Resounding victories for Reagan and Carter [in Illinois] would leave their opponents with little breathing room, even with the convention months away."[5]

"Invisible" and "Blind" Primaries

Modern presidential campaigns begin years in advance of the election. Arthur Hadley believes that most nominees are determined during an "invisible primary" which precedes the New Hampshire primary:

Far from being decisive politically, the primaries appear more as a ritual encounter, a symbolic show whose results reinforce a victory already decided. That is why candidates were on the road for 1976 as early as 1973. History proves them right. Modern political polling began in 1936. Since then, the active candidate who ranks as most popular within his own party in the Gallup Poll taken over the month before the New Hampshire primary has won his party's nomination 85 percent of the time.[6]

Philip Crane was the first candidate to announce for the 1980 presidential nomination, in August 1978. Crane, Bush, Connally, and Reagan had actually been at work speaking, fund raising, and planning long before that. In early January 1979, nearly two years before the election, John Anderson sat down with his key aides to discuss the formation of a presidential exploratory committee. Nevertheless, the effort was characterized by the strategists as an "extremely late start."

This period which precedes the Iowa caucuses and New Hampshire primary is virtually unnoticed by the public, but it is watched closely by political columnists, party leaders, political consultants, and readers of the *New York Times* and *Washington Post*. These participants can bestow or withhold the initial credibility so critical to successful fund raising and media attention, both of which further enhance credibility.

During the invisible primary a candidate works to enlist to his cause the longest list possible of prominent party leaders, elected officials, established contributors and fund raisers, and veteran strategists. These supporter lists become the rough measures by which the national political columnists and senior reporters begin to establish the odds in the race. These odds are reflected in the amount of attention given the respective candidates by the media.

In turn, the more mentions and feature stories a candidate receives the more successful he becomes in adding to his stable of supporters and in fund raising. Near the end of the invisible primary the actual dollar amounts raised become indicators to all observers of credibility and success.

In addition to this invisible primary, Illinois in 1979 created another interesting but difficult hurdle for presidential hopefuls, the so-called blind primary. House Bill 2618 was introduced into the Illinois General Assembly on April 6, 1979, by Representative Edward McBroom, the GOP county chairman of downstate Kankakee County. The bill would simply have prohibited the use of any nicknames on the election ballot that implied that a candidate possessed some title, degree, or professional status. It was considered by several legislators on the house elections committee to be a "shell bill," i.e., a bill that could be used at a later time as a vehicle for an amendment of greater substance. The shell bill passed the House on May 21 on a unanimous roll call.

The Senate sponsor for HB 2618 was James (Pate) Philip, like McBroom a Republican county chairman, of suburban DuPage County. On June 22, 1979, eight days before expected adjournment of the spring session of the legislature, Philip offered an amendment to his bill which would allow a party state central committee to preclude the listing on the ballot of presidential candidate preferences by the national convention delegate candidates. In other words, the electorate would be blind about whom the delegate candidate would support at the national convention.

Several reasons were given for seeking this option. Republican state central committee leaders said it would allow Illinois to take an uncommitted delegation of experienced party leaders to the national convention in Detroit. Philip said it would enhance Governor James R. Thompson's chances of being selected as the vice-presidential nominee. Thompson noted that it did not make much sense to require delegate candidates to declare a preference in December 1979 (prior to the January 21, 1980 filing deadline) for presidential candidates who might not even be in the race by the Illinois primary, or by the national convention. Moreover, by allowing delegate candidates to designate their presidential preferences on the ballot, many political unknowns displaced party leaders who ran as "uncommitted" or who designated less popular presidential candidates. For example, in 1976 Congressman Philip Crane, who designated Reagan, was defeated in his delegate bid by a less-well-known candidate who designated President Ford. Experience showed that prior to 1972 when the designations were first allowed, Republican congressmen were invariably elected delegates since they had the highest name recognition in their districts.

In addition to these public reasons for the blind primary bill, there was a not so public one. Governor Thompson and his advisors had determined that everything possible should be done to block Governor Reagan's nomination. The advisors felt Reagan could not win the election if nominated. While Thompson proclaimed strict neutrality during the invisible primary period, it appeared that he and numerous party leaders felt John Connally was both attractive and most likely to emerge as the major alternative to Reagan. This, however, would not be determined before delegate candidates were required to file their petitions in January 1980.

The answer to the dilemma was the blind primary. Under this system, well-known party leaders, many of whom were impressed by Connally and nearly all of whom favored some alternative to Reagan, would have much better chances for election than under the designated system. Conversely, Reagan delegate candidates, most of whom were not expected to be well known to voters would have greater difficulty being elected in a blind primary. Furthermore, should Connally not emerge successful, an uncommitted delegation of party leaders would be able to broker in behalf of a non-Reagan candidate and in behalf of Illinois interests.

With the help of seven Democratic votes, Philip got the amended HB 2618 out of the Senate with the bare minimum of thirty votes necessary for passage. Pro-Reagan senators David Regner and Mark Rhoads vigorously opposed the bill, which still had to go back to the House for concurrence in the blind primary amendment. Pro-Reagan Republican forces in the House, led by Donald Totten and Philip W. Collins, felt they had generated enough opposition to deny the bill the eighty-nine votes needed to send it to the governor. As a reflection of the governor's determination to achieve the blind primary, however, his aides requested support from the Democratic House leadership. More than twenty Democrats were included among the ninety-four votes in support of the blind primary on the concurrence motion on June 30, even though Democratic National Committee rules prohibited their party from ever invoking such an option.

This legislation added a new challenge for presidential candidates. In addition to winning the advisory "beauty contest" at the top of the ticket and electing delegate slates, they now needed to recruit delegate candidates with high name recognition in the respective congressional districts. This new task was all the more difficult in 1979 for unproved candidates such as Bush and Anderson. Well-known Republican politicos who wanted to be in the Illinois delegation as well as with a winner hesitated to commit themselves prematurely to anyone with little chance of success.

In the blind primaries that were traditional prior to 1972, GOP party organizations in most congressional districts would get together and endorse delegate slates. Few slates were challenged. In 1979–80, wherever a prospective party slate appeared unfavorably disposed to a candidate, that candidate's campaign tried to recruit delegate candidates on its own. For example, the Reagan campaign went along with the regular organization slate in the Fourth District, filed a partial slate in the Third, and a complete Reagan slate in the neighboring Seventeenth District, using well-known state legislators as candidates wherever possible.

The Connally campaign claimed forty-two committed delegate candidates, including many well-known persons such as Cook County GOP Chairman J. Robert Barr and Illinois Senate Minority Leader David Shapiro. In addition, at least thirty uncommitted party organization candidates were considered strongly in favor of Connally, should he do well in the primaries.

The Bush campaign organized late in Illinois, in the fall of 1979, and found few big names willing to commit to him, as the invisible primary momentum then belonged to Connally. Nevertheless, most candidates for delegate found Bush at least acceptable. Therefore, their strategy became one of working with the party organizations, on the premise that nearly all the delegate candidates, uncommitted and committed, would support Bush after the primary, should he emerge as the dominant alternative to Reagan.

Anderson faced the greatest challenge. With only 300 names on his Illinois mailing list in the fall of 1979, Anderson's state campaign manager Jeanne Bradner had few from whom to choose; most were little known to the voters. Several active liberal Republican women eschewed candidacy out of concern that a commitment to a "can't win" maverick might affect their own political futures. Even so, forty-four delegate candidates were filed by the Anderson campaign.

The Primary Campaigns

The Illinois Republican presidential primary was but part of the national campaign. Campaign staffs were selected and directed by the national headquarters; dollars, candidate appearances, and major paid media were controlled from the national offices. Success in Illinois was heavily dependent on successes generated in earlier primaries; indeed, even participation in Illinois depended on those earlier primaries. Dole, Baker, and Connally had run out of money and voters prior to Illinois; they had formally withdrawn, though their names remained on the ballot.

Bush, who upset Reagan in the January 21 Iowa caucuses, had early momentum, and for a short time the phones were ringing off the wall in the offices of Illinois Bush coordinator George Kangas. Then Reagan rebounded in New Hampshire on February 26 by getting as many votes as the other six candidates combined. Illinois interest in Bush plummeted.

The national media spotlight rapidly shifted away from Texan Bush, who was also losing badly in southern states to Reagan. After Bush's drubbing in New Hampshire, former President Gerald Ford even suggested that he himself might be available to challenge Reagan. He took himself out of consideration the weekend before the Illinois vote, however, leaving the field clear for Reagan and his only two remaining challengers, Bush and Anderson.

Meanwhile Anderson had startled everyone the week following the New Hampshire primary by running second to Bush in a photo finish in Massachusetts, 31.3 percent to 31.0 percent, and losing to Reagan by a nose in Vermont, 31 percent to 30 percent. Suddenly, the small two-person Anderson office in Illinois was overwhelmed by volunteers and was hard pressed to add phone lines quickly enough to unjam the circuits. According to Jeanne Bradner, "The whole place erupted; it was crazy. All of a sudden, the press beseiged me with requests for background interviews." As a result of doing much better than expected, direct mail contributions came pouring in at $150,000 per day, in contrast to a total of $456,000 raised in all of 1979.[7]

Reagan, and then Anderson, were the cover stories in advance of Illinois' March 18 primary. The *Chicago Sun-Times* published a poll the week before the Illinois election showing Anderson leading Reagan; Bush was trailing badly. This created great expectations which Anderson was now obliged to achieve in his home state.

The Illinois campaign operations and volunteers had little to do with all this. The momentum, the expectations, the visibility were all transmitted by the national television networks, news magazines, and news services. Illinois was a part of the national electorate and would step forward in its turn on March 18. In the two weeks between Massachusetts and Illinois there was little time for candidates to meet Illinois voters directly other than through limited appearances scheduled primarily for the benefit of the traveling national media.

Meanwhile the Illinois-based campaign operations of the presidential candidates were focusing most of their efforts on electing delegates in the blind primary. Here was an important, tangible task, dealing with real people living in Illinois, to which the armies of volunteers could direct their energies. Here traditional grass roots organizing and communications could have an impact.

The Anderson campaign provides a good case in point. In those suburban Chicago congressional districts where there were full Anderson slates, Anderson volunteers raised their own funds (there were none available from the national campaign) in order to print sample ballots and brochures identifying their slates and to communicate this information to as many voters as possible. The Ninth District (Chicago's North Side) Anderson volunteers held a "My Heart Belongs to JBA" Valentine's Day fund raiser at a popular restaurant. In the north suburban Tenth District Anderson volunteers distributed 400,000 pieces of delegate identification literature and defeated such well-known names as former Secretary of Defense Donald Rumsfeld and popular former state senator Bradley Glass.

The Reagan campaign conducted an even more thorough and effective delegate identification campaign, utilizing a large statewide network of committed volunteers.

These campaign efforts were aided by a strong reaction among voters offended by the absence of delegate presidential preferences on the Republican ballot—information that was available on the Democratic ballot. "The blind primary backfired on its perpetrators," declared state representative Philip W. Collins, a Reagan campaign official. "Our offices were deluged with calls from outraged voters wanting to know our delegate candidates." Anderson manager Bradner concurred: "We could never get enough phones to handle all the calls from people who wanted to know our delegate slates."

Results and Conseqences from Illinois

Governor Thompson and other Illinois GOP leaders did not achieve their original objective of taking an uncommitted delegation to Detroit. Indeed, even with the impediment of the blind primary, Reagan and Anderson elected delegates not far short of the numbers they would have been apportioned under pure statewide proportional representation. As table 3.1 indicates, Reagan won the Illinois primary decisively, taking nearly half of the 1.17 million votes cast, capturing forty of the ninety-two delegates elected, and probably persuading many of the twenty-one uncommitted delegate winners. Anderson made his strongest showing yet in terms of percentage of the vote, garnering 37 percent and winning twenty-six delegates, but this was disappointingly short of the *Sun-Times* poll that had suggested he might win. Bush ran a poor third, with 11 percent of the vote.

Consequently, Governor Thompson and such Republican leaders as national committeeman Harold Byron Smith, Jr., were forced to negotiate with the cohesive Reagan forces at the May 10 state convention and within the delegation itself. Several Reaganites, including their leader Don Totten (who had been defeated in his delegate race by Anderson candidates), were appointed to coveted at-large delegate seats. Moreover, Reagan delegates defeated a move by Governor Thompson, the delegation chairman, to have Anderson delegate and campaign manager Jeanne Bradner appointed to the national platform committee.

Another interesting aspect of the 1980 Republican primary was the fact that the turnout was the largest since 1952. Table 3.2 suggests that a substantial number of people who might have voted in the Democratic primary in earlier years crossed over to participate in the interesting Republican contest. Almost identical numbers of voters went to the primary polls in 1976 and 1980, yet Democratic turnout decreased by more than 340,000 while Republican participation increased by 360,000.

According to a *New York Times*/CBS "exit poll" taken after voters had cast their ballots, 46 percent of the Republican vote comprised "crossovers," i.e., people who had not voted in the preceding Republican primary. Anderson won a majority of the crossovers polled, but Reagan took about 30 percent of these

Table 3.1

Republican Presidential Primary in Illinois, March 1980

	Preference Vote	Percent of Vote	Delegates Won	Hypothetical Apportionment by PR
Reagan	547,355	48	40	44
Anderson	415,193	37	26	34
Bush	124,057	11	2	10
Crane	24,865	2	3	2
Others	18,611	2	0	2
Uncommitted			21	. . .
Total Elected			92	92

SOURCE: Illinois State Board of Elections

Table 3.2

Presidential Primary Election Turnouts in Illinois

	Total Votes Cast	Democratic Vote	Republican Vote	Republican Vote as Percent of Total Vote
1964	2,154,941	1,062,320	1,092,621	51%
1968	1,573,173	833,498	739,675	47%
1972	2,228,605	1,563,193	665,412	30%
1976	2,480,243	1,668,745	811,498	33%
1980	2,493,518	1,321,810	1,171,708	47%

SOURCE: Illinois State Board of Elections

Table 3.3

Distribution of Candidate Votes in the 1980 Republican Primary

	Total Vote	%	Downstate[a] Vote	%	Collar Cos.[b] Vote	%	Chicago Vote	%
Reagan	547,355	100	300,495	55	214,267	39	32,593	6
Anderson	415,193	100	140,681	34	218,296	52	56,216	14
Bush	124,057	100	57,576	46	58,535	47	7,946	6

SOURCE: Illinois State Board of Elections

[a]Downstate: Ninety-six counties outside metropolitan Chicago.

[b]Collar Counties: DuPage, Kane, Lake, McHenry, Will and the thirty townships of Cook.

voters. The *New York Times* of March 19 reported that Reagan took three out of five of the regular Republican primary voters.

As Everson and Parker have suggested, Illinois may have convinced Anderson that he could not win the GOP nomination but that he had wide appeal among ticket-splitters.[8] Table 3.3 shows that Anderson carried the Chicago suburbs where ticket splitting is high, and Chicago. In the remainder of downstate Illinois he was thrashed by Reagan.

Even before the Illinois primary, Anderson supporters in the East had been urging an independent or third-party candidacy. By the end of March Anderson stopped ruling out such a bid; one month later he abandoned his quest for the GOP nomination and began exploring the independent candidacy.

If the importance of a primary can be measured by the intensity of the rhetoric from the national press, then Illinois was very important. The *New York Times* reported that, ''As the first major testing ground in the industrial Midwest, Illinois was an important, perhaps decisive, prize for both President Carter and Ronald

Reagan."[9] In the immediate wake of Illinois, *Time* reported that, "Suddenly the primary campaign seems about over, and it looks like Carter v. Reagan."[10] The same issue of the magazine went on to quote prominent pollster Lance Tarrance, who talked about Illinois as a kind of threshold to the nomination: "This is one of the most clear cut races we've had in a decade. It's like a Monopoly game. Once Reagan passed Illinois, he passed Go!"

Conversely, as the *New York Times* said, "Bush's poor showing left him severely damaged, especially since he had planned to emerge from the Illinois race as Mr. Reagan's chief competitor."[11]

Another measure of the importance candidates attached to Illinois is reflected in state-by-state expenditures. Anderson spent more of his limited funds in Illinois than in any other primary state, while Bush spent more than $1 million. Anderson's strategy of focusing on New England states and Illinois while bypassing the South is reflected in expenditures as shown in table 3.4.

Delegation Voting and Behavior at the Convention

The Illinois delegation comprised the largest bloc of Anderson delegates and was headed by two prominent moderates, Governor James R. Thompson and Senator Charles H. Percy. Nevertheless, these combined forces were unsuccessful in their efforts to moderate the Republican platform.

Table 3.4
Candidate Expenditures in the First Four Major Primary Elections in 1980

	New Hampshire (February 26)	Massachusetts (March 4)	Florida (March 11)	Illinois (March 18)
Federal Limit	$294,000	$1,001,666	$1,562,204	$1,883,453
Anderson	246,395	433,336	500	646,726
Baker	268,764	274,966	82,499	191,201
Bush	240,448	752,757	1,257,552	1,206,824
Connally[a]	. . .	. . .	. . .	. . .
Crane	133,916	164,620	114,982	157,527
Dole	96,453	335	3,695	1,853
Reagan	279,321	591,745	1,168,779	669,217

SOURCE: Federal Election Commission, July 1980
[a]Connally did not participate in the federal matching fund program, and thus was not bound by federal limits or state by state reporting requirements.

As the nomination of Reagan was a foregone conclusion, the Illinois Anderson bloc of twenty-three delegates focused its energies toward amending the platform planks on the Equal Rights Amendment, abortion, appointment of federal judges, and urban policies.

Drawing upon the analogy of the Americans who were held hostage at that time in Iran, Anderson's bloc leader declared at the convention "they were holding their votes for Reagan hostage, in return for changes in the platform."[12] Their objective was not to further the campaign of Anderson, who was by then an announced independent candidate. When interviewed, Bradner and other Illinois Anderson delegates emphasized their desire to represent the moderate wing within the Republican party.

Before the full convention would consider opening a proposed platform plank to debate and a roll-call vote, rules required that three state delegations request such action. Thus the Anderson bloc requested and received from delegation chairman Thompson the opportunity for an Illinois caucus on the four platform topics of concern to them.

For three hours the Illinois delegates debated the topics openly. Percy sided with the Anderson bloc on all the issues and became a highly visible opponent to the proposed plank that sought to delimit appointment of federal judges to those "who respect traditional family values and the sanctity of innocent human life." Thompson concurred in Percy's position and joined the Anderson delegates in their efforts to garner platform support for the ERA and to reject the plank that called for an antiabortion amendment to the United States Constitution; the governor did not support the Anderson bloc desire to reconvene the platform committee to address urban problems, poverty, health, and crime.

All four proposals to open the platform were soundly defeated in the caucus. The closest margin was a 62–37 vote against opening the ERA issue for debate and roll-call vote on the floor.

Percy and the Anderson group were unable to convince other states to support what Illinois had rejected. The platform as proposed by the platform committee was adopted overwhelmingly by the convention on a single voice vote.

Even though John Anderson's name was never placed in nomination, twenty-one Illinois delegates cast their votes for the announced independent candidate. This was done as "a symbolic vote . . . to protest [the fact that] there is no room for moderates in the party," said Jeanne Bradner, leader of the Anderson delegates.[13]

Some Assessments

Blind primaries can now see. The assumption that people would not know whom they were voting for in the delegate races was incorrect to a large extent. While it was true that all nine Republican congressmen who ran were elected delegates, many well-known legislators and other party leaders were beaten by unknowns who ran in behalf of Reagan or Anderson. Anderson delegates tended to win where Anderson also won the preferential vote; the same was true for Reagan.

Conventional wisdom among Illinois political observers has held that political party elites will be represented more heavily in delegations selected in truly blind primaries than in those where presidential preferences are identified, whether by formal designation or by aggressive political marketing, as in 1980. As reflected in table 3.5, limited opportunities for comparison suggest this may not prove to be true. Should there be any blind primaries in the future, it can be expected that potentially strong presidential candidates and well-known politicos, i.e., party elites, will try to match with one another in marriages of mutual advantage.

Early designation of preference is hazardous. As Thompson argued, it makes little sense to state a presidential preference prior to the January 21 deadline for 1980 for delegate petition filing, for candidates who might not be in the race in March. Indeed, Dole, Baker, and Connally had withdrawn by the Illinois primary and Crane was out of the running, even though he had not withdrawn publicly.

Illinois law schedules the primary on the third Tuesday in March. Delegate candidates must file no later than sixty-two days before the primary. This two-

Table 3.5
Political Elites in Elected Delegations to Republican National Conventions[a]

Year	Type of Primary	No. Elected	No. Elites	% of Elites
1960	Blind	50	25	50
1964	Blind	48	15	31
1968	Blind	48	29	60
1972[b]	Designated Preference	48	24	50
1976	Designated Preference	96	33	34
1980	Blind	92	40	43

[a]Party elite defined here as persons sitting as members of Congress, elected state officials, state legislators, state central committeemen, county chairmen, and ward and township committeemen in Cook County.

[b]Richard M. Nixon was the uncontested candidate in 1972. Party organizations slated two candidates who designated Nixon in every district and there were no contests, so this primary election is not indicative of any differences that might occur between designated and blind primaries.

month period cannot be shortened appreciably, as absentee ballots must be available at least forty-five days in advance of the primary date.

Prior to 1970, the Illinois primary had been held in June. A later primary date would make it easier for experienced party leaders and other prospective delegates to designate viable preferences, but Illinois' impact on the nominating process would be diminished.

There is no Illinois Republican primary as such. There is a national primary process of which Illinois is an important component. What preceded Illinois was more important to the outcome in Illinois than what transpired within the state itself.

Political participation has intensified. There appears to be a more intense participatory ethic, at least among those who do participate, than existed prior to 1972. Of course, the process is also more extended than it used to be. The 1980 Illinois primary was held before the time when in 1952 General Eisenhower had even decided to become a candidate. Thus there is now more opportunity for participation. Nevertheless, in this day of weakened party identification there is greater willingness to challenge local party organizations by mounting, and winning, delegate campaigns against party slates.

The vehement public outrage at the blind primary is another manifestation of this participatory ethic. Even though the designated primary had been used in Illinois only in 1972 and 1976 in recent memory, the denial of information about candidate preference generated an angry reaction that GOP politicians clearly felt. Within two weeks after the March 18 primary three bills were introduced or amended by House Republicans to repeal the blind primary. Governor Thompson announced he would sign into law a repeal of the blind primary option.[14] Two of these measures passed, by votes of 130–1 and 145–0, respectively, but became stuck in Senate committee, kept there by the Democratic majority which enjoyed seeing the Republican leaders discomfited by their miscalculation.

It is a safe bet that Illinois Republicans will not hold another blind primary in 1984.

★ ★ ★ ▬▬▬▬▬▬▬▬▬▬▬▬▬▬▬▬▬▬▬▬

★ ★ ★ ▬▬▬▬▬▬▬▬▬▬▬▬▬▬▬▬▬▬▬▬

★ ★ ★ ▬▬▬▬▬▬▬▬▬▬▬▬▬▬▬▬▬▬▬▬

Chapter 4 The National Conventions of 1980

Paul T. David

As almost everyone knows, the Republican National Convention met in Detroit in July and the Democratic National Convention met in New York City in August of 1980.[1]

The Republican decision to meet in Detroit was controversial; it passed by a vote of ninety-five to fifty-two in the Republican National Committee. Members from the South and the West, the more conservative parts of the country, were opposed. Bill Brock, the national committee chairman, favored Detroit as part of his effort to broaden the appeal of the Republican party for blacks and blue collar workers.[2] In any event, the choice of Detroit seems to have worked out successfully, although several state delegations had to be housed in Windsor, Ontario, and others were in hotels quite distant from the convention center.

The choice of New York City by the Democrats was much easier, although four other cities were bidding for the convention. The facilities were considerably more ample in New York than elsewhere and certainly more adequate than in Detroit, which became the main other contender.[3] The hotel and convention hall facilities in New York proved to be excellent, and the New York City police had less trouble with demonstrations around the convention center than they had expected.

The choice of dates in July and August was not accidental. Both parties have learned by experience to avoid the dates on which the Olympic Games are held. There has never been any definite agreement between the parties on which will go first, according to Josephine Good, the long-time staff expert on conventions at the Republican National Committee. But there seems to be a tacit understanding that the party out of power will be the first to hold its convention, since it needs more time in which to prepare its campaign. That custom prevailed in the arrangements in 1980.

Both conventions were held pursuant to calls which had been sent out to the states by their respective national committees. Both calls specified the number of delegates and alternates allocated to each state and reproduced the complex rules under which these numbers had been determined. Both parties have greatly increased their numbers of delegates in recent years, with all the complications that result.

The Republicans have been more conservative than the Democrats in increasing their numbers, but the totals for both parties are formidable—just short of 4000 for the Republicans and more than 5400 for the Democrats, as table 4.1 shows.

The conventions of the two parties differed not only in size but also in composition. The Republican convention, as usual, was mainly white, Anglo Saxon, and Protestant, with few blacks, ethnics, or Catholics. Undoubtedly the ideological right was heavily represented. The Democratic convention was more diversified, with many more blacks, substantial representation from the major ethnic groups in the American population, and large contingents of Catholics and Jews.

Under new rules of the Democratic party in effect in 1980, each state was required to allot half of its places to women, and this rule was generally enforced. Every state was also required to pursue an affirmative action plan to assure adequate representation of blacks and other minorities. Table 4.2 reflects some of the major differences in the composition of the two conventions, including the emergence of the teachers in the National Education Association as an influential minority in the Democratic party.

Public interest in the two national party conventions generally centers on the selection of the candidates for president and vice president but this year, except for the choice of Ronald Reagan's running mate, most of the suspense was attached to other actions. The first-ballot nominating vote for Reagan at the convention, a nearly unanimous 97 percent, was a foregone conclusion. In effect, the lengthy procedures of the nominating process before the convention, with the

Table 4.1
Size of the 1980 National Conventions

	Republican National Convention	Democratic National Convention
Full vote delegates	1994	3224
Part vote delegates	. . .	159 (107 votes)
Alternate delegates	1994	2053
Totals	3998	5436

SOURCE: The calls for the conventions as supplemented by later sources. Democratic rules provide for a smaller number of alternates than delegates.

Table 4.2
Composition of the 1980 National Conventions

	Republican National Convention	Democratic National Convention
Women	29%	50%
Blacks	3	14
Hispanics	?	6
NEA members	?	9
Other union members	?	6–9

SOURCES: *New York Times*, August 11, 1980, p. B3 and other news reports.

media amplication of the results of state primaries, had foreclosed the action at the convention.

Weeks before the Democratic convention met, it had become clear that the front runner, President Carter, had more than enough votes to insure his nomination, but his determined opponent within the party, Senator Ted Kennedy, refused to concede defeat. The contest between them was finally settled in the fierce battle over the rules which took place—during prime viewing time—on the first evening of the convention.

The nominating campaigns are discussed at greater length in a previous chapter by Professor William J. Crotty of Northwestern University. Here we are mainly concerned with the other functions of the conventions, of which there are at least three in addition to the nominating function. These have been defined, initially in my own writing of twenty years ago, as the "governing body function," the "platform drafting function," and the "campaign rally function."[4] It is through the governing body function, which includes the drafting and enforcement of party rules, that the conventions largely control the nominating process. The platform drafting process is obvious enough as a distinct activity, and has been going on in national party conventions since the Democratic national convention of 1840. The campaign rally function has been implicit in convention organization and behavior ever since the decision was made, in preparation for the election of 1832, to hold the party conventions as public gatherings with the press in attendance.

The Governing Body Function in 1980

The governing body function was illustrated most specifically in 1980 by the contest over the Report of the Rules Committee at the Democratic national convention, which occupied the attention of press and public for weeks before the convention met, and in the early roll call vote on binding delegates.

Action on Rules by the Democratic Convention

In recent years, the Democratic party has organized to conduct as much of its convention committee work as possible several weeks before the actual meeting of the convention. The committee on rules was therefore scheduled to meet in Washington, D.C., on July 8 and 9, 1980, and did so. The committee reviewed the accumulation of rules that has come out of various reform efforts of the Democratic party since 1968, most recently from the Winograd Commission of 1976–78, and added a few new ideas of its own in preparing a comprehensive report to the convention. This was printed and mailed to the delegates in advance of the convention.

The most important issue with which the rules committee was confronted had come out of the Winograd Commission in 1978 and had been approved by the Democratic National Committee without much concern or argument in either forum. This was a new provision, which read as follows:

> (c) All delegates to the National Convention shall be bound to vote for the presidential candidate whom they were elected to support for at least the first Convention ballot, unless released in writing by the presidential candidate. Delegates who seek to violate this rule may be replaced with an alternate of the same presidential preference by the presidential candidate or that candidate's authorized representative(s) at any time up to and including the presidential balloting at the National Convention.[5]

This provision became objectionable to the Kennedy supporters when it became apparent at the close of the primary season that the senator could only be nominated if several hundred Carter delegates could be persuaded to change their votes. The issue was argued in terms of freedom of conscience and the virtues of an open convention on the one hand, and the values inherent in carrying out the mandate given by the voters on the other, but the political significance of the issue was clear to all. After the debate was over in the rules committee, the Carter forces won by a vote of 87.25 to 65.5, a vote that closely followed the representation of Carter and Kennedy people on the committee, a proportionate representation that was itself required by the reformed rules of the Democratic party.[6]

The Kennedy people thereafter filed a minorty report on the issue. After intensive negotiations between Kennedy and Carter representatives on the scheduling of this and other controversial issues, it was agreed that one hour of debate on the issue would take place at 6:30 p.m. on the first evening of the convention, Monday, August 11. This assured that the vote would be in prime time with a maximum television audience. In the debate, all of the previous arguments were repeated by prominent party members. The roll call vote followed and was won decisively by the Carter forces, 1936.42 to 1390.58[7] (see table 4.3). The regional breakdown of the vote shows the Kennedy forces winning heavily in the Northeast and also winning in the West, mainly because of California, but losing heavily in the Middle West and even more so in the South.

Carter had come to the convention with 1981.1 committed delegate votes to Kennedy's 1225.8. The vote on the rule to bind delegates followed the split in delegate commitments, with possibly as many as 50 Carter delegates defecting. The Kennedy people apparently picked up 10 Carter delegates from Illinois and 11 from Pennsylvania, and they were also supported by most of the 122 uncommitted delegates,[8] who were probably the only members of the convention who were voting the issue on its merits. For the most part the vote was a clear power struggle. A Carter victory had been assumed by most observers before the event, but the size of the victory was a surprise, in view of the previous claims of the Kennedy people.

Several other minority reports on the rules were filed by the Kennedy people and were carried in the printed report of the rules committee. Most of these were withdrawn or compromised by agreement, but the Carter people conceded on one Kennedy proposal that was important and controversial. This was a proposed rule under which each proposed nominee would be required to submit "a written statement of views on the approved Platform; including a pledge to carry out the recommendations and fulfill the principles contained therein, along with any reservations to specific provisions."[9] This written statement was to be provided after the platform had been approved and before the nominating procedure was initiated. The provision was obviously intended to embarrass

Table 4.3
The Vote by Regions on Minority Rules Report No. 5

Region	Yes, to Adopt (Kennedy)	No, to Defeat (Carter)	Abstain
Northeast	57.9%	42.0%	0.1%
Middle West	37.6	62.4	. . .
South	19.5	80.5	. . .
West	51.6	47.9	0.5
Other Areas	46.5	53.5	. . .
Total Convention	41.7	58.1	0.2

SOURCE: Calculated from *Congressional Quarterly Weekly Report,* August 16, 1980, p. 2437.

President Carter, but he agreed to it anyhow and the convention accepted it.

Thereafter the action on the rules committee report was routine, but in this process some important proposals for the future were adopted. Provision was made for another midterm party conference like those of 1974 and 1978, to be held in December 1982, with at least a full day of plenary debate and adoption of policy resolutions. This continues a recent practice that was first recommended by a group of political scientists in 1950 and which was approached initially by the party with considerable timidity. It now seems to be agreed that midterm conferences do no harm, although they may not be as helpful as their sponsors had hoped.

The most important future-looking provision, however, was a set of instructions for the Executive Committee of the Democratic National Committee, a regionally diverse body of about thirty members. The committee was told to consider the implications of the anticipated decision by the United States Supreme Court in the case of *Democratic Party of United States v. La Follette*. In this case, the State of Wisconsin has challenged the authority of the national party to adopt rules that override its state law requirement for an open primary. The decision of the Court would have significant consequences for the fate of state presidential primary laws. (Note: the Court decided in favor of the national committee.) The committee was also instructed to reconsider the length of the delegate selection process and to think again about increasing the participation of public and party officials in the work of the national party conventions, a change that a number of political scientists have advocated recently, as noted in chapter 1.

Action on Rules by the Republican Convention

The Republican national convention also considered a report by its committee on rules, which had met during the week before the convention. The report was adopted on July 15 without controversy, with no debate and by voice vote. But the report did include some interesting features.[10]

One action was the reversal of a binding rule on delegates, in which the Republican convention took action exactly opposite to that of the Democrats. In 1976, President Gerald R. Ford's supporters had been fearful that some of his delegates from primary election states might defect, despite their pledges under state law. The Ford people therefore put through what was called the "justice resolution," requiring all delegates pledged under state law to vote accordingly. In 1980 the Reagan people got their revenge, and repealed the rule. Something similar may happen in the Democratic case in 1984.

The most important action by the Republicans, however, was the creation of a committee or commission to consider an overhauling of the presidential nominating process during the coming four years. This body is also supposed to reconsider the rules for allocation of Republican delegates among the states, rules which presently heavily favor the states that vote Republican in presidential elections or elect Republican governors, senators, and representatives in Congress. The net effect of the existing rules is to favor the most conservative parts of the country in convention representation. The Ripon Society, a reformist organization, has challenged these rules in court (unsuccessfully) and elsewhere for several years and was successful this time at least in initiating a study.

Prospects for Further Reform of the Nominating Process

Before leaving the discussion of party rules, a few words further may be said about reforming the nominating process. This is not the place for a full discussion of that problem, which is discussed in other chapters. But the position of the conventions in reforming the process is certainly relevant. It is because of instructions given by the conventions or actions taken directly by them that most of the reforms of recent years have taken place. Insofar as those reforms are either ill-considered or insufficient, it is probably within the power of the conventions to change them.

Neither party was likely to move much further until after the decision of the United States' Supreme Court in the previously noted case of *Democratic Party of United States v. La Follette*. The case was decided on February 25, 1981, and the Court ruled again that convention decisions on delegate selection can override state law, as it did in *Cousins v. Wigoda,* the case involving the Daley delegation from Chicago in 1972. It can now be expected that the Democratic National Committee will move further to bar open primaries in which Republicans can vote for Democratic delegates, as in Wisconsin and Montana. The road will also be open to other changes to increase the uniformity of state presidential primary laws.

Everyone agrees that the presidential nominating process should be clarified, simplified, and shortened. Few students of the problem would go all the way to a national presidential primary, held in every state on the same day. The immediate pressure for action is to reduce the length of the period during which primaries are held and delegates are selected, to bring about more uniformity in the procedures of the different states, and to reduce if possible the total number of state presidential primaries. Texas abandoned its presidential primary in 1980, and the Michigan Democrats took party action to select their delegates totally without regard to the state's presidential primary law. Other states may follow suit in future years, especially if pushed in that direction by the national conventions and the national party committees. This could result in a reduction in the number of state presidential primaries and an increase in the number of states that rely on caucus and convention procedures. In 1980, as already indicated, both national party conventions took steps to insure that the nominating process will be the subject of recommendations by appropriate party bodies during the next four years. It can be expected that this task will be taken seriously and that important action may flow from it. We can look forward with some anticipation to the results.

The Platform Drafting Function in 1980

The party platforms of 1980 were the occasion for the usual snide comments by the press and the media. Platforms are said to be forgotten as soon as the conventions are over, to have little binding effect as far as the incoming president is concerned, and even less effect on congressional voting. Members of Congress frequently assert that they will not be bound by platform provisions with which they disagree.

In my view, much of the adverse commentary on platforms seems unjustified. Platforms involve the investment of an enormous amount of work by people who value their time highly and who obviously think that platforms are important. Moreover, platforms have been found to be clearly predictive of later action. One well-known political scientist, Professor Gerald Pomper of Rutgers University, has produced an analysis dealing with party platforms since World War II. He checked especially on the extent to which platform pledges are carried out. He found that the pledges on which the two parties agreed reached some form of fulfillment in about 76 percent of the cases from 1968 to 1978. Pledges by the party winning the presidency were found to reach fulfillment in 66 percent of the cases. Even the losing party was able to make good on its pledges about 56 percent of the time.[11]

Platform Action by the Republican Convention

The platform committee of the Republican convention met as usual during the week before the convention. The committee was heavily dominated by Reagan supporters, many of whom were even more conservative than their preferred candidate. It had before it the result of work that had started in January when the chairman, Senator John Tower of Texas, had opened platform hearings in Washington, D.C., taking testimony from members of Congress and former officials of the last Republican administration. Other platform hearings were held in nine other cities during the winter and spring. By the time the committee met in Detroit, the staff had prepared a complete platform draft, which was divided into sections for work by each of seven platform subcommittees. That draft was said to have been agreed to by top Reagan advisers, congressional leaders, and the executive committee of the platform committee, which included the chairmen of all the seven subcommittees.[12]

The subcommittees and the full committee nevertheless worked hard on revisions of wording and substance throughout the week before the convention. The issue receiving the most public attention at this time was the committee's new-found opposition to the Equal Rights Amendment (ERA), which had been favored by Republican platforms since 1940 but was now opposed by Governor Reagan. A CBS poll found that only 24 members of the current 108-member committee were in favor of ERA, with even fewer wanting it in the platform.[13] In compromise drafting suggested by Governor Reagan, the platform omitted direct opposition or support for the ERA, saying that this was a matter to be left to the states, but included an extensive statement on other action that should be taken to assure equal rights for women.[14]

Similar heat and a similar division of views occurred on the issues of abortion, with the committee voting seventy-five to eighteen for the following language: "we affirm our support of a constitutional amendment to restore protection of the right to life for unborn children. We also support the Congressional efforts to restrict the use of taxpayers dollars for abortion."[15]

On defense and foreign policy, to which a major section of the platform was devoted, the platform committee, working from the hard-line position that had been prepared by the staff, made it substantially more extreme. Many changes in this section were initiated by Senator Jesse Helms (R-North Carolina), who told a reporter: "In terms of the voters out there, I don't think it's possible to go too far on defense." Helms, for example, provided language calling for defense expenditures "sufficient to close the gap with the Soviets," and urging military superiority in the platform as an ultimate goal.[16]

Tax cuts were mentioned forty-six times throughout the platform according to a *New York Times* writer.[17] Tax cuts were stressed especially as a means of achieving economic stimulus and growth. The Kemp-Roth plan for annual tax reductions of 10 percent across the board for three years was specifically mentioned and endorsed.[18] Budget balancing was also favored, along with an increase in defense spending, which, with the tax cuts, produced a combination of features that the Democrats were prompt to label as impossibly incompatible with each other.

The completed platform ran to about 40,000 words or 78 printed pages, with no minority reports—a sign of the impressive degree of unity in the committee. Copies were on the delegates' seats when they entered the hall for the convention session at 5:00 P.M. on the second day. An unsuccessful attempt was made by a delegate from Hawaii to secure open debate on the platform. Shortly after this still-born effort, the platform was approved by voice vote and became official. The aim of the convention management to prevent any semblance of conflict or disunity on the floor of the convention had been almost completely successful.

Platform Action by the Democratic Convention

Detroit Mayor Coleman Young was appointed as the acting chairman of the Democratic platform committee several months before the convention. He announced in January that the committee would hold hearings beginning March 18 in Washington, D.C., at which time it would take testimony from the advisory groups on various issues that had been elected at the 1978 midterm conference. The following day, March 19, the committee was to hear Democratic mayors, and on March 20, Democratic governors. Four regional hearings at cities around the country were to follow in April and May, with a final set of hearings in Washington, D.C. on June 5–7, when members of Congress and representatives of national interest groups were to be heard.

While these hearings were going on, the actual writing of a first draft of the platform seems to have occurred in the White House staff, as is usual for the party in power. The Kennedy organization also prepared a first draft. A drafting committee of fifteen was then composed for further work under the chairmanship of South Carolina Governor Richard W. Riley, with nine members (including Riley) who supported President Carter, five members who supported Senator Kennedy, and Senator Daniel Patrick Moynihan of New York, who was not committed to either candidate. This committee met from June 17 to 20 and produced a revised draft which was made available to the press. Stuart Eizenstat of the White House staff claimed that it "fairly represented a cross section of this party and this country."[19]

The full platform committee of 158 members met in Washington, D.C. from June 21–24, nearly two months before the convention in New York City and immediately after the June 17–20 draft was available. The committee divided itself into five panels on as many sections of the platform for working purposes, and then followed up with debate in the full committee under Coleman Young's chairmanship. In its working sessions, which were open to press, television, and public (unlike the GOP), the committee looked much like a small national party convention. Much of the time only some of the members were seated and paying attention, while others were in the aisles talking to each other and the pressure group members who were present. Hundreds of minor changes were made in the text of the successive drafts by voice vote or unanimous consent, but major points were heavily debated, with more than fifty recorded votes.[20]

The vigor of the debate and voting in the platform committee foreshadowed what was to come in New York, but not always with the same results. The most important issues of concern to both Carter and Kennedy forces were those related to economic conditions and what to do about them. Kennedy's main economic plank, which called for immediate wage and price controls and a twelve-billion-dollar jobs program to relieve unemployment, was rejected, after full debate, by a vote of 83 to 59. A separate vote taken later concerning just the jobs program received one of the highest votes on any Kennedy proposal, but was defeated 84.5 to 63. Complex negotiations between Carter and Kennedy people softened or changed much of the drafting throughout the platform, but substantially all of the Kennedy proposals that came to a clear issue were defeated by votes of around 80 or more to about 55.[21]

The most important issue on which the Carter forces were defeated was initiated by defecting Carter members. This was on nuclear power, which the earlier platform drafts had favored as necessary. The original language was rejected, and in new compromise drafting a commitment was approved to "retire nuclear power plants in an orderly manner" as alternative fuels become available. This was accepted without a divided vote after Eizenstat had conceded that "It was the best language we could get." He had been surprised by the depth of the antinuclear sentiment in the committee.[22]

On issues of women's rights, the platform drafting at all stages favored the Equal Rights Amendment (ERA), without going as far to mandate support as some women would have preferred. The women wished to penalize Democratic candidates who opposed ERA. On abortion, the original language merely opposed a constitutional amendment to reverse the Supreme Court decision allowing abortion. The human rights task force added language supporting a woman's "right to choose whether and when to have a child," which the Carter representatives accepted, and which was accepted by the full platform committee by a vote of 88.5 to 22, with many members abstaining. A more controversial proposal by Gloria Steinem, a committee member, would have allowed federal funding of abortions for the poor. The Carter representatives refused to compromise on this and it was defeated by one of the closest votes in the committee, 76.25 to 66.25, with several Carter members abstaining.[23]

Another issue on which the Carter forces came close to defeat in the platform committee was that of the MX missile system. This had been supported by the Carter administration as necessary for national defense, but was strongly attacked by a western Carter delegate, R. P. "Joe" Smith of Portland, Oregon. Smith proposed to delete from the draft all references that favored the MX missile system, and was supported by the Kennedy people. Although around 20 Carter members defected on this issue, the Joe Smith amendment was defeated by the relatively close vote of 76.5 to 69.[24]

Three days after the platform committee finally closed its lengthy sessions, twenty-four minority reports had been filed, eighteen of which were originated by the Kennedy people, and two by the organized feminists on the committee, which was 50 percent women as required by the Democratic party rule for equal representation that went into effect in 1980. Each minority report was required to be signed by 25 percent of the membership of the platform committee, a rule that generally has the effect of restricting the number of minority reports reaching the floor of the convention. In this year's division of the party between two strong factions, however, it was easy to secure signatures for minority reports. The platform committee report, with all of the minority reports, was distributed to all of the delegates well in advance of their sessions in New York.

When the delegates arrived in New York, they learned that it had been agreed by the convention managers that Minority Reports numbers one through four, all dealing with economic issues, would be considered on Tuesday evening during prime television time, with Senator Kennedy scheduled to speak to the convention in support of his economic positions. But platform discussion was still scheduled to begin at 11:00 A.M. on Tuesday, August 12.

So the convention began its platform debate, "one of the longest and most wide-ranging in party history," as CQ observed with minority reports mainly on noneconomic issues.[25] The proposal to favor the Kennedy version of a national health program, rather than the more limited Carter program, was the first subject of a roll-call vote after debate and was defeated by the relatively narrow margin of 1573 to 1349. Shortly after this, a Kennedy amendment referring to jobs policy came up, providing as follows: "This jobs policy—and the need to guarantee a job for every American who is able to work—is our single highest domestic priority, and will take precedence over all other domestic priorities."[26] The debate on this issue was confusing, with question as to whether fighting inflation was not as important as fighting unemployment, as the Carter administration evidently believed. But on a telephone roll call, the minority report on jobs creation was passed by a vote of 1,790.6 to 1,394.8. This was the first clear defeat for the Carter forces in the full convention and was a signal of other defeats still to come.[27]

The next two minority reports were those on women's rights, both of which brought on heated and emotional debate before their eventual approval. The first provided that: "The Democratic Party shall withhold financial support and technical campaign assistance from candidates who do not support the ERA."[28] This passed on a voice vote with an overwhelming chorus of "ayes." Next came the Gloria Steinem proposal on federal funding of abortions for poor women. On this, the Carter people asked for a telephone roll-call vote and when it was over they had lost heavily.

The convention then moved on to the agreed evening program, with Senator Kennedy scheduled to speak last in favor of Minority Reports numbers one to four. His speech was outstanding in content, delivery, and reception, a statement of his fundamental beliefs. It was perhaps the greatest speech of his career. Certainly and ironically it was a far better performance than any he had achieved during his long struggle for the nomination, from which he had finally withdrawn the previous evening.

A forty-minute huddle then transpired at the podium, while the permanent chairman, House Speaker Thomas P. O'Neill, listened to arguments between Carter and Kennedy representatives on voting procedure. According to the television reporters, Kennedy representatives had been promised a roll-call vote on the jobs program plank, which it now seemed certain they would win. Eventually they agreed to a voice vote on that issue if the speaker would rule that they had won. In a dramatic moment of convention action, O'Neill then brought the convention to order and in rapid succession took voice votes on Minority Reports numbers three, two, one, and four in that order. On each vote the volume of noise on each side seemed about the same, but O'Neill ruled successively that number three, the twelve–billion–dollar jobs program, had passed; number two, the pledge to avoid actions that would significantly increase unemployment, had passed; number one, the most comprehensive pledge, which included wage and price control, had failed; and number four, against high interest rates and unemployment as a means to fight inflation, had passed.

Next day the convention resumed the consideration of the remaining platform minority reports, and the Carter forces were successful in regaining control of the convention, helped in part by the lobbying of various Cabinet members who had been rushed to New York. Various Kennedy proposals on oil company taxation and energy were defeated, the first by a margin of almost 400 votes on a roll call. Some of his proposals were compromised and accepted. Eventually the convention reached the Joe Smith proposal to drop support for the MX misssile system, on which the Kennedy forces had withdrawn a similar proposal. Paul Warnke, a former director of the Arms Control and Disarmament Agency, attacked the MX as "an unworkable and inordinately expensive solution to a virtually nonexistent military threat." Defense Secretary Harold Brown then defended MX plans from the podium while Carter forces lobbied the delegates on the floor. Reproductions of a handwritten letter by President Carter, calling on the delegates to support the administration on MX, were distributed throughout the convention. When the vote came, the anti-MX position was defeated, 1873 to 1276.[29] The convention then defeated a plank against nuclear weapons testing on a voice vote and accepted a compromise plank on draft registration, thus disposing of all minority reports. The platform was then adopted as a whole by voice vote, in late afternoon of the third day of the convention.

At this point the new rule came into operation that requires a proposed nominee to submit a written statement of views on the platform, including any reservations on specific provisions. President Carter, by his own agreement to this unprecedented rule, was required to submit such a statement before the nominating procedures could begin, a requirement that produced an almost impossible timetable. The convention waited for the statement from about 6:30 P.M., when the platform was adopted, until 8:40 P.M., when copies became available at the podium and on the floor. The statement proved to be a lengthy restatement of familiar Carter positions, but was conciliatory in tone while declining to accept the Kennedy twelve–billion dollar jobs program that had been voted into the platform, and reiterating Carter's personal opposition to abortion. A summary of the statement was read to the delegates, and the nominating vote then proceeded.

The Democratic platform was at least as lengthy and detailed as the Republican; the platform committee draft ran to 114 printed pages. Few if any issues of significance were omitted. More than in most years, the two party platforms were sharply different. The Republican platform was solidly conservative on most economic issues, while radically innovative on tax policy. The Democratic platform retained a Carter strain of fiscal conservatism, but had absorbed major features of the Kennedy liberalism on economic issues. The Republican platform was opposed to national programs for health care; the Democratic platform favored them. On women's rights, the ERA, and abortion policy, the platforms were in direct and specific opposition. Other differences could be listed at length.

Insofar as major party platforms can give voters a clear choice, the party platforms of 1980 did so. This result was largely because of the Kennedy success in changing important platform provisions and the Carter willingness to make concessions in the interests of party unity. The outcome was much like that in the Republican convention of 1976, when an incumbent president, Ford, fighting for his nomination, made concessions to the insurgent candidate, Reagan, in an effort to achieve some degree of party unity for the fall campaign. Platform action probably becomes increasingly important when it becomes clear that the nominating issue has been settled. Those who have lost on the nomination become even more intent on making gains on the platform, and are sure to remain disaffected if they are completely denied. In what may have been a quixotic search for consensus, President Ford allowed the Reagan forces to control platform drafting to a large extent in 1976. President Carter made concession after concession to the Kennedy forces in 1980 and was defeated at several points where the issue was most sharply drawn.

The Campaign Rally Function in 1980

Both political parties planned their 1980 conventions as openers for the 1980 election campaign. This was easier for the Republicans than the Democrats who, in contrast, knew that they would be required to spend many hours in debate and voting on rules and platform, during much of which time the convention would hold little interest for the public.

Both conventions were designed and scheduled as fully as possible with the television audience in mind. The Republican convention met almost entirely in the evening from Monday through Thursday, except for a brief opening session on Monday morning and routine action on committee reports in the late afternoon

Tuesday. The Democrats began in the afternoon on Monday, scheduled long and full days beginning at midday on Tuesday and Wednesday, and were able to finish between 5:00 P.M. and midnight on their fourth day, Thursday. For the most part the networks gave the conventions full coverage only during the evening hours from 7:30 until the sessions concluded at midnight or later, thus omitting much of the duller part of the business.

As usual, the networks were on the lookout for the more humorous and dramatic aspects of the conventions. Delegates with funny hats were frequently on camera when speeches were dull. Crowd scenes of the demonstrations were interspersed with the efforts of television newsmen to conduct interviews on the floor. Crowding in the aisles was ever present, brought on as much by the media people as the delegates.

The Republican Convention as a Campaign Rally

The Republican convention was planned and produced as a striking demonstration of party unity and of enthusiasm for its candidates. Former President Gerald R. Ford, who had defeated Governor Reagan in the bitter contest for the nomination in 1976, was scheduled as the most important speaker of the first evening. He made his own contribution to party unity and support for Reagan in a stirring speech. ''We cannot stand four more years of soaring inflation, sky-high interest rates, rising unemployment and shrinking take-home pay,'' he said. ''We cannot stake our survival on four more years of weak and wavering leadership and lagging defenses.'' Ford's speech undoubtedly contributed to the later pressure to put him on the ticket for vice president.[30]

A long list of party leaders from all regions, including all who were said to be seriously under consideration for the vice presidency, were called on for speeches during the first, second, and third days of the convention. Most overran their allotted time—George Bush was a noteworthy exception—and the timing problem was accentuated by the addition of Benjamin Hooks, executive director of the National Association for the Advancement of Colored People, to the list of speakers. This was arranged at the specific suggestion of Governor Reagan as part of his effort to come to terms with the black delegates at the convention.

Throughout these proceedings it was conspicuously evident that the television networks were giving little time or attention to the prepared speeches from the podium. A few speakers were given full network time; these included President Ford, Senator Nancy Landon Kassebaum, Benjamin Hooks, Senator Barry Goldwater, former Secretary of State Henry Kissinger, keynote speaker Guy Vander Jagt, and George Bush.

The acceptance speeches by the candidates were the final high point of the convention. George Bush was extremely brief, speaking incisively but only for five minutes. Ronald Reagan was then introduced by a ten-minute biographical film, received an enthusiastic demonstration, and delivered an address in which he went out of his way in an effort to promote party unity—a striking contrast with the Goldwater acceptance speech of 1964. He began by seeking to calm the irritation of the women who had been offended on ERA, and he sought the support of urban minorities, who he said were victimized more than anyone else by Democratic economic failures. He was on the attack throughout in dealing with the Carter administration, and produced a strong reaffirmation of his own conservative credo, but the speech as a whole was a significant attempt to broaden the base of the Republican party and the appeal of his own candidacy. Especially noteworthy were his references to Franklin D. Roosevelt in his appeals to Democrats.

The convention probably improved the public image of the Republican party. Whether the extreme conservatism of the party platform was helpful is doubtful, but it did display a new willingness to try to cope with the economic problems of the nation. The choice of George Bush for vice president and the tenor of Reagan's acceptance speech were both major signals of a desire to retain moderate Republicans and to win over independent voters and Democrats. Throughout the convention in minor ways there was evidence not only of a strong desire to win, but a willingness to make concessions in order to do so.

The results were apparent in various ways in the public opinion polls taken before and after the convention. On candidate standings, the Gallup Poll findings before and after were as indicated by table 4.4.

The Democratic Convention as a Campaign Rally

By the time the Democratic convention committee work was over in July, the Democratic convention planners knew well that they would have a problem in trying to make their party look unified. The Kennedy supporters were showing every sign of strength, energy, and determination to fight on a considerable number of issues. Whether Senator Kennedy himself would make any contribution to party unity seemed doubtful.

Table 4.4
Standing of the Candidates in the Gallup Poll

	June 27–30	August 1–4
Reagan	41%	51%
Carter	32	33
Anderson	22	16

SOURCE: *Public Opinion*, Dec./Jan. 1981, p. 19.

The Carter people met this threat as fully as they could in at least three ways. They began making concessions on Kennedy issues; in the end they accepted or compromised about half of the Kennedy minority report proposals on rules and platform. They adopted a variety of conciliatory tactics, which included letting the Kennedy people take over the convention for the Kennedy speech and their demonstrations on the second day and also included the conciliatory tone of the Carter commentary on the platform and his repeated invitations to Senator Kennedy to join in support of the ticket. They kept as much of the conflict as they could away from television prime time, handling as many issues as possible in the midday and afternoon hours of the sessions when the conventions were not being covered by the networks. This tactic was only partially successful, since the Kennedy people insisted on prime time for the major debates on rules and platform.

Along the way, and despite the pressure of business, there was the usual amount of speech making by party leaders. After the rules fight was over, the first day, Congressman Morris Udall delivered an amiable but corny keynote speech to a hall that was nearly half empty. The Kennedy speech the following night was delivered, in contrast, to what was probably the biggest audience in the hall during the four days. Later that evening there was a moving tribute to the deceased Senator and Vice President Hubert Humphrey. The following day produced the nominating speeches for president, in which the lead-off speaker, the governor of Florida, did not distinguish himself.

Finally, on the fourth day, came the acceptance speeches. Vice President Mondale called the convention "the most representative convention in American history," comparing unfavorably the Republican convention in Detroit, and made both a strong attack on the Reagan candidacy and a strong defense of the Carter record. President Carter followed, after a film on his presidency and a demonstration. In his speech he paid tribute to the party's heroes—FDR, Truman, Kennedy, LBJ, Humphrey—and was graceful in his remarks about Senator Ted Kennedy and Governor Edmund G. Brown, Jr., of California, his unsuccessful opponents for the nomination. He developed the theme of two possible futures—one dark and gloomy if the Republicans were to win, the other bright and promising if the Democrats were allowed to continue. He delivered a strong attack on some positions taken by Governor Reagan. But the speech was much too long, running more than fifty minutes, and much of it was dull in content as well as delivery. The ending of the speech was accented by the failure of the balloons to drop from the ceiling of the convention hall.

As the convention neared adjournment, party notables gathered at the podium to congratulate Carter and Mondale. Throughout the convention there had been speculation, avidly pursued by the television networks, on whether Senator Kennedy would join in this ritual. He did indeed do so, but he did not leave his hotel until after the celebration had started, stayed at the podium only five minutes after he had arrived, and was conspicuously lacking in enthusiasm for the ticket, although he had announced that he would support it. Shortly after the benediction was delivered by the Reverend Martin Luther King, Sr., and the convention adjourned.

The convention's effect on the party image was certainly mixed and not entirely helpful. It nevertheless seems to have produced at least a momentary upward movement in President Carter's standing in the public opinion polls. This effect was most strikingly revealed in the Gallup Poll results before and after the convention, as shown in table 4.5.

Many Kennedy supporters undoubtedly left the convention disheartened and alienated, and no doubt many other Kennedy loyalists thoroughout the country had similar feelings when the convention was over. Whether they would move to the support of the John Anderson campaign, stay home on election day, or finally vote for President Carter in antipathy to Governor Reagan was one of the great unsettled questions of the 1980 election campaign.

The Conventions as Representative Institutions

Part of the purpose of this study is to assess the processes and institutions that enter into the choice of a president. The national party conventions are a key factor in that choice. They have been criticized often enough for their behavior, lack of decorum, and results. Generally the losing side in every convention struggle tends to doubt the validity of the result. The conventions surely need to be assessed as objectively as possible in terms of their quality as representative institutions.

First of all is the matter of convention size. Political scientists have been saying for years that the conventions are too large to function adequately as deliberative bodies. The House of Representatives in Washington, with 435 members, strains the limits of size for many deliberative purposes. This year the Republican con-

Table 4.5
Standing of the Candidates in the Gallup Poll

	August 1–4	August 15–18
Reagan	51%	42%
Carter	33	43
Anderson	16	14

SOURCE: *Public Opinion*, Dec./Jan., 1981, p. 19.

vention had 1994 voting members, the Democratic 3383, as well as all those alternates sitting in the galleries (see table 4.1). So much size is clearly the result of pressure for delegate status, which in turn relates to the function of the convention as a campaign rally. So much size is unnecessary for any other reason and unhelpful in most respects. But it seems impossible to roll back the scale or magnitude of either convention to some earlier, smaller limit. As the matter is seen currently in both parties, the problem is to find ways to make the conventions work in spite of their size. On this there has been some success in the adjustments of recent years, especially in pushing more of the work into the convention committees meeting in advance.

Another issue is that of the apportionment of convention votes among the states. This has been argued intermittently in both parties in recent years. Some years ago the Democrats arrived at an apportionment formula that gives equal weight to the electoral college distribution and to the average of the Democratic vote for president in recent elections. This formula has been well regarded by objective students and seems to be settled as a matter of party policy. For many years, the Republican party supplemented an electoral-college apportionment with a system of bonus votes that were awarded to states with Republican victories without regard to state size. This was obviously unfair to the big states, and eventually the formula was revised to give some weight to the size of state in awarding bonus votes. The small states are still favored, and the formula as a whole certainly favors the more convervative parts of the country—the ones most likely to vote Republican. The formula is again under study and may conceivably be changed.

Another related issue is the apportionment of votes in the convention committees on rules, credentials, and platform, where so much of the convention business is now given final form. Historically both parties started their convention committees with equal votes for each state, regardless of state size. The Republicans still retain this practice, with two votes in each committee for each state. This can and has produced results that are out of accord with sentiment in the full convention and which may be upset if brought to a vote on the floor of the convention. The conservatism of the Republican platform committee this year was undoubtedly due in part to the malapportionment of the committee, which short-changed all of the big industrial states. The Democrats, in contrast, adopted a rule some years ago under which the votes in the committees are proportional to the size of the state's delegation in the full convention. Under that rule this year, California had 14 votes in each committee, New York 13, Illinois 8, while 19 smaller states had 1 vote each in committees each of which had a total of 155 votes.[31]

In past years, both party conventions have been torn by vigorous conflict over the credentials and seating of some state delegations, as in the case of the Daley delegation from Chicago in 1972. In response, both parties have elaborated their rules for early assessment and resolution of credentials disputes. The results indicate a degree of success in both parties. This year the credentials disputes were all relatively minor, many were settled before they reached the convention credentials committee, and there was no such dispute that reached the floor of either convention.

The demographic composition of the conventions has been an issue in both parties in recent years. The Democrats have moved to the 50 percent rule for women delegates and have taken strong action to increase the representation of blacks and Hispanics. They seem to have given up on the efforts of ten years ago to increase the representation of young people, who have taken little action on their own behalf in the meantime. Blacks, in contrast, are still not satisfied with their representation, but have not been successful so. far in achieving a formal quota, while getting some strengthening of affirmative-action provisions. The Republicans have pressed for more representation of women without giving them a quota and have mainly relied on strong words about affirmative action for minorities without providing any enforceable rule.

The parliamentary procedures of the conventions have frequently been critized in the past. Delegations have sometimes failed to receive recognition when legitimately seeking it under the rules. The powers of the presiding officer are great in a body so large and in which there is frequently widespread confusion as to agenda, issues, and applicable rules. This year there were few problems of that kind at the Republican convention. The Democratic convention, in contrast, was afflicted with many procedural problems that had to be settled by the presiding officers, as in voting procedures on the minority platform reports. Almost all of these problems were apparently solved in negotiations between representatives of the Carter and Kennedy camps. There were no major accusations of unfairness that came to public attention.

The obligation of delegates to vote for their candidate was much debated at the Democratic convention. The adoption of the binding rule was in effect a voicing of suspicion of the responsiveness and responsibility of the individual delegate. It almost certainly was unnecessary, was derogatory to the dignity of the delegates, and would be harmful in any year in which there really is a relevant change in the situation between the election of the delegates and the convening of the convention. In my view, the rule should be revoked, as it probably will be in 1984.

The vote on the nomination for president is the most important decision of each convention. Historically this decision has been protected by regularly insisting upon a full, public roll call vote of the state delegations, with provision for polling each delegation individually if its reported vote is challenged. These customs prevailed as usual in 1980 and there was no doubt as to the authenticity of the nominating votes.

For many years, the conventions have made their nominations on the first ballot; the Democratic convention of 1952 was the last in which it took more than one ballot to achieve a presidential nomination. Partly this is the result of tests of strength that come earlier in the convention when there is any doubt. The conventions have nonetheless begun to take on some of the appearance of the electoral college so far as the nominating function is concerned, in that they often meet merely to ratify a previous decision. But the other functions of the conventions remain important, as this chapter has attempted to show. With the shrinking of the nominating function, the platform drafting function especially has become more important. It is at least debatable that the Republicans might have improved their image in 1980 if they had been more willing to let the debate on the platform occur in public; most of it took place in closed sessions of the platform committee.

Despite these caveats, it can be said that every national convention makes its own contribution to the identity and survival of the party that it represents. This year there was no doubt that both party conventions were contributing effectively in that regard. They were successful as representative institutions within the political parties, and should be so judged.

★ ★ ★ ▪▪▪▪▪▪▪▪▪▪▪▪▪▪▪▪▪▪▪▪▪▪▪

★ ★ ★ ▪▪▪▪▪▪▪▪▪▪▪▪▪▪▪▪▪▪▪▪▪▪▪

★ ★ ★ ▪▪▪▪▪▪▪▪▪▪▪▪▪▪▪▪▪▪▪▪▪▪▪

Chapter 5 The Presidential Campaign of 1980

David H. Everson

This chapter examines the national presidential campaign in 1980 with particular attention to the following subjects:

(1) campaign themes and issues,
(2) the effects of the debates,
(3) the apparent instability of the electorate in 1980; and
(4) the quality and significance of the campaign.

In general, there is much cynicism about American presidential campaigns. Many seem to believe that style overwhelms substance in the campaign. To what extent does the record suggest that cynicism is justified? How does the 1980 campaign fit into this picture? We begin with a consideration of the policy significance of presidential campaigns.

The Significance of the Presidential Campaign in Policy Terms

Presidential campaigns, much like party platforms, have long been deprecated in terms of alleged differences between campaign *promises* and actual *performance* in office. It is often assumed that campaign promises are "made to be broken." An off-cited example is the 1964 campaign during which LBJ preached peace and planned war. It is widely assumed that presidential campaigns are personal struggles in which policy positions play *only* tactical roles. Nevertheless, just as in the case of party platforms,[1] the truth is different from the widespread perception. The presidential campaign, viewed in its totality, has served to foreshadow in reasonable detail and accuracy the content and direction of future administrations. Although there may be a tendency for the general election to introduce more generality and ambiguity in the positions of candidates than during the prenomination campaign, the record of fulfillment of campaign pledges from the Kennedy through Carter years is actually quite impressive.[2] It is therefore not a waste of time to examine the 1980 general election campaign in terms of the more general themes articulated as well as the more specific policy positions set forth. We shall find good clues to the future character of the Reagan administration in the substance of the campaign. (This assumption has only been reinforced by the direction the Reagan administration has taken since assuming office.)

Campaign Themes and Issues

The American voter is reported to be more issue oriented these days.[3] While it may not appear so in media coverage, presidential campaigns respond to the issue concerns of voters. The platforms adopted by the two major parties in 1980 expressed clear differences on many issues.[4] And, as we have noted, platform differences are meaningful after the election. In addition to platforms, the campaigns themselves articulate specific issue positions. But apart from specific issues, each campaign attempts to communicate favorable images of candidates with respect to broad campaign themes. These images are *suggestive* of proposed policy directions or imply criticism of opponents' policy directions. National security (defense) provides a good illustration on both sides. The contest between incumbent president Jimmy Carter and challenger Ronald Reagan resulted in efforts by both sides to portray their candidate in a certain light and to caricature the opponent.

> Carter: Portrays himself as tough but sensible, ever anxious to negotiate arms agreements with the Soviet Union yet as willing to oppose Soviet adventurism with an Olympic boycott, a grain embargo or draft registration.
>
> Reagan: Portrays himself as the clear-sighted guardian of freedom and uncompromising foe of communism, committed to preserving world peace, but determined to restore what he calls the nation's military "margin of safety."
>
> Carter on Reagan: He paints Reagan as belligerent, confrontational, eager for an arms race, perhaps willing to risk the horrors of a nuclear war.
>
> Reagan on Carter: Carter's administration is . . . one of "weakness inconsistency, vacillation and bluff," and Carter himself is a naive appeaser[5]

This mutual caricaturing is, of course, a staple of many political campaigns. The crux of President Carter's reelection strategy was to frighten the nation away from voting for Ronald Reagan. As one Carter aide said: "If Reagan doesn't make it . . . it will be because people are afraid of war."[6] While this strategy may seem to be excessive and a distortion of Reagan's views, the fact is that there were real differences on the ways in which the United States should approach national security issues.

The broad campaign themes of the Carter campaign can be classified in positive and negative terms. Each positive Carter theme had its negative Reagan counterpart. The most general Carter theme seemed to be the "two futures"[7] developed in his acceptance speech to which Carter returned throughout the campaign. The "two futures" can be glimpsed in the pairing of the following themes:

Pro Carter Themes		*Anti-Reagan Themes*
Experience	vs.	Inexperience
Unity of nation	vs.	Divided nation
Realistic command of	vs.	Simplistic solutions
complex problems		

Carter hit hard at the division theme. At one point, in a remark widely criticized, Carter said that the election would decide whether "America will be separated black from white, Jew from Christian, North from South or rural from urban."[8] In combination, these themes are not unusual for the incumbent president in that they stress the virtues of stability, continuity, and experience. In its emphasis on the peace issue, there were distinct echoes of the Johnson campaign against Goldwater in the Carter themes.[9]

The Reagan campaign themes emphasized change, again a familiar refrain for a challenger. The major appeals of the Reagan campaign, all linked to change, were:

(1) Carter's view of the future (in terms of energy, etc.) amounted to giving up on future economic growth and development;
(2) Carter's economic policies had produced economic misery;
(3) Carter defense policies had weakened the United States military position vis-à-vis the Soviet Union.

These themes are an artful mix of traditional Republican/conservative positions and appeals to independents and Democrats. The Republicans had gained the initiative as a party of ideas as illustrated by Kemp-Roth tax cut proposals during the late 1970s.[10] These broad Reagan themes take on the character of "valence"[11] issues—it is difficult to be against *progress, development, jobs* and *military strength.*

But there are also constituencies to appeal to on the basis of specific issues. One of the most talked about aspects of the political climate of 1980 was the emergence (or reemergence) of religiously based issue politics. One manifestation of this phenomenon has been the growing activity and influence of the Christian right. Four major organizations in this group are the Moral Majority (whose president is the Reverend Jerry Falwell), the Religious Roundtable, the Christian Voice (best known for its moral "report card" on Congress) and the National Christian Action Coalition.[12] The issues which appeal to the Christian right include the right-to-life, opposition to the Equal Rights Amendment, restriction of prayer in the schools, an anticommunist foreign policy and heavier defense spending. Whether coincidentally or not, the Republican platform bore a close resemblance to the issue positions articulated by the Christian right and early in the campaign Reagan made "an open play for the evangelical vote, typified by his statement to a thunderously friendly crowd in Dallas that 'I endorse you and what you are doing.'"[13]

On the Democratic side, the "guns of incumbency" were targeted toward groups hard hit by recession. For example, on August 28 President Carter produced a new economic game plan (his fourth in twelve months), which included "a temporary Federal Supplement Benefits program providing an additional thirteen weeks of unemployment compensation." He also asked for additional money for loans to industries and areas hard hit by industrial change, investment credits for investing in areas of high unemployment and additional money for aid to local communities.[14] Both candidates also attempted to woo women's votes with the president attempting to capitalize on the Republican platform's opposition to ERA.[15]

Some Moderation

It also should be kept in mind that the need to appeal to specific groups also causes candidates to moderate their previously held positions. Reagan did so frequently in the campaign. In general, conservative Republicans have favored a free market in agriculture. Reagan, however, pledged "not to dismantle Federal agriculture price-support programs if elected President."[16] He also dropped his opposition to a federal bailout for New York City. President Carter, meanwhile, criticized the Federal Reserve Board chairman for "following precisely the restrictive course [on monetary policy] that the President put him there to adopt."[17] A presidential campaign requires a balance of clear and fuzzy appeals.

When all was said and done, the two broad issues of the campaign were the economy and the war-peace issue. To a degree, both are valence issues. Everyone is for prosperity and peace. In both instances, although the initial difference in method between the two candidates seemed clear, the waters muddied. In its September 20 issue, *Congressional Quarterly* reported that "once the 1980 campaign moved into its final phase, both President Carter and his Republican challenger found it expedient to modify their economic policies so that each now occupies a safe middle ground."[18] CQ cited Carter's late August advocacy of tax cuts and Reagan's scaling back "the size and timing of his economic initiative." While substantial differences remained, the differences were ones of emphasis and timing. There was a similar blurring of the differences on the defense side. Although Carter pledged in 1976 to cut defense spending, both sides now wanted to increase defense spending. How much more Reagan would spend was unclear: when discussing the issue he "generally stays away from specifics."[19] Moreover, as we shall see, Reagan worked assiduously to remove the impression that he was impetuous and apt to lead the nation into war. One reasonably clear distinction between the candidates on the defense-spending issue was that Carter accepted the notion of "essential equivalence" with the Soviet Union in nuclear capability while Reagan called for superiority.[20]

In the campaign, Reagan was careful to moderate his views and to attempt to avoid the charges of extremism which plagued Goldwater in 1964 and to strengthen his appeal to disaffected Democrats. As a final example, the *New York Times* reported that Reagan switched positions on two union issues (OHSA and antitrust) to make legitimate his proworker appeals in Pennsylvania and Ohio.[21] Nevertheless, when all the shifting was done in the campaign, the issue differences between the candidates remained about as clear, or more so, than they generally are in American politics. The election of Reagan over Carter would be bound to move the nation in directions indicated by the campaign differences between the two candidates.

Regional Bases, the Electoral College, and Electoral Coalitions

The fascination with national opinion polls and the popular vote in presidential elections often makes us neglect a fundamental truth: "A presidential election is not only a national referendum, but also a combination of 51 elections choosing 538 presidential electors."[22] In fact, it is first of all a series of 51 elections, the object of which is to gain a majority of 270 in the electoral college. Two facts about the electoral college are of preeminent importance for presidential election coalition building. The first is that the number of electors a state has reflects (albeit imperfectly) its population.[23] Second, all states but one award their electoral votes on the basis of a unit rule—the candidate with a plurality of the popular vote in the state wins all of the electoral votes.[24] The effects on presidential campaign politics are significant.[25] For our purposes, it is sufficient to note that candidates will concentrate their time and financial resources on competitive states with large numbers of electoral votes.

The 1980 campaign drew attention to the fact that regional strategies are still significant despite nationalization trends in contemporary American politics.[26] Both candidates started the campaign with what they felt were reasonably secure regional bases of support. In 1976, Jimmy Carter carried all of the South except Virginia. At the same time, President Ford made a strong showing west of the Mississippi. It was anticipated that Reagan would duplicate or better Ford's performance. Early estimates showed him carrying every state in the West with the exception of Hawaii.[27] Reagan's staunch conservatism might make him a threat in Carter's Southern base where, in some instances, Carter's 1976 victories were narrow.[28] At the same time, it was thought that Carter might challenge Reagan's supremacy in some Western states such as Oregon, Washington and even perhaps California.[29] Outside their bases, Carter was expected to be strong in the (now) traditionally Democratic Northeast and Reagan in the heartland. Carter won the presidency in 1976 by putting together a coalition of Southern and Northeastern states plus several key Midwestern states such as Ohio and Wisconsin. As the 1980 campaign began, both camps analyzed the electoral college situation similarly: the large competitive, industrialized states of the Northeast and Midwest would be the crucial battleground in this election.[30] In particular, one could point to Illinois, Michigan and Ohio (with a combined one-quarter of the electoral votes needed for victory) as pivotal. The economy would be the important issue in these states, particularly Michigan with the highest unemployment rate in the nation.

Several other states emerged as crucial for both candidates. These would include two in Carter's base, Texas and Florida, two in the Northeast (New York and Pennsylvania) and, of course, one in Reagan's base, California. It was reported that Reagan would devote an extraordinary 40 percent of his campaign schedule to Ohio, Pennsylvania, Illinois, Texas and Florida. Pundits were wont to say that Carter could not win without New York and Texas; equally, it was difficult to imagine a Reagan win if he lost California.

Groups as Electoral Coalitions

If one reality of presidential campaigns is the focus on key states, a second is the effort to build majority coalitions out of disparate minority groups of various kinds. There have been clear tendencies, tracing back to the New Deal and beyond, for various groups to line up in support of Democratic and Republican party candidates. For example, key elements in the normal Democratic presidential coalitions have been residents of large central cities, blacks, Jews, Catholics, labor union members, and southerners.[31] One of the long-standing problems of the Republican party has been its lack of support among various minority groups.

But for some time, it has been questionable whether the old economic security issues which generated the New Deal coalition were any longer potent enough to produce Democratic majorities. Although a Democratic president was elected in 1976, the viability of the coalition has been in doubt from 1968 on. The 1980 campaign and election would provide another test of that view.

Conversely, the 1980 election would provide another chance (one which was thrown away after the Nixon landslide of 1972 by the Watergate scandal) for the Republican party to alter the long-standing partisan balance by seducing some traditional elements of the New Deal coalition. As unlikely as that might have appeared, given the nomination of the party's most conservative candidate since Barry Goldwater, that is precisely what the Republican party and Ronald Reagan tried to do. This strategy, not exactly new in the course of modern Republican politics, was nevertheless given fresh impetus by two developments in the party itself prior to the nomination of Ronald Reagan. One was the chairmanship of Bill Brock of the Republican National Committee. A good portion of Brock's efforts at revitalizing the Republican party at the grass roots had gone into wooing minorities.[32] Second, Republicans who accepted the Kemp-Roth position advocating major tax cuts for individuals, which Reagan did in his campaign for the nomination, had an issue on which they could appeal to job-hungry Democratic groups. Reagan made appearances in the heart of normally Democratic strongholds. He kicked off his campaign at an ethnic picnic in New Jersey on Labor Day where "before the largely working class audience, Mr. Reagan invoked the name of George Meany, the late AFL–CIO leader."[33] Reagan also made early campaign appearances before the Urban League and in the South Bronx. During the campaign, he visited other Democratic enclaves in Michigan, Ohio, and Pennsylvania.

But the opportunities for seduction went beyond economic self-interest. The Republican nominee made strong appeals for the Jewish vote. There was, of course, a good deal of uncertainty and dissatisfaction among Jews over Carter's policies toward Israel.[34]

If the Reagan campaign was noteworthy for its efforts to appeal to normal Democrats, the Carter problem was to stem the tide of possible defections. For example, repeatedly, Carter pledged "steady support for Israel."[35] In his debate with Reagan (discussed later), Carter made specific appeals to virtually every major Democratic constituency.[36] The Democrat candidate, however, also set his sights on the suburbs, normally thought of as Republican territory. David Broder explained why the Democrats had to broaden their vision to the suburbs. Central cities have lost population, the urban machines are no longer as reliable in terms of turning out a Democratic vote, and the Reagan threat, discussed earlier, to the Democratic constituency all made an appeal to the independents, moderate Republicans (and even a few Democrats) in the suburbs attractive.[37] Part of the winning coalition Carter constructed in 1976 was based in the nation's suburbs.

The Debates: Round 1 (Reagan vs. Anderson)

With the revival of presidential debates in 1976 (the only previous ones had been held in 1960), a climate of expectations developed for 1980 involving two assumptions: (1) that debates would be held; and (2) that they might well be decisive in the election. Theoretically, both major party candidates wanted to debate. There were vast differences between them however, over the timing and make-up of the debates.

The independent candidacy of Congressman John B. Anderson complicated the debate picture. His candidacy forced the debate sponsors, The League of Women Voters, to formulate criteria for inclusion in the presidential debates. Eventually, the League established a 15 percent standing in national opinion polls as the condition.[38] At the tactical level, the two major party candidates each had to decide whether the inclusion of Anderson would help or hurt their effort. Polls which appeared to show Anderson taking more from Carter than Reagan undoubtedly influenced the president's decision to refuse an initial three-way, debate.[39]

Reagan and Anderson squared off in Baltimore on the evening of September 21. The two responded to questions from a panel of print journalists. Inquiries ranged from inflation to energy supplies to organized religion in politics. This debate seemed crucial to the Anderson candidacy for it was one of the few opportunities he would have in the early fall campaign for national television exposure. Toward the end of the debate he expressed the wish "that we had more time to talk about some of the other issues that are so fundamentally important."[40] This would be Anderson's last chance to address a national audience on an equal footing with a major party candidate. A summary of the debate indicated that the two Republicans, from opposite wings of the party, differed on most issue positions.[41] Surveys taken just after the debate indicated that Anderson was the "winner" in the eyes of the public.[42] Nevertheless, he got no boost in the presidential polls from the encounter.[43] Round 1 of the debates proved inconclusive.

The Debates: Round 2 (Carter vs. Reagan)

The Reagan camp held out against any presidential debate excluding John Anderson until mid-October. The trends of the campaign, however, forced a change in position: "When a number of newspaper polls as well as the Reagan campaign's own surveys began to show Mr. Reagan's lead narrowing in key states . . . the consensus began to shift. Some aides were reported concerned . . . with charges that Mr. Reagan would be too quick to use force in international disputes."[44] Fortunately for Reagan, Anderson had slipped well below the minimal 15 percent criterion in the national polls. After a general staff meeting, the recommendation was made to go ahead and debate. Stuart Spencer noted that Reagan "took about 10 minutes to make the decision. . . . I have the impression he had wanted to do it for some time."[45] Of course, the Carter camp had always wanted a one-on-one confrontation with Reagan. As Robert Strauss put it: we are ready "at any reasonable date, at any reasonable place, under any reasonable format."[46] After considerable wrangling over format, the two candidates met in Cleveland on the evening of October 28.

Both debaters had preset agendas for the debate. As suggested earlier, Reagan's major task was to defuse the "warmonger" issue. Early in the debate he declared "that I believe with all my heart that our first priority must be world peace, and that use of force is always as only a last resort, when everything else has failed, and then only with regard to our national security."[47] Reagan's other primary goal was to spotlight the economic record of the Carter administration. He asked "are you better off than you were four years ago?"[48] President Carter also had two messages to deliver. One was to raise doubts about Reagan's judgment in defense and economic matters. He also made repeated efforts to "call out" the various elements of the Democratic party's coalition: minorities, Southerners, older citizens, women committed to the ERA and so on.[49] Carter wanted to encourage turnout among groups predisposed to vote Democratic and to cut down on partisan defections.[50]

Assessments of the outcome of the debate varied. Several observers saw it as a crucial event in the Reagan victory. Three plausible interpretations could be made about the debate: (1) that the debate made little difference; (2) that the debate slowed Carter's momentum and thus turned the race for Reagan; and (3) that the debate was a clear-cut victory for Reagan and a decisive factor in the ultimate Reagan landslide. The first view was a common one immediately following the debate: "Neither candidate knocked the other out rhetorically nor committed a fatal gaffe, in the opinion of most analysts." A CBS Poll found that the public perceived Reagan to be the winner by a narrow plurality.[51] In the light of the Reagan's election victory and some predebate, postdebate polls, however, a different interpretation emerged: that the debate was decisive. Reagan's pollster Richard Wirthlin argued that "the debate was successful in conditioning the environment for the take-off."[52] A Gallup report argued that "Carter's momentum was stalled by the Oct. 28 debate."[53] Gallup's data are in table 5.1. The figures would seem to suggest the debate was decisive in that the positions of the candidates reversed after the debate. Other polls, however, did *not* show Reagan trailing before the debate.[54] In any case, the debate alone could not account for the magnitude of the ultimate Carter defeat, so the third interpretation seems implausible.

In light of the conflicting views and the ambiguity of the evidence, the most sensible interpretation of the debate may be that it tipped "undecideds" in the direction that they were already leaning by showing that Reagan was "different from the image that Carter tried to create for him."[55] In the absence of the debate,

Table 5.1

Gallup Poll Predebate and Postdebate Results (in Percentages)

	Reagan	Carter	Anderson	Other/Undec.
Predebate				
Oct. 25–26	42	45	9	4
Postdebate				
Oct. 29–30	44	43	8	5
Change =	+2	−2	−1	+1

SOURCE: George Gallup, "Reagan Win Sparked by Debate," *Bloomington Daily Pantagraph*, Nov. 12, 1980, p. A–7.

the larger electoral tides (inflation, unemployment, general dissatisfaction with the incumbent) may well have moved those voters in precisely the same direction anyway. The debate, however, helped to crystalize that decision.[56]

The Anderson Factor

At the beginning of the 1980 campaign, perhaps the most intriguing aspect was the independent candidacy of Congressman John B. Anderson of Illinois. His candidacy was one episode in a recurring series of efforts by third parties and independents to break the two-party monopoly in American presidential politics. One unusual aspect of Anderson's candidacy was its centrist nature. Such a center challenge to the major parties had not been launched since 1912.[57] Most often, third party efforts have come from the extremes of American politics. The positioning of Anderson might have been a deterrent to a Carter strategy of moving to the center in the manner of LBJ in 1964.

Beyond the fact of a centrist candidacy, there were two "what ifs": (1) What if Anderson won enough electoral college votes to prevent a majority in the electoral college? (2) And even more improbably, what if an independent were elected president? These "what ifs" did not appear completely outrageous in the Summer of 1980. For example, at the peak of his public support in June, Anderson received 23 percent in a three way race with Carter and Reagan (only about 10 percent behind).[58] During and after the two-party conventions, Anderson slipped sharply in the polls.

The Anderson campaign revived, however, in early September. Several developments sparked the revival. Among these were:

(1) He moved toward meeting the legal requirements for being on the ballot in all fifty states and the District of Columbia;

(2) He received a Federal Election Commission ruling which qualified his campaign for retroactive public financing if he received 5 percent of the vote;

(3) He chose a running mate, former Governor Patrick Lucey, a Democrat (and previous Kennedy supporter and Ambassador to Mexico in the Carter administration). Lucey had strong ties to organized labor in Wisconsin;

(4) He received the endorsement of the Liberal party in New York; and

(5) He met the League of Women Voter's criterion of 15 percent in the national polls for presidential debates.[59]

The debate afforded Anderson an opportunity to obtain badly needed public exposure. But, as we have seen, the debate did not visibly improve Anderson's standing in the presidential polls.

The decline in Mr. Anderson's fortunes following the debate could probably be traced to two factors: (1) His inability to obtain bank loans to launch a television advertising campaign (it was not until Oct. 17 that Anderson ads began running); and (2) The effects of the relentless anti-Anderson campaigning by the Carter forces who argued that a vote for Anderson was a wasted vote.[60]

Despite the fact that Anderson had, as indicated earlier, sunk to 8 percent in the Gallup Poll by mid-October, the effects of his presence in the race were uncertain. Depending upon which polls one used, and where they were taken, Anderson could be shown to have no effect, to give advantage to Carter, or Reagan.[61]

Why did the Anderson campaign falter after a promising beginning? One obstacle afflicts all third-party efforts in the United States. There can be only one winner in the presidential race; therefore, the supporters of third parties are "wasting their votes." The second reason is that Anderson was never able to find a theme or set of issues that expanded his constituency beyond a narrow band of independents, younger voters and college graduates.[62] The Anderson campaign ultimately withered because it did not represent a clearly compelling alternative point of view for a broad range of the electorate.

Events and Nonevents: The Hostage Crisis

Throughout the campaign, the Reagan forces feared an "October surprise"—the announcement of some significant presidential initiative or success. The holding of American hostages in Iran seemed to hold the potential for such a dramatic event—their release—which would aid the president. Previous research on foreign policy crises suggests the public reacts with a "rally round the flag"[63] response which bolsters presidential popularity. Thus it was possible to assume that if the hostage crisis became a focus in the latter stages of the campaign, that this would help the president. Rumors were rampant in the week prior to the election that a release was imminent. At first the administration encouraged and then, fearing an adverse reaction, attempted to dampen such hopes.[64] Nevertheless, a climate of optimism emerged (as it had so often during the year of captivity) which ultimately proved illusory.

Again, as with the debates, the interpretations of the effects of these events varies. Reagan's pollster, Richard Wirthlin did not "think there was a sudden change in opinion about Carter because of the hostage news." In contrast, Pat Caddell, Carter's pollster, argued that "the president was the victim of a sudden welling up of national frustrations, catalyzed by the last-minute roller coaster developments involving the hostages."[65] It should be pointed out that both of these interpretations served the self-interests of the respective candidates. If the size of the defeat were due to the "accident" of the hostage disappointment, then the Reagan mandate would be diminished and the Carter record not as tarnished.

Substantial numbers of voters did decide in the last week of the campaign, and a clear plurality of those decided for Reagan.[66] The "nonevents" of that week, the fact that expectations were dashed again, may have placed *in focus* the inability of the Carter administration to achieve a resolution of the crisis. In that sense, the hostage situation may have been the final undoing of the Carter administration *but* it is important to keep in mind that without a previous record of failure, both on this issue and the economy, the "nonevents" of the final week would not have been as significant.

The foregoing discussions of the putative effects of the hostage crisis and the debates points up the fact that the campaign in 1980 was widely thought to have major effects. This runs counter to much political science lore about presidential campaigns. Was 1980 an exception?

The 1980 Electorate

For many years, political scientists have derided the idea that a presidential campaign represented a rational debate between candidates for the votes of large numbers of "undecided" voters who were waiting to be convinced of the merits of the opposing arguments.[67] This skepticism was introduced in an early voting study in which the authors concluded that "the open-minded voters who make a sincere attempt to weigh the issues and the candidates dispassionately for the good of the country as a whole—exist, mainly in . . . campaign propaganda, in textbooks on civics, in the movies, and in the minds of some political idealists. In real life, they are few indeed."[68] Presidential campaigns aroused and rallied the party faithful, brought some waywards back to the fold and reinforced the choices of those who always intended to support the party's candidate. Major changes by the voters during campaigns were unlikely. Campaigns were holding operations first and foremost, and only secondarily efforts to attract undecideds or convert the opposition. In fact, it would be argued that the actual campaign has changed the outcome of the election in only one instance since 1952. That would be 1960 where JFK surged from behind to win narrowly.[69]

Relatively fixed voting choices in presidential campaigns were, of course, strongly influenced by a partisan electorate. To the degree that party affiliation represented a "standing decision," to that degree campaign strategy would be tied to the tasks of arousing and reinforcing existing party loyalties.[70] If partisanship has waned, as many suggest,[71] then the nature of political campaigns in the United States would also be expected to change.

Survey data on the time of the vote decision has suggested that about two-thirds of the electorate has normally made up its mind before the political campaign ever begins.[72] The 1976 election was a clear exception, however, perhaps forecasting the fabled volatility of the 1980 electorate. In 1972, 63 percent of the voters made up their minds as to how to vote before the campaign began. Only 14 percent made up their minds in the final two weeks, including 6 percent on election day. In contrast, in 1976, only 52 percent had made up their minds just after the conventions while one-quarter of the electorate decided in the last two weeks and 8 percent on election day.[73]

The greater instability of presidential electorates in recent years would certainly be consistent with the suggestions of a decline of American political parties. The events of 1980 would appear to provide an excellent example of the new instability in presidential preferences. In mid-September, George Gallup, Jr., estimated that 60 percent of the voters were still "up for grabs" in this year's election.[74] Although many state polls showed nearly one-quarter of the electorate "undecided" in mid-October, the important point seemed to be that even those who had made up their minds were uncertain. On November 3, a Gallup survey, reported in *Newsweek,* found only 9 percent undecided but "the lightly committed voters represent[ed] a quarter of Carter's total, a fifth of Reagan's. Combined with the truly undecided, this group amounts to about one-third of the electorate."[75] The significance of this uncertainty is that there was more room for "campaign effects" in 1980. This does not mean that the ideal citizen of the textbooks, regarded as an endangered species, had been reborn. Delay in decision, or uncertainty, was no sign that voters would ultimately choose on the basis of dispassionate, rational analysis. Nevertheless, an electorate which weighed its decision until the end ultimately decided in a direction which the flow of events would have predicted.

As in all recent presidential elections, the vagaries of public opinion have been tracked assiduously. The polls and projections were a major story of the 1980 campaign.

Polls and Projections

Continuous public opinion polling, by both candidates and the news media, has become a staple of presidential campaigning. This activity fuels speculation on the "horse race" aspects of the campaign. These same projections, however, can deepen our understanding of the dynamics of the campaign. At this point, we will examine how the polls and projections changed over the campaign.

Let us first consider the national opinion polls for the full year to see exactly how fluid voter preferences were in 1980. At the height of the Iranian crisis, in January of 1980, Carter lead Reagan by nearly 2–1 in a two-man race. In the two-way pairing, Reagan moved ahead in June and widened the lead in July. After the Democratic convention, however, the two candidates were virtually in a dead heat.[76] Gallup Polls (see table 5.2) taken in mid-September and mid-October of "likely voters" showed the sharp decline of the Anderson candidacy with neither Carter nor Reagan gaining a marked advantage from that fall. As the election approached, polls suggested an extremely close race. A *Newsweek* poll of Oct. 17–20 showed Carter slightly in the lead.[77] As we noted above, on the eve of the election, most polls were saying that the election was "too close to call."[78]

Despite the national polls, it seemed that the election would be won or lost in several key states. Assessments at the beginning of October were that Reagan had a substantial electoral vote lead but, as Broder noted, his support was "almost twice as broad as Carter's . . . [but] it is—almost literally—only half as deep."[79] Let us turn to a brief analysis of the state races.

At the end of September after nearly a month of full-tilt campaigning and after the Anderson-Reagan debate, a consensus emerged that Reagan held a clear, but not uncatchable electoral vote lead: the *"Washington Post, the New York Times* and *Newsweek* magazine put Reagan over the top at this point with leads in 28 states with 283 electoral votes *(Post)*, in 29 states with 314 electoral votes *(Times)* and in 30 states with 321 electoral votes *(Newsweek)."*[80] Although these projections were hedged as indicated, they ultimately proved to be more accurate than the polls taken immediately prior to the election. In retrospect, the important aspect of the state-by-state analysis was that, to win, Carter had to nearly sweep

Table 5.2

Candidates

	Reagan	Carter	Anderson	Other
Sept. 12–15	41	37	15	7
Oct. 10–12	45	42	8	5
Change =	+4	+5	−7	−2

SOURCE: *Chicago Sun-Times,* Oct. 16, 1980, p. 5.

all of the large electoral vote states. The national media did a reasonably good job of analyzing various key states. The national pollsters, however, in declaring the race "too close to call" ignored the available state-by-state data.[81]

Ohio can serve as an example of a key state placed under the journalistic microscope in 1980. The economy was the major issue in the state and the problems of "jobs, inflation and interest rates"—those are the "cross that threatens to bear Carter to the ground in eastern Ohio."[82] A *New York Times* Poll, conducted in early October, showed that (1) 23% of the registered voters in Ohio were undecided; (2) nearly one-quarter of the labor union vote was going to Reagan; (3) female voters were the most undecided (31%); and (4) that 56 percent of Democrats intended to vote for Carter.[83] This latter figure was not encouraging for Carter's chances although the *Times* noted that many of the "undecideds" were from union families and might revert to the President. Ohio, which Carter won by only about 11,000 votes in 1976, had a strong state labor organization pushing hard for President Carter. Here, as in the rest of the nation, the success of Reagan in appealing to traditional Democratic voters would be critical. Scrutiny of other key states would, from different sets of conditions, yield very similar conclusions: an election in which Reagan was ahead, but the outcome was uncertain. Assessments that Carter was gaining, or that Reagan's momentum was slipping, began to pop up in mid-October. Again, as noted previously, this undoubtedly influenced Reagan's decision to debate "one-on-one."

The Quality of the Campaign

A constant refrain accompanying the 1980 campaign was a negative evaluation of the quality of the candidates, their campaigns and the whole process: "As the 1980 campaign nears its end . . . the process is beginning to resemble a funeral procession with the American voters gnashing their teeth as they proceed to the moment of decision. They march with all the enthusiasm of the convicted murderers who once got to choose between the gallows and the firing squad."[84] The lack of enthusiasm for the election ultimately showed itself in declining voter turnout.[85]

There are good reasons for wondering why this negative evaluation should be so widespread. The election was perceived to be closely contested and to involve clear choices. In addition, for those disaffected from the two parties, John Anderson provided a (seemingly) attractive third alternative. As it finally worked out, all three major candidates got to participate in debates which informed voters of their positions on a range of issues. Moreover, it was possible, with a minimum of effort, to find out detailed information about the candidates and their positions on issues.[86] In contrast to 1976, the 1980 election seemed a lively and interesting contest.[87] Nevertheless, there was a constant refrain that the campaign presented unattractive choices. This type of evaluation seems endemic to commentary on presidential campaigns regardless of ''objective circumstances.'' The mass media, which do so much to trivialize the campaign, also popularize the view that the choices are unattractive.

Another popular theme during the campaign was that President Carter showed a ''mean-streak'' and that the campaign itself was unusually harsh. With respect to the president, this may have seemed significant because of his reputation for decency. By any fair historical standard, however, neither Mr. Carter nor Mr. Reagan ran a particularly mean campaign.[88] Harry Truman's ''give 'em hell'' campaign of 1948 is now regarded as courageous but evidently not to be repeated. In 1964, President Johnson ''insinuated that the Republicans election would mean the end of social security, farm subsidies, and strong labor unions'' and ''just might lead the nation into war.''[89] In 1972, Republican commercials devastated McGovern's judgment on the economy and defense. All presidential campaigns have their moments of harsh, personal, and unfair invectives and exaggeration. And 1980 does not stand as unusual in that respect.

Perhaps the greatest problems of the modern campaign are its length and the nature of the coverage given in the mass media. The length results in boredom and the mass media, particularly television, trivialize the election.[90] The result is a widespread impression, only partially accurate, that campaigns lack substance.

The 1980 presidential campaign represented as wide a variety and clarity of choices as we have seen in American politics in many years. The response of the press, television, and the public was overwhelmingly negative. This is a critical problem for the functioning of American politics, as the continued decline in voter turnout shows.

★ ★ ★ ▆▆▆▆▆▆▆▆▆▆▆▆▆▆▆▆

★ ★ ★ ▆▆▆▆▆▆▆▆▆▆▆▆▆▆▆▆

★ ★ ★ ▆▆▆▆▆▆▆▆▆▆▆▆▆▆▆▆

Chapter 6 Minorities in the Politics of 1980

Lois B. Moreland

"We hold these truths to be self-evident, that all men are created equal, that they are endowed by their Creator with certain unalienable Rights, that among these are Life, Liberty and the pursuit of Happiness.—That to secure these rights, Governments are instituted among Men, deriving their just powers from the consent of the governed."

These words are taken from the Declaration of Independence, which declares to the world the justification for the American Revolutionary war. The words are inspiring, hopeful, and affirm that all men are endowed by God with certain unalienable rights—that all men are equal and are entitled to life, liberty, and the pursuit of happiness.

One group of people, however, was omitted from this declaration of rights to freedom. That group was the black slave population. Thomas Jefferson, the principal writer of the Declaration, in his first draft of the document, had sought to include them. That paragraph was omitted. The institution of slavery was too profitable to give up. Since that omission, it has been the struggle of blacks and other minorities to be included in the mainstream of American life.

The Declaration of Independence is not the document which protects citizens' rights; the Constitution of the United States does this, but the Declaration does set the moral tone in which the rights are to be protected. But blacks were even excluded from protection by the Constitution. The 3/5 clause in Article I characterizes the black slave as 3/5 of a person.

Inclusion of blacks and other minorities into the American political-legal system began with the Thirteenth, Fourteenth and Fifteenth Amendments. The slaves were freed by the Thirteenth, given the rights of citizenship by the Fourteenth and given the right to vote by the Fifteenth. The rights of the Fourteenth Amendment are still in the process of being realized and have not been fully implemented.

One right of American citizenship is to participate in the selection of the president of the United States. This paper will examine the participation of three minority groups in the political process as they exercise this right. The three minority groups are blacks, Hispanics, and Jews. The continuing status of blacks as a minority group affects black participation, especially in the political institutions and processes employed in presidential selection.

Political Parties and the Electoral College

Political parties, though viewed as divisive instrumentalities by the writers of the Constitution, have developed as the means in this country by which the governing power of one group is peacefully transferred to another group. The peaceful transfer of power from the Democrats to the Republicans in the 1980 presidential election powerfully confirms the value of political parties in the American two-party system.

Development of political parties profoundly changed the operation of the electoral college as outlined in the Constitution. The electoral college was to nominate and elect a President of the United States. Political parties now nominate the president, at least formally. The presidential electors in the electoral college now vote for the candidate who received a plurality of the popular vote in their respective states. Under the "winner take all system," the candidate who received a plurality of the state's popular vote, receives all of the state's electoral vote. Under this system, sometimes if a few thousand more people had voted for the losing candidate in two or three states the electoral college vote would have been changed and a different person would have been elected president. Because of the way the electoral college operates, minority groups, if they bloc vote, can have a significant impact upon the selection of the president. This happened in the election of President Carter in 1976 when blacks gave him 90 percent of their vote.[1] Without this heavy black vote, Carter would have lost several states that he carried and probably would have lost the election. (This is equally true, however, of other blocs of voters, e.g., Southern whites.)

The Direct Primary and the National Convention

In an effort to wrest control of the presidential nominating process from the political party "bosses," the presidential primary was instituted. Thirty-five states,

Puerto Rico, and the District of Columbia used primaries in 1980, more than double the number in 1968. This growth in use was, in large measure, a response to charges that too few minorities, women, and youth were delegates to the national party conventions. If sufficient numbers from these groups are not elected in the primaries, the affirmative action requirements of the Democratic party allow appointments of delegates at large from these groups. The Republican party's affirmative-action goals have not been implemented to the same degree as the Democratic party's. "Of the 1,993 delegates to the 1980 Republican National Convention, 55 are black."[2] This was the lowest participation since 1968. "Of the 3,331 delegates to the 1980 Democratic National Convention, about 481 or 14.4 percent are black."[3] This was the largest number of black delegates ever to attend the Democratic Convention.

While affirmative-action obligations work to the advantage of blacks by increasing the numbers of delegates, if quotas were established for Jews, their numbers at the conventions would probably be greatly diminished. They are only 2.7 percent of the total population. In former times, Jews were able to exercise power at the convention by their disproportionately large number of campaign workers for candidates and their large share of political contributions.[4] Because of the direct primary, however, conventions now are mainly confirmations of nominating decisions made at the polls; political bargaining or "brokering" is no longer often practiced.

Blacks and Direct Primaries, Election 1980

Of four major early Democratic presidential primaries analyzed by the Joint Center for Political Studies in 1980, President Carter won a solid majority of the black vote.[5] In Florida: 67.4 percent for President Carter, 29.6 for Senator Kennedy, 1.2 for Governor Brown. Greatest support for President Carter came from low-income areas.

In Alabama: 67 percent of the black vote for President Carter, 29 for Senator Kennedy, 3 for Governor Jerry Brown. (These were projections since all data were not available to the Joint Center at press time.)

In Illinois: 59.4 percent for President Carter, 33.9 for Senator Kennedy, 3.9 for Governor Jerry Brown. Blacks in metropolitan areas voted 58 percent for Carter, 34.2 for Kennedy. Blacks in suburban areas voted 66.5 percent for Carter, 32.1 for Kennedy. Further analysis of Illinois results indicated President Carter received more support in affluent black Illinois areas than in low-income areas. This was the reverse of the case in Florida.

In the Illinois Republican primary, Congressman John Anderson received 59.2 percent of the black Republican vote, Governor Reagan 17.2, George Bush 9.4. Fourteen percent split among other GOP candidates.

In New York: Senator Kennedy, 48 percent of the black vote, President Carter 52. They split the black vote almost evenly in the suburbs, but Carter won 52.5 percent in metropolitan areas, Kennedy 47.5.

There were too few black votes to analyze in Republican presidential primaries in Florida, Alabama and New York.

In Pennsylvania[6] Senator Kennedy received 51.2 percent of the black vote, President Carter 44.4. The remaining 4.4 either voted for Governor Jerry Brown or cast a "no preference" vote on the ballot. In the Republican primary, George Bush received 45.9 percent of the black vote, Governor Reagan 33.7 and the remaining 20.3 split among other GOP candidates.

At the Democratic National Convention, 68 percent of the black delegates and 66 percent of the black alternates were pledged to President Carter; 32 percent of the black delegates and 34 percent of the black alternates were pledged to Senator Kennedy.[7]

As will be shown in discussing the election outcome, this split among blacks over support of President Carter (⅔ support) or Senator Kennedy (approximately ⅓ support) melded together at the general election. Solid cohesion was demonstrated by blacks then.

Campaign Issues

What were the campaign issues? What were the concerns of minorities?

The Hispanic Community

Like blacks and Jews, Hispanics also want a greater voice in governmental decision making. The Carter administration appointed over 180 Hispanics to subcabinet, White House, and other top level government positions—more than any other administration. Employment, health concerns along the United States-Mexico border, bilingual programs, relations with Cuba, social services, e.g., food stamps, social security, immigration, and economic development, were among the issues in the Hispanic community.

The Jewish Community

The Jewish vote was split in the 1980 election, with less than 50 percent going to the Democratic Party. What were the issues?

A perennial issue in the Jewish community is America's support of Israel. The Carter administration had achieved great success in the Camp David accords, which resulted in a peace treaty between Israel and Egypt.[8] But the Carter administration made a "bad mistake" on a vote on Israel, March 1, 1980 in the United Nations Security Council. This "mistake" is listed as the first of a series of issues of concern to the Jewish community during the 1980 presidential campaign.[9] This listing of issues, determined by "countless interviews conducted over many months" reveal "the political cross-currents vying in the Jewish community." According to Robert Strauss, President Carter's campaign manager, the Security Council vote cost President Carter the Jewish vote. The "mistake" was that the administration at first supported the Resolution to rebuke Israel for having Israeli settlements in Arab claimed territory and then "disavowed it." Strauss said the United Nations vote also caused Senator Kennedy to win the New York primary. He said the administration never "fully recovered" from the Kennedy challenge.[10] Stuart Lewengraub, Southeastern Director of the Anti-Defamation League, also cites this vote as a concern in the election.

Illustrative of the fact that there are, indeed, "crosscurrents" within the Jewish community, is the statement by Earl Raab, Director of the Jewish Community Relations Council of San Francisco that the "primary reason that Jews . . . see the Democratic Party as a fading ally is not in foreign policy but domestic policy."[11] It is not that government is too big, he says, but that it is "bad" and intervenes in ways "antithetical to Jewish interests," e.g., as in many of the affirmative action requirements for other minorities.

The *New Leader Special Edition* devoted to the survey of issues in the Jewish community is valuable, not only for its illuminations on specific political issues, but because it allows the reader a glimpse into the heart of the community. It describes the pervasive and deep fear that grips American Jews. It is a fear for their safety—indeed, very survival. It is a fear grounded in the memory of the Holocaust when six million Jews were annihilated. It is a fear rekindled everytime an anti-Semitic demonstration is allowed to take place. It is a fear described by Cynthia Ozick, the Special Edition's author, as a "sort of touchiness, hysteria, paranoia (whichever best characterizes the anxiety of insecurity)." She says, "The truth is that most American Jews live their lives feverishly attuned first to the words themselves and then to the words behind the words. The Jewish temper rises and falls by every gesture, remark, aside, tone, question mark; by every failure to acknowledge Jewish safety and acceptance."[12]

Insight into the intensity of the fear and the "touchiness' which is pervasive enables others to understand better why Andrew Young and his role in attempting to facilitate communication between the Arabs and Jews was listed as an "issue," and why the Carter administration's handling of the Andrew Young dismissal was viewed as exacerbating already strained, black-Jewish relations.[13] It was not Ambassador Young's mere speaking to the Arabs which was so disturbing. The Jewish community saw his act as an implied endorsement of the PLO. The community perceived the Arabs as representatives of the PLO, a terrorist organization dedicated to the destruction of Israel and the killing of Jews. This insight helps to explain the intense anti-Brzezinski attitude.[14] The insight into the "anxiety of insecurity" brings more understanding into the reasons why less than 50 percent of the Jewish vote went to President Carter:

1) despite that community's recognition that he had appointed more Jews to key governmental positions than any other president.

2) despite the fact that under his administration Israel received more loans and military and economic aid than in all other administrations combined.

3) despite the fact that President Carter created the National Holocaust Commission and activated it; that access to the president was no problem.[15]

President Carter, himself, was an issue.[16] "Camp David: He is good for the Jews. The UN vote: He is bad for the Jews."[17] "He is not the first President to be both good and bad." It was stated that President Franklin Delano Roosevelt also had appointed more Jews to high level governmental positions than his predecessors but he is linked to responsibility for the Holocaust by refusing to allow fleeing Jews haven in the United States, among other things. Thus, despite President Carter's positive activities, he was suspect, especially because of the people who surrounded him—especially Zbigniew Brzezinski.

The Jewish community couches its interests in traditional American values. Ozick writes, "The Jews are the touchstone of the American enterprise—of the Bill of Rights, of the American Conscience, of the American promise."[18]

The Black Community

What were the issues in the black community during the presidential campaign? "The traditional civil rights issues of the 1960s are rapidly giving place to a more complex array of social and economic concerns," so states the Joint Center for Political Studies.[19] In its *Platform Analyses—1980 Election*, the NAACP categorizes the issues under the broad topics of employment and economic growth, education, energy, voting and the political process, housing, health care, welfare reform, civil rights enforcement, criminal justice, military justice, foreign affairs. This listing cites a multiplicity of interests. Yet, some are of greater concern and are given priority over others. The priorities herein are deemed to be those most frequently espoused by black leaders. Most of these leaders endorsed President Carter. Near the end of the campaign, a few well-known blacks endorsed candidate Reagan.

The Carter supporters included Mrs. Coretta Scott King, Jr., wife of the slain civil rights leader, Dr. Martin Luther King, Jr., Reverend Martin Luther King, Sr., the father of the slain leader, Maynard Jackson, Mayor of the City of Atlanta. These three were prominently seen at the Democratic National Convention during prime-time TV as strong supporters of the president. Other leaders who were very visible during the campaign were Carl Rowan, nationally syndicated columnist, Andrew Young, former Ambassador to the United Nations, Reverend Jesse Jackson of Operation PUSH, based in Chicago, who gave very limited support to the President in 1976, and a host of other prominent blacks, including Muhammed Ali. Some supporters spoke up early and forcefully, others late and with reservations.

The issues most frequently addressed by these personalities were issues on which the president had taken some action. Their statements were given as supportive evidence that the president had made great strides in some areas or had done what was possible, given the political circumstances, or that he promised to continue his past efforts on behalf of blacks and would strive to do more.

The biggest drift away from support of the president came during the primary elections, when Senator Kennedy challenged President Carter's renomination.

Domestic issues clearly received top priority in statements by black Carter supporters, although foreign policy issues were sometimes discussed, including the fact that he had kept us out of war. Two areas were particularly prominent: 1) employment; 2) opportunities for blacks to participate in the governing and decision-making processes of this country. Repeatedly cited was President Carter's employment record, to the effect that 8 million more jobs were created, more than under any previous administration[20] or that 8½ million more jobs were created and 95 million Americans were working.[21] Repeatedly cited was President Carter's black appointments record, bringing the number of black federal judges up to 40, 13 in the South. In less than four years President Carter changed the numbers from 16 to 40, from 0 to 13 in the South. He had appointed more black judges than all other Presidents combined.[22]

Responses to President Carter's black critics concerning promises he didn't keep may be summarized in Carl Rowan's statement that President Carter could not "remedy a now chronic situation where black unemployment runs double to white joblessness." In Rowan's view, President Carter didn't keep his promises because he couldn't keep them. He could not control the Congress, which was becoming more conservative. The public itself had grown "disenchanted with social programs for the poor."[23]

In mid-October, several persons well known in the black community announced their support for Governor Reagan: Reverend Ralph Abernathy and Hosea Williams, both former civil rights protest leaders, and later Mayor Charles Evers of Fayette, Mississippi. They said they supported Governor Reagan because President Carter had not kept his promises to blacks.

"Poor black people cannot make it under this system for another six months," Abernathy said.[24]

Because the Republican Party has long been perceived as hostile to or opposed to the interests of blacks, disclaimers of the Republican endorsement came from sectors of the black community. A rally was held by students in the Atlanta University Center in Atlanta, Georgia, at which they rejected the idea that Reverend Ralph Abernathy and Hosea Williams were their "leaders." Both are residents of Atlanta. In a straw vote on television, ABC's "Nightline," televised immediately after the Carter-Reagan debate, one interviewee said, "In fact, Ralph Abernathy's trip to Detroit, endorsing Reagan was already enough to get blacks out to vote for Carter." Abernathy and Williams had gone to Detroit where Governor Reagan and Ambassador Bush were on hand to receive the endorsement.

Governor Reagan, himself, had not seemed to be as much of an issue as the Republican Party until he went to Philadelphia, Mississippi, where three civil rights workers had been killed, and announced his support of states' rights. To blacks, "states rights" are "states wrongs," (wrongs perpetrated against blacks) as stated by Jesse Jackson in his endorsement of President Carter. While Governor Reagan may not himself be a racist, in the words of Rev. Joseph Lowery, chairman of the Southern Christian Leadership Conference, the black community perceives that racist forces have gravitated towards him.[25] But Governor Reagan made himself an issue when he said during the TV debate with President Carter, that when he was years younger, this country did not "know it had a race problem."

As important as the employment issue is, the perception that the Republican party and perhaps its leader are not in favor of the interests of blacks is more important. The alternative in this two-party system is the Democratic Party. Nonetheless, the Joint Center's statement that the issues are more complex than employment and party perception, may be true as evidenced by an increase in the number of blacks who voted Republican in 1980.

Issues in Perspective

It becomes abundantly clear from an examination of the issues that minorities cannot be treated alike on all issues. Their respective concerns diverge, conflict, and converge at points. For example, for blacks, the primary concerns are economics and education. For Jews,[26] economics and education are not the primary issues, since "sociological surveys report that Jews are now the most affluent group in America."[27] As a group, Jews are both affluent and educated. Jews are concerned about Israel.

The Hispanic community cannot be treated as a single entity. Cubans, e.g., unlike Mexican Americans, are concerned about Castro and Cuba. Like Jews, their concerns are not primarily economic. Alfredo Duran, former chairman of the Florida Democratic Party, said that Cubans do not analyze political issues like other minorities. Their concern is "foreign policy" which will "get rid of Castro." He said, the Republican party "insinuates" it will do so.[28] The Republican party also is perceived by Jews as the party which will give ideological, if not economic support to Israel and will recognize the PLO as a terrorist organization, largely sponsored by Russia.[29] Cuban-Jewish interests here converge on their perceptions of the Republican party as being supportive of their foreign policy concerns.

Blacks and Mexican Americans share common economic and educational interests. On this basis of common interests, they would likely share the view that the Democratic party, with its tradition of using the federal government to aid citizens, is the party that best represents their interests. An example of government aiding citizens stems from the government's "affirmative action" policy. This is one of the conflicts between the minority groups' interests: while blacks, 11 percent of the population, are allotted goals or "quotas," Jews, 2.7 percent of the population, are not allotted goals or quotas. Since they already have a disproportionate share of, e.g., educational slots (85 percent go to college),[30] their positions, obtained by individual merit, are perceived by them as being cut back and allocated to other minorities when quotas are imposed. Thus Jews are opposed to affirmative-action programs as they have developed and describe them as infringing on individual liberty—a long cherished American value.[31] This is one of the reasons for the strained relations between blacks and Jews.

Given these differences in their perceived interests, why have Jews historically been supportive of blacks? One obvious reason is that both groups are the objects of racism, active and latent—objects of racial hatred and hostility which exist independently of what the group does—good or bad. What affects one minority in this area, affects all minorities. Thus civil rights creates a common bond. For example, both groups were concerned with a "Reagan Court" and what this will mean. Civil rights protection is a "group" right. Yet there is within the Jewish community a feeling that protection of minorities as a group, in areas other than civil rights, undermines the interests of Jews. Their interests are generally best protected, they feel, when individuals, not groups are protected.

Demographics and Strategies

"Blacks constitute the largest and most cohesive minority within the American electorate."[32] Blacks are about 11 percent of the population and according to the 1980 census, are now 10.6 percent of the voting age population. While more than half live in the South, and are 16.8 percent of its voting age population, the greatest increase in growth has been in the Northwest and North Central sections, where blacks are now 9.1 and 8.2 percent of their respective voting age populations.

Blacks are heavily concentrated in 19 states, 14 below the Mason and Dixon line. The 14, including the District of Columbia, are: Alabama (22.5), Arkansas (13.9), Delaware (13.8), District of Columbia (66.5), Florida (11.6), Georgia (23.9), Louisiana (27.3), Maryland (20.1), Mississippi (31.2), North Carolina (19.6), South Carolina (27.7), Tennessee (14.0), Texas (11.3), Virginia (17.4). The percentage of the state's black voting age population in 1980 is given in the parenthesis. The remaining five states are key industrial areas and are pivotal in presidential elections: New York (12.8), New Jersey (11.4), Illinois (12.8), Michigan (11.7), Missouri (10.8). Two additional pivotal states are Pennsylvania (8.4) and Ohio (9.4).

While blacks have been heavily concentrated in central cities, the black suburban population increased by 41 percent from 1970–77.

The twenty largest cities with their respective percentages of the black voting age population are: New York (18.2), Chicago (27.7), Los Angeles (15.9), Philadelphia (29.7), Detroit (38.9), Houston (23.2), Baltimore (42.3), Dallas (21.4), Washington, D.C. (64.0), Cleveland (34.6), Indianapolis (14.5), Milwaukee (11.5), San Francisco (11.1), San Diego (6.3), San Antonio (7.8), Boston (13.2), Memphis (34.1), St. Louis (35.0), New Orleans (39.0), Phoenix (4.0).

A greater percentage of the black community is below voting age—36 percent—than in the white community—27.2 percent. There are proportionately more blacks between 18–24 years old than in the white community.

For a variety of reasons, blacks do not vote in as large numbers as whites. In 1976, only 49 percent indicated they had voted in the presidential election, while whites reported that 61 percent had voted. Northern blacks, however, voted at rates equivalent to northern whites. Overall since 1968, there has been a constant decline in voting. In 1976 there was a 54 percent turnout of all voters.

Turnout has continued high in the Jewish community, which constitutes 2.7 percent of the population and has a constantly diminishing birth rate.[33] "Nobody has to 'get out' the Jewish vote; 95 percent of the Jews show up at the polls."[34] Jews also are concentrated in six states with a heavy electoral college vote—New York (41), New Jersey (17), Florida (17), Illinois (26), Pennsylvania (27) and California (45). These are pivotal states in the electoral college. The electoral college count is given in the parenthesis. New York, New Jersey, and Illinois are states with a more than 10 percent black voting-age population.

The Hispanic or Latino population is estimated to be 12,708,800[35] or 5 percent. Of the total Spanish origin population, the breakdown for origin is: Mexican Americans, 59 percent; Puerto Ricans, 15 percent; Cubans 6 percent; Central South American, 7 percent; other Spanish, 12 percent. Fifty-nine percent of the total population lives in six states in the southwest; Arizona (16), California (17),

Colorado (12), New Mexico (39), Texas (22), Utah (4). Two other states with heavy percentages of Hispanic populations are New York (10) and Florida (8).

The Southwest Voter Education Project estimated that there would be 5.8 million voting age Hispanics by November 1980. Of this 5.8 million, they estimated that 59 percent would actually be registered to vote. Having assumed there would be an increase in voter turnout in 1980 over the 1976 voter turnout, the Project thus estimated the Latino vote would be significantly greater.

Sixteen states were targeted for Latino voter registration and turnout: Arizona, California, Colorado, Florida, Illinois, Indiana, Iowa, Michigan, New Jersey, New Mexico, New York, Ohio, Pennsylvania, Texas, Utah, and Wisconsin. Note that California, Florida, Illinois, New Jersey, New York and Pennsylvania were states where blacks and Jews are concentrated, and were targeted by both blacks and Hispanics. It appeared likely that these states would vote for President Carter. Hispanics had voted 75 percent for President Carter in 1976,[36] blacks had voted 90 percent for Carter in 1976,[37] Jews had voted 64 percent for Carter in 1976.[38]

What do these statistics mean? Because the president is elected by majority vote of the electoral college, and not by popular vote, the candidates and the minorities target those areas with the largest voting-age population and the largest number of electoral-college votes. The strategy is to get the potential voters registered and then get them out to vote. This was the strategy of both the black and Hispanic communities. Both had massive voter registration campaigns. In the black community it was "Operation Big Vote" which targeted seventeen states.

The Count Down

As much as 75 to 80 percent of all black registered voters actually voted in the 1980 presidential election, according to the NAACP.[39] Black voting reached an all-time high. Black registration had increased to almost 11.5 million or 67 percent of the black voting-age population. It was better than the 63.8 percent registered in the white voting-age population. The size of the black vote was contrary to predictions that many blacks would stay at home, as would other Americans. Blacks voted over 82 percent for President Carter, 14 percent for Governor Reagan, 3 percent for Congressman Anderson.[40] Blacks gave President Carter 21 percent of his popular vote count.[41]

Hispanics voted 54 percent for President Carter, 36 percent for Governor Reagan, 7 percent for Anderson.[42] It had been projected that Hispanics would "stay at home."[43] It was reported in Florida that the Latin community's number of registered voters had increased from 83,000 in 1976 to 125,000 in 1980. They were said to be "still passionately anti-Castro and enthusiastically pro-Reagan."[44] In Texas it was reported that the Southwest Voter Education Project had increased the number of registered voters by 53 percent since 1976: 488,000 to 750,000. If they actually voted, it was estimated they would give President Carter 70 percent of their vote. President Carter lost both Florida and Texas.

It was only in the Jewish community that Congressman Anderson, perceived as a liberal, received a significant vote from the minorities. The Jews voted 45 percent for President Carter, 39 percent for Governor Reagan, 14 percent for Congressman Anderson.[45] For the first time since the 1930s, the Jews gave the Democratic candidate less than 50 percent of their vote.[46] The Jewish 1980 vote was 5 percent of the total nationwide, nearly twice as much as their percentage of the total population—2.7. In New York, it was estimated that 18 percent of the state's vote or 1 in 5 voters in New York was Jewish.[47]

The dichotomy between black interests and Jewish-Cuban perception of the Republican party helps to explain part of the break-up in the 1980 election of the Democratic party's coalition, which had held since 1932. In that 1932 election, called a "realigning election," the electorate made lasting party identification changes. The majority party became the Democratic party, which was composed of a coalition of blacks, Jews, and other minorities, Catholics, blue collar workers, urban dwellers. The defection from the Democratic party in the 1980 election, leads to speculation as to whether it will be a "realigning election," which will make the Republican party the majority party.

In an analysis of the election, two of President Carter's close associates cited the loss as related to a mistaken strategy of targeting minorities. Former United States Attorney General Griffin Bell said, "the Democrats went overboard trying to attract black, Jewish and Hispanic votes. 'I think all those other people voted for Reagan.'"[48] Adviser and close friend, Charles Kirbo, said that President Carter had followed policies that were right, but not popular. It took courage for the president to "make an issue of appointing women, blacks and Hispanics."[49] He said that Senator Hubert H. Humphrey had told President Carter it would kill him politically, but the President did it anyway. Now it will be easier for other presidents to appoint women, blacks, and Hispanics, he said.

In his concession speech President Carter said, "We've tried to deal fairly with all people, with those who speak Spanish, with women, for those who've been deprived in life. . . . Sometimes it's aroused the displeasure of others and sometimes it's been politically costly."[50]

The electorate gave Ronald Reagan a landslide victory in the electoral college, though he received only 51 percent of the popular vote. The Republican party is now the majority party in the United States Senate. There are five Supreme Court Justices over 70 years old. This means that President Reagan most likely will have the opportunity to change the composition of the highest court in the land.

What this portends for racial minorities is of urgent interest, but that topic is beyond the scope of this paper. Carl Rowan likens the Republican administration to a trip back to the 1920s. Early indications are that "states' rights" will again have its day.

Chapter 7 Financing the Campaigns and Parties of 1980

Herbert E. Alexander

The 1980 presidential prenomination and general election campaigns were notable for the dissatisfaction they aroused over the long, grueling presidential-selection process and the discontent they stimulated with the laws that regulated the financing of the campaigns. Nevertheless, the 1980 presidential elections set records in the amounts of money raised and spent—well beyond increases due to inflation.

The 1980 presidential candidates, their committees, their political parties and independent committees, and individuals working on their behalf reported spending approximately $275 million on the presidential prenomination and general election campaigns, some $115 million more than was spent in 1976 to elect a president. Given a 35 percent rise in the consumer price index in the intervening years, the total amount spent in 1980 represented an increase of about $60 million in constant terms of value over amounts spent in 1976, and almost one-third of the increase was caused by the rise in independent candidate and minor party spending.

Of the $275 million total, some $106.3 million was spent during the prenomination period; approximately $10 million was spent to finance the parties' national nominating conventions; and $142 million was spent on behalf of major-party, minor-party, and independent general-election candidates. These figures do not include the cost equivalents of free broadcast time provided to some candidates during forums, debates, and other coverage of the campaigns, nor do they include delegates' expenses to and at the national conventions.

1980 was the second presidential election year in which public funding was provided. The largest contributor was the United States government, supplying about 37 percent, or $100.6 million of the $275 million spent. This money was derived from voluntary checkoff contributions that about 35 million taxpayers make each year by earmarking $1 each on their federal tax returns for the presidential election campaign fund. The checkoff receipts are aggregated over a four-year period but the payout is made only in the election year. The public funds this year were divided into about $29.7 million in matching funds for the Republican and Democratic candidates seeking nomination, $8.1 million for the major parties to hold their nominating conventions, and $58.8 million for Reagan and Carter in the general election. John Anderson qualified for about $4.2 million in postelection public funds by getting 6.5 percent of the vote (5 percent necessary to qualify), enabling him to pay off most of his debts.

The $275 million spent to elect the president in 1980 represents a sizable portion of the approximately $1 billion spent in behalf of candidates and political committees at all levels, federal, state, and local, during the 1980 election cycle. The consumer price index rises during the period between 1976 and 1980, accounted for much of the increase, but some campaign costs, such as television advertising, computer usage, and air travel, spiraled at a still higher rate than inflation.

The Prenomination Campaigns

The relatively high costs of the 1980 prenomination period may be credited to several factors; early announcements and early campaigning by an unusually large number of out-party candidates; an increase to thirty-six in the number of primaries plus a number of costly caucuses and, additionally, several straw polls in which some candidates felt obligated to participate; and a strong challenge to an incumbent president by a member of his own party.[1]

Federal Matching Funds

Under federal-election law, matching funds of up to one-half of the overall spending limit are available to candidates meeting a fund-raising requirement of $5,000 raised in individual contributions of $250 or less in each of 20 states. While the contribution limit for individuals is $1,000, only the first $250 of such contributions may be matched. Political action committee contributions are not matchable.

Of the approximately $106.3 million spent by the major presidential candidates to finance their 1980 prenomination campaigns, some $29.7 million—about 29 percent—came from federal matching funds. In 1976 the matching funds helped Jimmy Carter; in 1980 the public money helped candidates such as George Bush and John Anderson, who were, like Carter, not well-known, and did not have ready access to significant campaign funds, to stay in the prenomination race long enough to generate sufficient enthusiasm among the electorate to mount substantial campaigns. In this way the Federal Election Campaign Act has opened up the electoral process to candidates who otherwise might not have been factors in the prenomination contests.

Republican Candidate Receipts and Expenditures

In August 1978, nearly two years before the Republican nominating convention, Rep. Philip M. Crane of Illinois became the first major candidate to announce for the presidency. With his early announcement, Crane continued a trend toward increasingly early entry into the prenomination contest by little-known candidates seeking name recognition and a head start in fund raising and campaign staff organization. The success of early-announced candidates George McGovern in 1972 and Jimmy Carter in 1976 encouraged the trend. At the same time, the movement toward mass participation in the nominating system has led to more primaries and other prenomination contests. The changes in campaign financing laws have eliminated large contributors and placed a premium on carefully planning how to raise and spend limited amounts of money. Thus early announcements and key solicitation networks became necessities for many candidates.

In time Crane was joined by six other Republicans who remained in serious contention at least through the early stages of the primary season: Representative John Anderson of Illinois, Senator Howard Baker of Tennessee, George Bush, John Connally, Senator Robert Dole of Kansas and Ronald Reagan. Anderson, of course, dropped out of the race for the Republican presidential nomination in late April and announced as an independent candidate for the presidency. Two minor candidates, Ben Fernandez and Harold Stassen, also ran for the Republican nomination but failed to garner sufficient support and did not qualify for public funds.

Figures for receipts and expenditures of the nine Republican contenders are shown in table 7.1. Together the nine candidates reported receiving $71.1 million, of which $49 million, or 69 percent, was raised from individual contributions. Federal matching funds accounted for $19.1 million of the Republican candidates' receipts, or 26.7 percent of the total. Among the major candidates only John Connally decided not to accept the federal funds. And, once John Anderson opted for an independent route, thereby withdrawing from the Republican contest, he no longer was eligible to receive matching funds; he received $2.3 million in matching funds. Republican candiates spent $70.2 million.

Democratic Candidate Receipts and Expenditures

In the 1976 presidential prenomination period, an incumbent president met with a strong challenge from a member of his own party. The exceptional character of

Table 7.1

*Prenomination Receipts and Expenditures of Major Republican Contenders,
1980 (in millions)*

Candidate	Adjusted Receipts	Individual Contributions	"PAC" Contributions	Matching Funds	Adjusted Disbursements
Anderson	$ 6.6	$ 3.9	$ .02	$ 2.3	$ 6.5
Baker	7.1	4.2	.13	2.5	7.0
Bush	16.7	10.9	.13	5.7	16.7
Connally	12.7	11.6	.20	0.0	12.7
Crane	5.2	3.5	.00	1.9	5.2
Dole	1.4	.9	.05	.4	1.4
Reagan	21.4	13.8	.29	6.3	20.7
Total	$71.1	$48.8	$ .82	$19.1	$70.2

SOURCE: FEC news release, November 15, 1981, includes contributions and expenditures
reported through December 31, 1981. Matching funds and adjusted disbursements revised through
March 1982.

this occurrence, however, was tempered by the fact that the incumbent, Gerald
Ford, had never been elected to the presidency. Neither had Ford been elected to
the vice presidency, from which he moved up to the chief executive's office. By
the time the 1976 prenomination campaigns were getting started, then, Ford had
been in office a relatively short time and perhaps had not fully enjoyed all the
advantages of incumbency.

In 1979–80, an incumbent president once again met with a strong challenge
from a member of his own party. This time, however, the incumbent, Jimmy
Carter, had been elected to the office and had occupied it for nearly three years
by the time his major challenger, Massachusetts Senator Edward Kennedy, formally announced his candidacy. Carter also was challenged by California Governor Edmund G. Brown, Jr., whose last-minute campaign in 1976 had stirred
considerable interest. Lyndon LaRouche, United States Labor party founder, and
Cliff Finch, former Mississippi governor, also ran as candidates for the Democratic nomination, but neither was much of a factor, although LaRouche qualified
for and received public funding. The unusual competition involving an incumbent
president and major in-party opponents served to increase the amounts of money
spent in the Democratic prenomination contests.

Receipts and expenditures for the four qualifying Democratic contenders are
shown in table 7.2. Together the candidates reported receiving $35.7 million, of
which $24 million—67.2 percent—came from individual contributions and $10.5

Table 7.2

Prenomination Receipts and Expenditures of Major Democratic Contenders, 1980ᵃ (in millions)

Candidate	Adjusted Receipts	Individual Contri- butions	"PAC" Contri- butions	Matching Funds	Adjusted Disbursements
Brown	$ 2.7	$ 1.7	$ .04	$ .9	$ 2.7
Carter	18.6	12.9	.46	5.0	18.5
Kennedyᵇ	12.3	7.8	.23	4.1	12.3
LaRouche	2.1	1.6	. . .	.5	2.2
Total	$35.7	$24.0	$ .73	$10.5	$35.7

SOURCE: ᵃFEC news release, November 15, 1981, includes contributions and expenditures reported through December 31, 1981. Matching funds and adjusted disbursements revised through March 1982.
ᵇDraft-Kennedy total of $538,454 was in addition to the authorized committees noted in table, expended prior to Kennedy's announcement of candidacy.

million—29 percent—from federal matching funds. All four candidates accepted federal matching funds and the corresponding expenditure limits. Additional money was raised and spent by various draft-Kennedy committees operating in various states prior to the Senator's announcement; draft expenditures amounted to $538,000. Democratic candidates spent $35.7 million in the prenomination campaigns.

Although it will be a long time before the ledgers for the prenomination campaigns are finalized, several features of the financing of those campaigns are noteworthy.

Fund Raising

As in years past the major candidates employed a variety of fund-raising methods to raise the money they needed to finance their campaigns. Personal solicitation, direct mail, dinners, concerts, and other special events were used in different mixes by the candidates with different degrees of success.

In addition, the Kennedy campaign innovated some interesting methods in fund raising. The campaign attracted donors to some fund raisers by offering as door prizes paintings donated by prominent artists such as Andrew Wyeth. Prints of original silkscreens and lithographs donated by artists also were offered to the public in exchange for "suggested" contributions determined by the appraised values of the prints.[2] Under an interpretation by the Federal Election Commission, an artist's time and effort in producing a work of art donated to a campaign is considered volunteer activity. Only the cost of the artist's materials is counted toward the legal contribution limit.

The Kennedy campaign also introduced a "Convention Sweepstakes" mailing, offering 10 lucky winners free rooms at the Waldorf Astoria Hotel and unlimited passes to the New York Democratic National Convention. Though contributions were not required, two-thirds of the entrants did contribute to the campaign, and the FEC ruled their contributions were matchable by about $62,000 in federal funds.[3] These innovations in fund raising helped to keep the Kennedy campaign going when other fund sources slackened.

Financial Constraints

The candidates, including some of those in the thick of the race, experienced difficulty meeting the financial obligations of conducting their campaigns. It is generally agreed that the $1,000 individual contribution limit prevented some candidates from raising sufficient funds to campaign effectively. A $1,000 contribution in mid-1980 was worth only about $641 when compared with the buyer power of $1,000 in 1975 when the limit went into effect.

After Senator Kennedy lost three contests in a row to President Carter, two of them in New England, Kennedy forces decided to cut their campaign payroll by 50 percent and spend the money savings on television advertising, particularly in the large industrial states thought to be partial to Kennedy.[4] A short time later a number of his key staff persons resigned, reportedly because they were not being fully paid.[5] Art works by Andy Warhol, Jamie Wyeth and Robert Rauschenburg, some of them uncompleted, were put up as collateral for bank loans, including a $100,000 loan from the Chemical Bank of New York.[6]

The Carter campaign never missed a payroll, but because of a perceived need to spend large amounts early in the campaign to counter opposition first from draft-Kennedy committees and then from the Kennedy campaign itself, there were some close calls as the campaign progressed. For example, the tightness of money caused some limitations on campaign strategy; the campaign was forced to scrimp in Maryland in order to have sufficient funds to finance efforts in large states holding primaries on "Super Tuesday," June 3.

On the Republican side, though George Bush was able to outspend Ronald Reagan in late primaries, limited prospects of new money, among other reasons, led Bush to withdraw prior to the June 3 primaries. When Bush withdrew, his campaign was $300,000 in debt. Reagan forces also felt the pinch. By the time of the New Hampshire primary, the Reagan campaign was compelled to lay off a number of paid campaign workers and to rely more on volunteers.[7] Chartered air travel was cut back,[8] and attempts were made to supplant paid media advertising with press conferences and private interviews.[9] The campaign, having spent heavily early, was approaching two-thirds of the overall expenditure limit with the rest of the primary season yet to come.

Straw Polls

Nonbinding straw votes conducted at the Democratic and Republican state party conventions in Florida in November 1979 attracted the most attention among a number of straw polls—and the most spending by the candidates. Reagan forces spent $300,000 in Florida in 1979, with most of the money earmarked to win the straw vote.[10] John Connally's campaign spent $250,000 in an unsuccessful attempt to outpoll Reagan in Florida.[11] Carter forces spent an estimated $250,000 mobilizing for the October 13 local caucuses, at which half the Democratic state convention delegates were chosen.[12] That expenditure, which offset an expenditure of $175,000 by draft-Kennedy forces,[13] enabled Carter to come out ahead in the caucuses and in the nonbinding state convention vote. Additional presidental straw polls were held in Massachusetts, Maine, and California.

Expenditure Limits

As in the 1976 campaigns, so in 1980, the federal elections laws had a significant impact on campaign strategies and, one suspects, outcomes. In particular, campaigns were obligated to adjust to the law's spending limits—both the overall prenomination period limit and the state-by-state limits.

Overall Spending Limit

The national spending ceiling of candidates accepting public funding was $14.7 million. Their campaigns were allowed to spend an additional $2.9 million for fund-raising costs, bringing the total to $17.7 million. This forced campaigns with a realistic chance to remain in the race for the long term to plan carefully when to spend available money. They could spend heavily early, hoping to gain enough momentum to help propel their candidate in the campaign's later stages when they would have to spend less in order to remain within the spending limit. Or they could pick and choose where to spend money early, saving enough for heavier spending later in the campaign when the majority of primaries in the most populous states were held.

The Reagan campaign invested large sums early; two-thirds through the primaries, the campaign had only $2 million left to spend before reaching the limit. The Bush campaign carefully husbanded its funds through the early primary season and then outspent the Reagan campaign by as much as ten to one in the later primaries of Pennsylvania, Michigan and Texas. Though Bush won in Pennsylvania and Michigan and did better than expected in Texas, Reagan had built sufficient recognition and support to carry him to the nomination; accordingly, Bush withdrew.

It is worth noting that if former President Gerald Ford, who maintained a national following, had entered the prenomination contest in March 1980, as was widely speculated, and if he would have been able to raise sufficient funds, as is likely, he probably would have caused Reagan great difficulty in the remaining primaries. He would have been able to spend liberally while Reagan would have been severely constrained by earlier heavy spending credited against his overall limit.

Among the Democrats, the Carter campaign had spent more than $9 million by the end of March while the Kennedy campaign had spent about $7 million and having won primaries in New York and Connecticut, was beginning once again to enjoy some fund-raising success. Though Carter was handicapped by the spending ceiling in the late primaries, the lead he had built up over his opponent proved insurmountable.

State-by-State Limits

The state-by-state limits, which vary according to the state's voting-age population, also affected strategic decisions in the campaigns. Candidates felt the need to do well in early contests, which customarily are assigned more importance by the news media than the number of delegates at stake would otherwise warrant. This need for early success was reinforced by the election law under which a candidate drawing less than 10 percent of the vote in two consecutive primaries became ineligible for matching funds thirty days after the second primary and could be restored to eligibility only by winning 20 percent of the vote in a later primary. The low spending ceilings in those early contests in less populous states forced the candidates to budget tightly. A number of them, including Bush and Baker, spent near the limit in the nation's first primary in New Hampshire; Reagan, Carter and Kennedy actually exceeded the limit and were fined by the FEC. One candidate, John Connally, chose to reject public funding in order to avoid state limits. More than one candidate resorted to one or more subterfuges to get around the limits in the hope of gaining early advantage; examples included: stopping overnight during a primary campaign in states bordering on the primary state so the cost of accommodations could be counted against the other states' limits; arranging flights during a primary campaign to pass through cities outside the primary state, thus becoming interstate trips which, unlike intrastate trips, do not fall under the primary state's spending limit; adding a fund-raising element with each primary campaign event so at least some of the cost of the event would be exempt from the primary state's limit (fund-raising costs of up to 20 percent of the overall candidate spending limit are exempted from the limit); soliciting funds in all mailings in order to allocate mailing costs against the 20 percent fund-raising average and not against the spending limit; purchasing television, radio, and print advertising in cities outside a primary state when the city's media market included that state, so costs could be applied to another state's limits; or placing a primary state's field director or other primary state staff on the candidate's national staff so at least a portion of their salaries could be excluded from the primary state's limit.

FEC audits of prenomination expenditures revealed that both Ronald Reagan's and Jimmy Carter's campaign committees exceeded certain limitations in the primaries. Reagan's committee exceeded the New Hampshire limitations by $137,738, while Carter's committee exceeded the limits in three states; $53,477 in Iowa; $35,782 in Maine; and $34,177 in New Hampshire. Reagan's committee also exceeded the overall spending limit of $14.7 million by $77,387. The FEC audits also revealed that Reagan had a surplus of more than $2.8 million at the end of the prenomination period.

Independent Expenditures

The spending limits, particularly the state limits, enhanced the potential effectiveness of independent expenditures, especially in early primary states with low spending ceilings. According to the 1976 Supreme Court decision in the case of *Buckley v. Valeo,* individuals and groups can spend unlimited amounts in behalf of a candidate provided the spending is not coordinated with the candidate's own campaign organization.

Such expenditures worked to the advantage of those candidates attractive to organizations and individuals willing and able to mount independent spending campaigns in behalf of the candidates. Thus the Fund for a Conservative Majority spent more than $60,000 in New Hampshire in behalf of Ronald Reagan when his campaign was approaching the state's $294,000 spending limit.[14] The Fund also spent more than $80,000 in the Texas primary, and $600,000 in all, to help Reagan. Unless the law is revised, and the court agrees, independent expenditures will play an even greater role in future campaigns as familiarity with the law becomes more widespread.

"Presidential PACs" and Exploratory Committees

The law's overall spending limits encouraged the formation of political-action committees by a number of potential candidates a year or more before they announced their candidacies. In 1977 and 1978 Republican candidates Reagan, Connally, Bush and Dole formed PACs which organized speaking tours for their sponsors and served as vehicles through which the potential candidates raised and contributed funds and offered services to a variety of federal, state, and local candidates and party organizations around the country. The most successful of these PACs was Reagan's Citizens for the Republic, which spent $6.5 million from 1977 until 1980, almost $700,000 of it in direct or in-kind contributions to candidates at federal, state and local levels.[15] The ''Presidential PACs'' allowed each of the four presidential hopefuls to raise money and spend it on activities that would enhance their standing and increase their name recognition among party activists, but without having to count their expenditures against the overall spending limit that would apply to each announced candidate who accepted federal matching funds.

Other political candidates, such as Baker, Brown and Carter formed exploratory committees that could raise and spend money in their behalf before they formally announced their candidacies. Expenditures by such committees, however, are counted toward the overall spending limit of the potential candidates who form them if the individuals later announce their candidacies.

Early Money

Early money has often been said to be worth much more than money received later in a campaign. While a large early campaign chest is necessary in mounting a major presidential campaign, it does not ensure success. In the 1976 election, Alabama Governor George Wallace, Washington Senator Henry Jackson and Texas Senator Lloyd Bentsen were the leading fund raisers early in the Democratic prenomination contest. Yet their campaigns came to an end in the middle of the primary season. In the 1979–80 campaigns, John Connally far surpassed all the others in raising money early. By the end of 1979, he had raised nearly $9.2 million, about $3.5 million more than any other candidate. Connally ended up spending $12.7 million and still came up with only a single delegate pledged to him. His poor showing at the polls forced him to withdraw after the South Carolina primary. Early money helps, but early prenomination contest victories are much more helpful.

Television Coverage

Television coverage of campaigns—or the lack of such coverage—continued to play an important part in the prenomination campaigns. Despite the fact that Reagan, Carter, and Connally were rebuffed by the three networks in their efforts to buy program time in late 1979 and early 1980, the major contenders all spent a significant percentage of their campaign treasuries on television advertising, including buying television time and paying production costs, which range from 20 to 33 percent of the cost of air time. In addition, campaign strategies were devised to get free network or local station coverage.

The Reagan campaign thought television coverage of Reagan's announcement of candidacy so important that when the national networks refused to sell the time it wanted in mid-November—maintaining it was too early for TV politicking—the campaign put together a makeshift network of about ninety stations to air the speech at a premium cost of $400,000. The Carter campaign also was unsuccessful in persuading the networks to sell program time for its candidate's December 4th announcement of candidacy. Finally two networks offered Carter time in early January, and he bought a half-hour on ABC at a cost of $86,000 for air time. The Carter prenomination campaign spent a total of $4,215,050 on media, most of it going for TV air time and production costs.

In deciding not to accept public funds for his campaign, John Connally made clear that television was a prominent factor. Connally believed only ample television exposure could project him into a competitive position vis-à-vis front-runner Reagan. When the national networks refused to sell him thirty-minute segments of prime time in November and December 1979, Connally shifted his strategy to buy the attention he sought in the primary states.

The money Connally spent on television advertising did not bring him the election victories he sought. Nor did television advertising result in success for most of the other candidates who felt the need to spend their funds on it. Yet the 1980 prenomination campaign confirmed that wise use of television remains an essential ingredient of winning.

A suit brought to require broadcasters to sell such early time to presidential candidates was decided by the United States Supreme Court in favor of requiring broadcasters to provide "reasonable access."

A series of three forums, sponsored by the League of Women Voters, was held among Republican candidates, at no cost to the candidates. And three newspaper forums also were held and broadcast, although Reagan paid for one following an adverse advisory opinion by the Federal Election Commission.

Polling

Polling remained important in prenomination campaign strategy, both the polling conducted by the candidates' own pollsters to determine how campaign resources were to be allocated, and the polling conducted by organizations publicly reporting on public opinion. The discoveries of candidate-hired pollsters helped determine how the candidates might most effectively spend the campaign funds they had available. The results of published public opinion polls, however, often determined whether the candidates would receive the funds they needed to carry on their campaigns. An Anderson staff member described the likely reaction to a candidate low in the polls when he or she seeks campaign contributions: "Lou Harris says you're stuck at two points. Why should I give you $250?"[16]

Campaign Debt Reduction

When the primary season ended, the losing Republican presidential candidates banded together with Ronald Reagan to help pay off the losers' campaign debts. Former candidates Baker, Connally, Dole, Fernandez and Crane joined Reagan as hosts of a series of four "presidential unity dinners." Former candidate George Bush lent his name to the fund-raising dinners, though his campaign did not seek a share in the dinner proceeds, preferring instead to pay off its estimated $300,000 debt through mail solicitations.[17] At the time the unity dinners were announced late in May, Connally's deficit was close to $1.5 million.[18] Baker's deficit as of May 19 was reported to be $890,586, Crane's was said to be $398,057 and Dole's was estimated at $113,000.[19] With the exception of Connally, the dinner cohosts were able to use the money they raised through the dinners to qualify for additional federal matching funds until their deficits were paid off.

The first of the dinners, a $500-a-plate affair held in Beverly Hills on June 13, brought in gross receipts of $550,000.[20] A substantial portion of the net proceeds from that dinner went for production of a thirty-minute television show drawn from the dinner, which was aired on CBS on June 21 and served as a fund-raising appeal, the proceeds of which were divided among the various candidates. Winning candidate Reagan, whose campaign paid only one percent of the cost of the program, benefitted from the exposure and from the endorsements of those he had defeated.[21] The program was not counted as an in-kind contribution to the Reagan campaign since it was reported to the FEC as part of a joint fund-raising operation by the unsuccessful Republican candidates to reduce their campaign debts. A Baker spokesperson said the response to the program was "very positive."[22] Other unity dinners were held in Chicago, New York, and Houston. Proceeds from the dinners—$1.4 million in all—had to be allocated in such a way that no donor exceeded the $1,000-per-candidate contribution limit, and the FEC played an important role in determining allocations. Most of the proceeds of the dinners and the videotape went to Connally and Baker, who had the largest debts.

Losing candidates also used a variety of other approaches to pay off their campaign debts. Like George Bush, Howard Baker used direct mail with good results.[23] John Connally wanted to sell donated art works through an art dealer with the sale exempt from the contribution limits, much as the sale of left-over campaign materials is exempt.[24] Adverse FEC and IRS rulings, however, severely limited the potential effectiveness of Connally's novel approach.[25]

On the Democratic side, Kennedy ended with a debt of $2.2 million, and Carter ended with a debt of $650,000, half of it incurred by the campaign itself and half by its compliance effort. The Kennedy and Carter campaigns struck an agreement whereby the proceeds of three unity dinners, scheduled for October 19, December 4, and December 12 of 1980 were to be split between the two candidates until both debts were paid up. Only one such dinner was held, however, and it failed to garner significant proceeds. For his part, Governor Brown paid off his $600,000 campaign debt through proceeds from a number of private fund-raising events. The Democratic fund raising for debt reduction was criticized in the general-election period when competitive funds were being sought by the Democratic national, state and local party committees for their support on behalf of the presidential ticket, and by the Carter-Mondale Committee for compliance costs.

Financing the Conventions

As in 1976, in 1980 the two major political parties received federal grants to finance their conventions. The 1979 FECA Amendments raised the basic grant to $3 million. When indexed to take into account the rise in the consumer price index, the federal subsidy amounted to $4.4 million for each convention in 1980, although the Democrats spent only $3.7 million. The federal grants are used to pay for such convention-related expenses as salaries and professional fees, platform hearings prior to the conventions, printing, telephone, and staff travel. They replace in large measure the previous mode of convention financing whereby host cities and local businesses furnished cash and services to the party conventions, and national corporations bought advertising space at considerable cost in convention program books. None of the federal grant money could be used to defray the expenses of any candidates or delegates participating in the conventions.

Since the federal grants do not provide sufficient funds to finance all aspects of the conventions, state and local governments where the conventions are held are allowed to provide the convention halls and certain services and facilities to the parties.

Money spent by the presidential candidates during the convention for such things as communications and living arrangements, came out of the candidates' own campaign funds and was counted toward the overall prenomination period expenditure limit. Money spent by delegates to pay their convention expenses—

travel, food, lodging and so on—generally came out of the delegates' own pockets.

Additional money was spent at the Republican convention in behalf of candidates for the vice-presidential nomination, such as Representative Jack Kemp of New York ($56,700) and North Carolina Senator Jesse Helms ($219,400).[26] About $100,000 were spent at the Democratic convention in an effort to free delegates from the rule binding them to vote on the first ballot for the candidates they were elected to support, thus seeking to "open up" the convention.[27]

The General Election Campaigns

Total spending in the 1980 presidential general election campaigns far exceeded the corresponding amount spent in 1976. In 1976 spending in behalf of the campaigns of major-party candidates Jimmy Carter and Gerald Ford totalled approximately $60.2 million.[28] Independent and minor-party candidates accounted for an additional $2 million in expenditures.[29] In the 1980 general election campaigns, spending in behalf of major-party candidates Ronald Reagan and Jimmy Carter came to about $115 million, almost twice the 1976 amount and an increase far beyond the 35 percent rise in the consumer price index between 1976 and 1980. In addition, spending in behalf of independent and minor-party candidates amounted to about $20.2 million, roughly a ten-fold increase over the 1976 amount.

Major-party Candidate Receipts and Expenditures

Each of the major-party candidates benefitted from a patchwork of funds amounting to $64.3 million for Reagan and $53.9 million for Carter (see table 7.3). Some of the funds were within the direct control of the candidates, notably the $29.4 million federal grant each received from the presidential checkoff fund, and which served as an expenditure limitation. That amount was supplemented by the approximately $4 million each national party committee spent in conjunction with the presidential campaign. The candidates also could exercise indirect control over allowable state and local party committee spending—$15 million in behalf of Reagan and $4 million in behalf of Carter—through the coordinating activities of the national party committees. Other funds were outside the candidates' control, such as independent expenditures of about $11 million and corporate, labor and other business spending of some $3 million in behalf of Ronald Reagan, and labor spending of about $15 million in behalf of Carter. Though labor's spending could not be controlled by the Carter staff, it could be coordinated with the campaign.

Table 7.3

Sources of Funds in 1980 General Election for Major Party Candidates (in millions)

Sources of Funds	Reagan	Carter
Federal Grant	$29.2	$29.4
National Party	4.5	4.0
State and Local Party	15.0	4.0
Independent Expenditures[a]	10.6	.03
Labor	1.5	15.0
Corporate/Association	1.5	-0-
Compliance	1.5	1.5
Transition Planning	.5	-0-
Total	$64.3	$53.93

SOURCE: Citizen's Research Foundation
[a]In addition, $209,781 were spent against Carter and $47,868 against Reagan.

In addition to money spent to further the campaigns of the two candidates, each major-party candidate's campaign committee raised privately and spent money to pay for the costs of complying with the election laws, amounting to $1.5 million each for Reagan and Carter. Contributions to each candidate's Legal and Accounting Compliance Fund are subject to the law's $1,000 individual contribution limit. Finally, each presidential candidate who accepts federal funding for the general election campaign is allowed to spend up to $50,000 of personal or family funds on the campaign, although neither did.[30]

Each major-party candidate spent more than half his federal allotment of $29.4 million on media advertising, with the lion's share going to pay for television advertising costs. Carter's media costs totalled $20.5 million, $15.8 million of it on television. An additional $2.6 million went to radio advertising, and the remainder was spent on the print media and production costs. The Reagan campaign spent $16.2 million in media costs, with $10.2 million on television, $1.5 million on radio, and $2.2 million on newspapers. Other categories of campaign expenditures were transportation costs, particularly air transportation for the candidates and their running mates and surrogates to conduct their nationwide campaigns; lodging for the candidates and their staffs; staff salaries and consultant fees; telephones; office rental, equipment and furniture; polling; and campaign materials.

The Reagan campaign was able to count on significant spending by the Republican National Committee and by state and local party committees to help cover the costs of volunteer-operated voter registration and get-out-the-vote drives and other such activities directed at the general public to further the national campaign.

The campaign committee's federal grant of $29.4 million, then, was available to be used primarily for media, salaries, travel, and lodging,

The Carter campaign, however, could not count on the same level of support from Democratic state party committees; consequently the Carter committee had to use part of its federal grant to pay for some of the things the state-party committees might have paid for, such as telephone banks and get-out-the-vote programs—or do without them.[31] Strains on the Carter campaign budget forced the campaign to cut down on many of its travel costs,[32] and to choose carefully the states in which to spend its limited funds.[33] The Carter campaign agreed to handle bills which had to be paid immediately, while some deferable bills were the responsibility of the DNC.

Rising Costs

Several factors account for the notable rise in 1980 spending in behalf of the two major-party candidates:

In 1980 the amount each national party was permitted to spend on the presidential campaigns was $4.6 million. The Republicans spent $4.5 million while the Democrats spent only about $4 million.

In 1976 state and local party committees were not permitted to spend more than $1,000 each on grass-roots efforts in support of their presidential ticket. The 1979 FECA amendments enhanced the role of state and local party committees by permitting them to spend unlimited amounts on voter registration and get-out-the-vote drives and on other volunteer activities that would benefit the parties' presidential tickets. The amendments also allowed the national party organizations to help the state and local party committees develop volunteer programs and coordinate them with the national campaigns.

In 1980 Republican state and local party committees spent an estimated $15 million in behalf of the Reagan-Bush ticket. Democratic state and local parties spent about $4 million in behalf of the Carter-Mondale ticket.

In 1976 independent expenditures played an insignificant role in the presidential campaigns of Jimmy Carter and Gerald Ford. In 1980, several independent committees and individuals spent about $10.6 million, largely on communications with the public, in behalf of Ronald Reagan's candidacy.

In 1976 labor union groups spent some $11 million on internal communications with their members, on voter registration and on getting out the vote. Most of that spending was not required to be reported even though it was carefully coordinated with the Carter-Mondale campaign. On the other hand, corporations and other business-related groups, many of which might have been expected to support Gerald Ford in the general election campaign, spent very little on internal communications, voter registration or get-out-the-vote activities.

In 1980 labor once again supported the Carter-Mondale ticket—however reluctantly and belatedly—spending about $15 million on reported and unreported communications costs directed at members and their families and on voter registration and getting out the vote. Corporations and other business-related groups including several supportive labor unions spent about $1.5 million on similar activities in behalf of the Reagan-Bush ticket.

Independent and Minor-Party Candidate Receipts and Expenditures

Spending in behalf of independent and minor-party candidates—$20.2 million—was not surprising, given John Anderson's candidacy. In contrast to the major-party candidates, independent and minor-party candidates must finance their campaigns entirely with private funds raised in accordance with the federal election law's contribution limits. Such candidates receive no federal funds in advance of their campaigns—unless their party's candidate received 5 percent or more of the popular vote in the previous presidential election—and may receive federal funds retroactively according to a complex formula only if they appear on the ballot in at least ten states and receive at least 5 percent of the vote in the general election. The independent candidacy of John Anderson so qualified.

John Anderson

John Anderson's campaign efforts were plagued throughout by financial difficulties and by the need to spend an inordinate portion of available funds on legal battles and on fund raising. Indeed, the Anderson campaign was waged almost as much in the courtroom and at the FEC as on the campaign trail.

When Anderson declared his independent candidacy on April 24, he faced formidable obstacles. The $1,000 contribution limit prevented wealthy contributors from providing "seed money" for his campaign. Initially he had no chance to receive federal funds, even retroactively, since the FECA provided for such funds only for candidates who were nominess of political parties.

Fund raising was slow and fell short of expected—and needed—amounts. Raising a total of $12.1 million in contributions and loans, the Anderson campaign conducted most of its fund raising through direct mail appeals prepared by Craver, Mathews, Smith and Company, of Arlington, Virginia. Other sources of the approximately 14.4 million spent were contributions in response to newspaper ads and telephone solicitations; fund-raising events that included personal appearances by the candidate, members of his family, and his running mate, former Wisconsin Democratic Governor Patrick Lucey; local grass-roots events; fund-raising concerts and special events featuring such Hollywood entertainers as singer

James Taylor and actor Ed Asner; and contributor loans. The Anderson campaign also sought to tap affluent donors with a national finance council composed mainly of wealthy professionals who gave $1,000 to the campaign and pledged to raise $10,000 more.[34] An Arts for Anderson program solicited original artwork from more than a dozen artists to be used as prizes in lotteries with chances sold at $1,000 a ticket.[35]

The Anderson campaign challenged the interpretation of the FECA that limited the possibility of retroactive federal funding to candidates of political parties. The campaign filed suit in a United States District Court in Washington, D.C., against the FEC on the matter, but before a decision could be rendered, the FEC itself decided Anderson's "national unity campaign" was the functional equivalent of a political party and on September 4 declared by a five to one vote that Anderson was eligible for federal campaign subsidies if he received at least 5 percent of the vote on November 4. The resultant sense of euphoria among campaign staffers dissolved quickly when the hoped-for bank loans were not forthcoming. Even though a subsequent FEC decision assured bankers that loans to the Anderson campaign would not violate FEC standards, the campaign was unable to negotiate any substantial bank loans. At the end of September, Anderson was forced to ask his more than 200,000 grass-roots donors for loans as small as $10 or $25, with 8 percent interest promised. His obligation to repay these loans ensured that he would remain a candidate to the end, to seek to qualify for public funds.[36]

There were no significant independent expenditures in behalf of John Anderson's general election campaign, nor did the candidate enjoy the benefit of corporate, business or labor spending in his behalf.

Just as Anderson had to rely on sources of funds quite different from those that financed his major-party opponents, he had to face different campaign costs. Though direct mail proved an essential source of funds, it also was an expensive fund-raising approach costing the Anderson campaign $3 million.

The Anderson campaign had to spend an enormous amount of money on organizing signature petition drives and legal assistance in getting on the state ballots—$2 million in all. Since such expenses did not leave much money to mount a television ad campaign[37]—a little more than $2 million—Anderson had to rely on free television time. His campaign included a large number of media interviews, especially on local television stations.[38] He readily agreed to take part in the September 21 nationally televised debate with Ronald Reagan and took Jimmy Carter to task for refusing to participate. And his campaign no doubt suffered from the decision excluding him from the October 28 nationally televised debate between Jimmy Carter and Ronald Reagan.

Lack of sufficient funds also caused Anderson to curtail travel plans, to cut back on his campaign staff and to ask some staff members to work for very low pay.

John Anderson concluded his independent campaign with a debt of about $5 million, including $2 million owed to individuals who loaned the campaign money in the closing days of the general-election period. By winning 6.5 percent of the popular vote, Anderson qualified for about $4.2 million in retroactive federal funds, which allowed him to pay off most of his campaign debts.

Minor-Party Candidates

A variety of minor-party candidates accounted for an additional $7 million in presidential general election campaign spending. The best financed of the minor-party campaigns was Libertarian party candidate Ed Clark's campaign. Clark, a lawyer on leave from the Atlantic Richfield Co., whose name was on the ballot in all 50 states, received a significant portion of his funding from his running mate, millionaire chemical engineer David Koch, and the Koch family, who had contributed nearly $600,000 to Clark's campaign by mid-August 1980.[39] Other sources of the approximately $3.3 million received by Clark's campaign were responses to monthly mailings to party sympathizers and to conference phone calls by Clark and Koch with potential donors.[40] The campaign also started a 52-city closed circuit television rally designed to raise money to pay for a number of 5-minute television spots.[41] This effort raised "in excess of $175,000," enough to pay for seven such spots.[42] Significant expenditures for Clark's campaign in addition to television advertising were travel costs of a candidate tour through most of the 50 states and salaries for a campaign staff of 25.[43]

The Citizens' party, founded in 1979, and its presidential candidate, environmentalist Barry Commoner, were also visible in the 1980 presidential campaign, though Commoner's campaign was not as well-financed as that of Clark. Still, after compiling the expenditures by various authorized and unauthorized committees, Commoner spent about $1.1 million, most of which went to pay for signature-gathering in ballot-access drives and some radio ads.[44] Almost $1 million was raised by other minor-party candidates, including those from the American Independent and the Socialist Worker parties.

General Election Campaign Finance Issues and Strategies

Observation of the 1980 general election campaigns and interviews with numerous presidential campaign finance officers and campaign committee staff members suggest several notable features of the financing of those campaigns.

Increased Private Giving

The apparent effectiveness of independent expenditures totalling $1.4 million in behalf of Ronald Reagan during the prenomination period and the conviction that contributors to Reagan's prenomination campaign would seek outlets to further his candidacy during the general election period encouraged several groups to begin organizing independent expenditure campaigns even before Reagan had been formally nominated. By mid-July five such committees had announced plans to make independent expenditures in Reagan's behalf. Three of the committees— the National Conservative Political Action Committee, the Fund for a Conservative Majority and the North Carolina-based Congressional Club—had been in existence and had proven direct mail fund-raising ability. Their fund-raising goals were relatively modest. Two other committees—Americans for Change and Americans for an Effective Presidency—were formed expressly to advance Reagan's candidacy, and their fund-raising goals were high. As the general election campaign developed, the committees were forced to scale down their overly ambitious fund-raising goals from a total of $30-55 million to a more realistic $10-15 million. Lawsuits by Common Cause and the FEC opposing the independent committees, and complaints filed with the FEC by the Carter-Mondale Committee early in the campaign undoubtedly slowed the committees' fund raising and dampened the enthusiasm of some contributors.

Despite the failure of the independent committees to reach their combined goal, however, they and other independent groups and individuals did account for a significant portion of the private funds—about $13 million—that helped finance all of the general election campaigns, apart from the private funds that went to independent and minor-party candidates. This private giving, largely absent in 1976, may signal a growing interest on the part of a number of citizens to become financially involved in the political process. It also may signal dissatisfaction with current election laws that prohibit private contributions to candidates who accept public funds in general election campaigns. This development encourages some rethinking of the place of pocketbook participation in presidential general election campaigns.

The Role of Television

As in 1976, television played a role of great importance in the 1980 general-election campaigns. Both major-party candidates devoted more than half their federal grant money to television advertising. They and independent candidate John Anderson planned much of their campaign activity around the possibility of its being broadcast on national and local television news programs, and Anderson, especially, placed great hope in what his inclusion and performance in televised debates with his opponents could do for his candidacy. He realized that participation in a televised debate—at no direct cost to his campaign—would give him more exposure than he could possibly buy. Even minor-party candidate Ed Clark launched a significant television advertising campaign, however modest it might have seemed in comparison with the efforts of the Reagan and Carter campaigns.

Incumbency

In the prenomination campaign incumbency proved to be an advantage for President Carter in his competition with Senator Kennedy. The president deftly used the perks of office, including the incumbent's ability to command media attention. In the general election period, incumbency functioned as a double-edged sword. Carter still was able to attract the media attention that goes only to a sitting president, as network coverage of his September 18 news conference indicates. He still was able to count on high-ranking administration officials to make political speeches on his behalf. Since many voters, however, tend to blame the incumbent and his administration for whatever woes the country may be suffering, the country's economic decline and its difficulties abroad made incumbency a heavy burden for Carter to bear.

Negative Advertising

Both major-party campaigns spent significant sums on negative advertising. The Reagan campaign aired ads intended to convey the message that Jimmy Carter was a failure as a leader and administrator. The Carter campaign aired ads that sought to discredit Reagan and to raise questions about John Anderson's congressional voting record. In addition, pro-Reagan independent committees sponsored ads that questioned Carter's religious integrity, and at least one pro-Reagan committee funded an anti-Anderson television ad.

Though negative ads may command greater attention from viewers and listeners than bland, positive pitches in behalf of candidates, they run the risk of arousing sympathy for the candidates they are meant to discredit and of appearing mean-spirited and vindictive. It is difficult to determine just what effect negative advertising had in the 1980 campaigns, but Carter was forced to admit he had to tone down his overall attack on Reagan in the face of criticism that he was taking the low road in campaigning. In addition, anti-Anderson radio and television ads sponsored by the Carter campaign, along with other Carter campaign and Democratic party efforts to stymie Anderson's campaign, angered the independent candidate and may have strengthened his resolve to stay in the race—despite low standing in public opinion polls.

The Importance of Party Organization and Support

Though there has been a trend throughout the past decade toward personal politics characterized by campaigns carried on independently of the political parties, the

1980 general election campaigns served to underscore the importance of party organization and support. The Reagan campaign owed much of its success to the formidable fund-raising and organizational skills of the Republican party, under the direction of Republican National Committee Chairman Bill Brock. From January 1979 through late September 1980, the national party committee recognized 965 gifts of at least $10,000 each for membership in the Eagles program of large contributors.[45] The committee set aside $5,000 out of each of those contributions until it reached the $4.6 million level it could spend in behalf of the nominee.[46] Despite the large amount of money it received from big donors, however, the RNC raised most of its money from small contributors. In 1979 the committee netted $12 million from 550,000 contributors who responded to direct mail appeals. The average contribution was $26.[47] In 1980 the committee netted more than $30 million from about 750,000 donors responding to further direct-mail appeals.[48]

The RNC spent a significant portion of the $4.6 million it was allowed to spend directly on the Reagan campaign to pay for "Commitment '80," a program designed to mobilize thousands of Reagan volunteers in a massive pro-Reagan get-out-the-vote drive. In states where it was best organized, the Reagan campaign itself oversaw the volunteer efforts and absorbed the expenses out of its $29.4 million federal allotment. In the remaining states the RNC supervised and state Republican committees paid for the volunteer program.[49]

The RNC also spent money in other ways that benefitted the Reagan campaign. The committee spent $8.5 million on television advertising urging voters to "vote Republican for a change," and to elect "the Republican team."[50] The national committee also spent $1 million on voter registration efforts.[51]

In addition to money raised and spent by the RNC in behalf of the presidential ticket, Republican state and local party committees raised some $15 million to fund volunteer activities that would further the national campaign. In fact, the Reagan campaign made raising money for state and local committees to spend on the Republican ticket a top priority and even encouraged potential donors to its compliance fund to give instead to the party committees. On September 29th, a series of 20 closed-circuit dinners were held, grossing $7 million.

In contrast, the Carter campaign expected the Democratic National Committee to spend the maximum $4.6 million in conjunction with the campaign, but the DNC was not able to raise the money early or easily. The national committee, which has never enjoyed the financial successes of its Republican counterpart, was stymied in its efforts to raise money during the primary season as the competition between Carter and Kennedy siphoned off funds the DNC might otherwise have received. Once the primaries were over, the DNC began a series of large fund-raising events through which it hoped to raise $8 million of its $14 million target. The remainder was slated to come from responses to direct mail appeals and from large contributions to the DNC's national finance council. Part of the monies it spent was for a modest volunteer program in conjunction with the Carter-Mondale campaign, and part was a DNC-conducted drive to identify and register probable Carter supporters in targeted states and to get out the vote on November 4.

The Carter campaign received only about $4 million of support from Democratic state and local party committees, even though both Carter and his running mate Walter Mondale spoke at events designed to raise money for the party committees. A main reason for the relatively low figure was the sometimes intense competition for available dollars among the Democratic National Committee seeking to raise its $4.6 million; various state and local party committees, the Carter-Mondale compliance fund, and a unity dinner committee seeking to raise money to help pay off Carter and Kennedy primary campaign debts.

The Impact of the Law

Low individual contribution limits, $1,000 per candidate per election, are one reason for the long prenomination campaigns, because candidates need to gear up their fund raising early in order to obtain "seed money" to get the campaign rolling. The finance laws put a premium on fund raisers who have access to lists of contributors and membership groups. The individual contribution limit should be raised to $5,000 per candidate per election.

No major-party candidate fund raising is permitted in the general elections for general purposes, but candidates do raise money for their compliance costs, for national and state party committees, and to help themselves and others erase prenomination debts.

The costs of compliance, while exempted from expenditure limits, impact on other fund raising needs, but in the prenomination period, some expenditures under the limits can be allocated to fund-raising or compliance costs, thus protecting the candidate's expenditure limit.

Expenditure limits require central control of spending, dictate strategy, force careful planning in the use of resources, and reduce spontaneity and flexibility in campaigning.

State-by-state expenditure limits forced candidates for nomination to undertake subterfuges in order to stay within the limits. John Connally refused public funding mainly in order to avoid expenditure limits. The 1979 Amendments gave the state and local political party committees a role they did not have in 1976, and brought more grass-roots campaigning in the general election period.

The national party committees no longer need to raise money for their conventions, but can do so in the general election period to supplement the spending by the nominated candidate.

Independent candidates are at a severe disadvantage, needing to raise money while the major party candidates receive theirs in flat grants from the government. The Federal Election Commission was innovative in recognizing John Anderson's independent campaign as the functional equivalent of a minor party, although the need to pay off debts and loans forced Anderson to try to qualify for public money, dictating his strategy till the end.

Money did not determine who won in 1980, either in the prenomination campaigns or in the general election, but expenditure limits were low in both cases. Low limits played a role in triggering independent expenditures, which violated the sanctity of both the contribution and expenditure limits. But still other spending occurred beyond the limits. The Carter people have pointed out still more indirect Reagan spending than has been accounted for, including $8.5 million in "anti-Democrat" TV spots paid for by the Republican National Committee but directed to help senatorial and congressional candidates as well, and "non-partisan" evangelical and "new right" spending that opposed programs of the Carter administration. Republicans point to federal government spending programs expertly used by the president to benefit his campaign. All the activity and accusations point to the United States as a pluralistic society with many ways, direct and indirect, to affect election outcomes. All the indirect ways raise questions about the effectiveness of election reform, and the Congress will need to address the reasons for the many forms of spending that occurred in the 1980 presidential elections.

While there is much reason for criticism of the presidential selection process and the financing laws, the system did not discourage potential candidates from running, the results did seem to reflect the popular will, and factors other than money played key roles in the outcomes.

Chapter 8   Media Influence in Presidential Politics

Robert D. McClure

The 1980 presidential election was predominately a mass-media election. The Carter-Reagan race also was shaped by some old-fashioned political organization, however, and some instinctual voter reaction that not even the powerful pulse of media politics could overwhelm completely. In short, while the 1980 election was *mainly* a mass-media election, it was not *solely* one. Other "outside" factors influenced events, and an understanding of these other influences rivals in importance an understanding of the media's impact.

By media election, I mean that the mass media is the *primary* (but not necessarily the sole) mitigating/organizing institutional link between candidates and voters. In this situation, the mass media becomes the dominant carrier of the dialogue between elites and the main vehicle through which voters get their political information: Quite simply, the mass media becomes the most preferred and frequently used *conduit* through which candidates seek to create and mobilize a majority. In other words, in modern elections, the mass media is the string between the Dixie cups of American politics.

It should be added that this definition of mass media election does not connote that citizens necessarily are more easily bamboozled because candidates can now use the media to manipulate voters more successfully or that media elites can now successfully conspire to control the outcome of presidential elections more completely. As the principal conduit of American presidential elections all that is meant is that the mass media, as an institution, naturally guides and shapes the content and strategy of the campaign and the citizens' perceptions of the candidates and issues, and therefore the mass media indirectly (at least) influences the whole process, including the outcome. In other words, it is the mass media that increasingly has the task of organizing the nation's political choices, and it is to the mass media that both candidates and voters first turn to play presidential politics.

Within this context, let me state precisely the broad theme of this analysis of the media in the 1980 election (for the theme goes beyond just commenting on and interpreting the 1980 presidential election): The mass media as an institution cannot execute adequately the major mitigating/organizational role that it has been assigned and has ACCEPTED. Bluntly, mass-media elections are flawed elections.

The mass media cannot play its newly acquired role because its traditional institutional habits and journalistic canons unwittingly, but inevitably, combine to present an unreal, cynical picture of politics which over the long run serves to corrupt the people's sense of good government and ultimately to diminish their capacity to meet the ordinary demands of enlightened citizenship. Thus, mass-media influence does not serve to organize national politics or to enhance popular control of government; it serves instead to aid disorganization and decay.

Make no mistake: The mass media does not corrupt the nation's politics intentionally; it does it out of the best, not the worst, of motives; it does it without, not because of, a conspiracy. The damage is done simply by the behavior that results from the laudable logic of the mass media as an institution (a logic created prior to its present burden in presidential politics) and the laudable logic of the legal and philosophic environment which produces the regulation in which at least the electronic media is forced to operate.

Implicit in this argument is the contention that political parties can better perform the primary role of organizing American politics and presidential elections. It is at least implied that prudent and responsible democracy with informed, involved citizens is served best by the activity of many mitigating institutions between candidates and voters. The most important of these institutional links is a strong party system. Political parties are the best mitigating/organizing institutions because their traditional habits and canons of conduct, unlike those of the mass media, combine to support a more accurate, responsible, and positive view of government and politics.

The remainder of this chapter will give detail to this broad theme. By making a number of observations about the media's coverage of the 1980 campaign and the candidates' relationships with the media in the 1980 race, I hope to build a fuller understanding of my general argument as well as add to our particular understanding of the media's role in the 1980 presidential election.

The Modern Media Tradition

The mass media was not always the principal mitigating/organizing institution in American politics. For more than a century, the political party played that role, but a series of forces combined to weaken the power of the party and to strengthen the power of the media.

One powerful factor in this change has been the great popular desire in America to lodge all power with the people. In presidential politics this desire has not been fulfilled easily because for a long time there was no straightforward, practical procedure for doing it. Beginning at the Constitutional Convention in Philadelphia, America first wrestled with the mechanical (technical) question: How, in such an extended, diverse country as this one, do you prudently and practically involve the people in the presidency?

The twentieth century found the answer—modern technology. Modern technology—including the mass media—suddenly made "all power to the people" possible both in theory and in practice. The conduit functions that the party and party elites out of necessity had once filled, but which had been curtailed sharply by twentieth-century progressive reforms, could be taken over quite fortuitously by the wizardry of a technology that could produce a mass media with the capability of instant, national communication.

The mass media could now be the conduit. Candidates could now appeal to the public directly—without elite interference, without a mitigating institution (or so it appeared)—and build political majorities directly—through the mass media. Politics could now be fair and open and much more consistent with the philosophy of America's liberal tradition. Individual citizens informed by the neutral mass media could register their independent, considered judgments, and individual candidates and officeholders freed from the yoke of party control could exercise their independent views based on principle and conscience. At last American presidential elections could become essentially huge town meetings—the mass media could make it so.

The mass media accepted the challenge and adopted new twentieth century standards of conduct. It embraced a set of journalistic canons that all concerned believed would meet the media's new obligations and serve the public interest in the postparty era. In some cases, such as Federal Communication Commission regulations, these canons became the law of the land.

As part of this change, the mass media adopted a stance of objectivity. In political terms, the media became nonpartisan. Of course, this contrasts sharply with the blatantly partisan newspapers of the nineteenth century. In that era, newspapers (particularly those outside the great urban centers of America) frequently were mere auxiliaries of the party organization. They printed the party line; they touted the party candidates, and they extolled the principle of partisanship. One study reports that in America in 1850 there were 1630 party-affiliated newspapers, and only 83 neutral ones.[1] Quite clearly, a century ago the media took sides. And in so doing, these partisan papers were extremely critical of (and often unfair to) about half of the nation's officeholders (the half belonging to the other party), but the nineteenth-century press also was extremely flattering and painted a quite positive picture of the other half of America's public officials (the members of their own party). What is important to stress is that this style of journalism included *both* good guys and bad guys. Politicians sometimes did get a bad press, but they also sometimes got a good press.

In the twentieth century, and particularly post-World War II with the rapid expansion of the electronic media, this relationship between press and party changed. The mass media was detached from party and became the objective observer of national politics, the one institution responsible for "telling it like it is."

Careful studies of the modern mass media demonstrate that to a remarkable degree this institutional goal has been realized. In fact, if objectivity is measured in terms of partisan neutrality (which after all is the bedrock, historical meaning of that journalistic claim), the mass media is, for all practical purposes, completely objective. Truly systematic studies of the partisan bias of national network television news have yet to uncover any partisan prejudice.[2] The networks are not Republican or Democratic, liberal or conservative; they report right down the middle. Indeed, parties as institutions are ignored almost totally on national television, except at national convention time. And America's national papers and news magazines are nearly as scrupulous about maintaining partisan neutrality in their news columns as the electronic media is careful to maintain nonpartisanship over the airwaves. It is simply of another era to cite a New York *Herald Tribune* or Chicago *Tribune* as a voice of the Republican party establishment.

With the advent of the electronic media, the operative meaning of objectivity expanded beyond partisan detachment. Objectivity also came to mean balance, equal time—for every pro, a con; for every McGovern minute, a Nixon minute; for every story in which someone advocates abortion on demand, a story with an advocate for right-to-life. In short, every point of view must be balanced with an opposite point of view that is given equal exposure.

Again the data demonstrate that this is not just an aim of the mass media, especially the electronic media, it is the practice as well. Richard Hofstetter's exhaustive content analysis of the network coverage of the 1972 election and several studies of the network coverage of Watergate all reveal a near perfect balance between opposing points of view.[3]

And finally, it is agreed upon by providers and consumers of news alike that the mass media's primary role in society is to chronicle the day's events, to report the news. But as Walter Lippmann made clear more than a half century ago, to understand what the media reports to us we need first to see reporting the day's events from the journalist's point of view based on his definition of news.[4] To a journalist, not every event is news, and no newspaper, not even the New York *Times,* reports everything that happens.

To a journalist, news is a chronicle of *today's unusual events.* News is about today, not yesterday. It is about the unusual happening, the new and different, not the old and familiar. News is about events and deals with circumstances that can be documented, backed up by look-see evidence.

The important point is that political news, presidential campaign news, is treated no differently in the mass media than any other news. What gets reported in the mass media about national politics must first meet the media's test of what news is.

The Mass Media Tradition and the 1980 Election

It is within this tradition that presidential politics get conducted. Recognizing that circumstance enables us to explain, at least partially, some of the broad trends associated with the past twenty to thirty years of American presidential elections as well as to try to explain some of the particulars of the 1980 presidential election.

Media Emphasis on the Horse Race and the Decline in Voter Information

The first trend spurred by this environment is the decline in the percentage of the election coverage given to a discussion of long-term, fundamental political and partisan issues and a corresponding increase in emphasis on what my colleague Tom Patterson and I call the "horse race" aspects of the campaign.[5] Horse race coverage focuses on who is winning and losing, on conducting polls and touting their significance, on the strategies and tactics associated with "the election game," and on the immediate circumstances surrounding the horserace—the next motorcade, the next primary, and the current "campaign issue." A campaign issue is a pseudo issue. It is usually a brief controversy—full of sound and fury— arising *and* disappearing within the campaign. Media emphasis tries to portray it as a significant issue, but no sooner is the claim of importance made than the media discovers another campaign issue of greater importance and replaces the former with the latter. Within a short while "musical issues" gets played again, and on and on it goes. Examples of campaign issues are Gerald Ford's misstatement, in 1976, about the Soviet Union's insignificance in Eastern Europe and Ronald Reagan's telling, in 1980, of a joke containing an ethnic stereotype.

The data on this trend are clear. Research demonstrates a marked change in media attention to questions of substance. Patterson reports in his book *The Mass Media Election:* "In the 1940s, Paul Lazarsfeld and Bernard Berelson found that about 35 percent of election news dealt with the fight to gain the presidency; a considerably larger amount, about 50 percent, was concerned with subjects of policy and leadership."[6]

Today, those proportions are reversed; or worse, substance may account for less than one-third of contemporary media election coverage. Reporting on the CBS *Evening News'* coverage of the 1980 presidential primaries (January 1 through June 4, 1980), Mike Robinson, Nancy Conover, and Margaret Sheehan write:

> The hollowness extends beyond the campaign coverage of the candidates themselves. We sifted through every campaign story to decide how many sentences were principally devoted to understanding, explaining or describing an *issue* versus a *candidate,* the horse race, or something else ("other"). The results reflected what Patterson and McClure learned in 1972 and what Patterson learned again in 1976: horse race always prevails. No less than 54 percent of the news time in all campaign news stories was given over to horse race—and only 17 percent to issues.

> Measuring stories instead of sentences, we found that the percentage of horse race stories rose to two thirds. It has been eight years since Patterson and McClure discovered that 66 percent of the CBS Evening News coverage in the 1972 general election was devoted to "hoopla" and "campaign activity." In 1980, as of June, the percentage of horse race in our study varied from theirs by only one point.[7]

Post-Labor Day, however, Robinson and Sheehan report a substantial upsurge in issue reporting on the *CBS Evening News:*

> But after Labor Day, issues come into vogue. Between the first phase of the campaign and the first three weeks of October, issue coverage more than tripled in percentage terms. If one takes into consideration the length of the issue pieces that were being broadcast in October, *practically* (my emphasis) as much time on *Evening News* was devoted to issues as to horse race."[8]

This upsurge in issue coverage in late 1980 is important to note. But several factors place substantial limits on the interpretation of the finding. First, issues received increased attention for seven or eight weeks out of the approximately forty weeks that constituted the formal campaign. Over the whole election year, the media's campaign emphasis still heavily favored the horserace. Second, even in the Labor Day period, issues "practically" received as much time as the horse race coverage. Even in this period, then, issues did not dominate. And finally, it is important to understand the type of issues that were being emphasized. In September, in descending order of amount of coverage, CBS emphasized "the debate-debate; security leaks concerning Stealth; Carter's personal slurs against Reagan; the economy; Reagan's remark about Carter starting his campaign in Tuscumbia, the alleged birthplace of the KKK."[9] Only the economic issue was of enduring importance. The other four were typical, transitory "campaign issues," and the debate-debate issue was a quintessential horse-race strategy story. In October, the five top issues were (again in descending order of emphasis) "the economy, the debate-debate, American military strength, social security, U.S. Middle Eastern relations."[10] In this period only one "campaign issue" was emphasized and the basic topic of the economy received the most attention. In this month alone, then, the media agenda contains mainly issues of enduring significance.

Robinson and Sheehan also point out, however, that the network's issue coverage of the candidates in this period was not necessarily reports of what they were saying on the campaign trail: "A good chunk of the issues coverage in September and October came as special segments and candidate interviews—stories that were not in any sense hard news. Done at the network's initiative, these items were *not* what happened today—reality—but were soft news."[11]

Judged as a whole, then, the evidence says media coverage of the 1980 presidential election followed (with a noteworthy, but limited, exception) the pattern established firmly in the 1970s—horse race dominated substance. An Albuquerque television reporter interviewing Barry Commoner captured perfectly the underlying tone of media politics when he asked the Citizens' party candidate, "Mr. Commoner, are you a serious candidate, or are you just running on the issues?"[12]

The change in emphasis is even more marked if we contrast the modern era with the media behavior of the late nineteenth century. Richard Jensen writes about the press of that day: "The papers, both daily and weekly, devoted their columns to political news and commentary, providing far more details than now reach modern readers."

"In 1896, for example, the three leading San Francisco papers printed twice as much political information as *the same* papers did in 1952, even though the number of pages per issue had increased fourfold."[13]

Why this change? Issues of substance continue to divide America. In fact, government plays a larger, more divisive, role in people's affairs today than in the nineteenth century. And candidates still address issues when they talk to voters. Listen to any stock campaign speech of presidential candidates; every one of these speeches is a litany of issue positions and program commitments.[14] And today, as in 1900, party platforms are full of issues and pledges. Indeed, they are more so. Party platforms are many times longer, far more detailed, cover a far wider scope, and just as a century ago, they address many important issues from clearly different perspectives.

Because of the media's definition of news, a significant factor in accounting for the changed emphasis is the shift from party organizations to the mass media as the primary conduit of political information. Since news is something immediate and different, a candidate's policy statement can be reported only once (at best, quite infrequently), no matter how many times he states it.

In fact, candidate issue positions tend to get far more coverage when the political figure says something different from his past statements, appears inconsistent, slips up, or changes his mind in some way, than when conviction and acumen cause complete consistency. Anything new and different (no matter how trivial or unintended) is more newsworthy than anything old and consistent (no matter how fundamental).

At each campaign stop, then, the traveling press corps, which has heard the stock speech repeatedly, must look for other news. Thus, the nature of the setting, the size of the crowd, the names of platform guests, the prominence of local dignitaries, the strategies that prompted the rally, all become more newsworthy than what is said by the candidate. Since the address the candidate makes is so predictable and to the journalist so tiresome, there is just not much news any more in the traditional political speech. With the emphasis shifted away from substance to strategy, public opinion polls become a particularly promising subject matter. Ideal in fact. Polls appeal to the modern journalist's commitment to objectivity and to "scientific" detachment. Polls can be up-dated and repeated; so they are always news. And finally polls can create excitement and suspense. They clock the horse race and provide the candidates' "split-times."

In 1980, election coverage was inundated with polls. Each television network and major national newspaper had its own poll, and each gave extensive, regular coverage to the results. This experience contrasts with Tom Patterson's finding that ten poll-based items would have been a newspaper's entire production of such stories in the 1940s.[15]

Notice, however, how the media emphasis on the horse races paints a distorted, indeed inaccurate, picture of the presidential-campaign trail. As a chronicle of the day's events it omits regularly the basic behavior of the principal figure—the speeches of the candidate. What the candidate does and says, what *he* emphasizes, the *media* deemphasizes. The media audience gets little exposure to the "real" campaign trail—to the main, live events of the day. This is particularly true when polls are the focus of the story. Commissioned and paid for by the media, the poll story is a true *contrived* event. In this instance, the event is not contrived by the candidate, but contrived by the media itself to "make news" and serve its own purposes.

When the political party acts as the conduit for political information, a significantly different diet of information is fed to voters. Because it has a different set of institutional goals and motivations, the party emphasizes old and realiable, not new and different, information. To build the credibility and consistency which is the base of an enduring political consistency, it is necessary to repeat the same line. In short, repetition is an essential political strategy. Put another way, parties are interested in selling voters on the organization's candidates and programs. As the savvy advertiser interested in selling consumers repeats his commercial over and over, so does the shrewd political party repeat its theme day after day, year in and year out. Thus, the party, unlike the media, has built-in incentives to reiterate the candidate and party message until voters know and remember it.

The point is that each of these institutions has different goals and values and those differences lead to important and dissimilar consequences. When the mass media conveys political information, it chooses a leaner diet of information than the party chooses, and the media feed that diet to voters intermittently in tiny crumbs which provide them mere subsistence.

The poor quality of information voters are exposed to leads directly to their having a lower level of political knowledge on election day. Again, the data are clear about the decline in voter information. If we compare voters in the mass media era with voters in the last pre-media, party-effort election where we have some measure of comparable data—1948, this pattern emerges:

> In general, however, the substantive side of the election seems to be losing ground in the bid for people's expressed interest. In this study of the 1948 election, Berelson, Lazarsfeld, and McPhee found that 67 percent of the voters' conversations were concerned with candidates; positions and qualifications. Only about a fourth of voters' discussions focused on the question which candidate was likely to win. In 1976, however, only 34 percent of people's conversations were concerned with the candidate's abilities and views. The game was the major topic of conversation of 1976.[16]

It is little wonder that "the game" is the major topic of public conversation in modern campaigns, because data from the 1972 election demonstrate that this is what voters remember from the media coverage that passes before them. When asked to recall stories they had seen or read in the media during he 1972 campaign, 54 percent of all regular network television viewers and 31 percent of all regular newspaper readers recounted a horse-race story.[17] For both groups of media users, the campaign horse-race recollection was the most frequently mentioned.

Tom Patterson points out the final consequence of this preoccupation with horse race: Voters in the modern era, even though the presidential campaign is longer and even though citizens have experienced more formal education, know less about the candidates and issues.

> The themes of election coverage also affect what voters do not learn about today's campaign. In their study of the 1948 election, Berelson and his colleagues found that, in August, two months before election day, 37 percent of the voters knew three-fourths of the issue positions taken by the candidates. In August 1976, however, only about 25 percent of the voters knew three-fourths of the candidates' positions.[18]

This decline of basic knowledge in the citizenry and the media's preoccupation with the horse race is of some help in trying to explain two particular circumstances in the 1980 election.

Voter Volatility in 1980 and Beyond

First, I believe, this state of affairs was a contributing factor to the voter volatility, the ups and down of attitudes about the candidates and the fickleness of voter support for candidates, that marked the 1980 election. With less meaningful information about the candidates, voters held less firmly anchored attitudes about the political contestants and held political judgments with considerably less conviction. Put another way, judgments about candidates and parties were formed around information too flimsy to sustain them, and therefore volatility resulted. In short, mass-media politics is unstable politics, and the fickleness that was a part of 1980 can be expected in mass-media elections of the future as well.

This line of reasoning also is useful in explaining (at least partially) why George Bush failed to capitalize on his Iowa caucus win and beat Ronald Reagan for the GOP nomination. Made a national figure and a surprise presidential contender only by the excessive media attention he received by his upset victory in Iowa, Bush was much more a creature, and a captive, of the media than Ronald Reagan. For Bush to be successful in the primaries after Iowa, he needed to patch together a new, national constituency. Unlike Iowa where Bush could woo voters face-to-face and build a traditional organization, the wins after Iowa out of necessity would have to be based on a constituency organized by mass media contact. Given Reagan's long quest for the presidency and the residual support that campaign had generated over the years, and given the new right's surging grassroots organization, the former California governor was not nearly so dependent on media hype and media-conveyed information to build and mobilize his electoral base.[19]

Bush, on the other hand, was the media's prisoner; his own battle plan made it so. His campaign strategy called for him to work hard to win the Iowa caucuses to gain media attention, which then would catapult him out of the pack of contenders into the prominence of frontrunner. At that point, Bush and his strategists believed he would be able to tell voters in some detail why he deserved to be president, and a winning coalition would be formed.

To a considerable degree, Bush's campaign plan succeeded. He won the Iowa caucuses, helped evidently by Ronald Reagan's decision not to participate in the statewide television debate of the Republican primary contenders. Immediately after his failure to appear, Reagan lost support in Iowa, apparently the victim of a media politics miscalculation. As the Bush forces' battle plan had predicted, the Iowa victory produced a spate of media coverage. From out of nowhere, Bush emerged as the alternative to Ronald Reagan. Immediately, he made enormous gains in national polls. In early January, before the Iowa caucuses, the ABC/Lou Harris Poll showed Ronald Reagan with the support of 32 percent of a nationwide sample of Republicans and independents. Bush trailed Howard Baker, John Connally, and Robert Dole, tying John Anderson with the support of 6 percent of those interviewed. Immediately after the Iowa triumph, Bush gained 21 points in the polls and tied Ronald Reagan, whose support dropped to 27 percent of the Republicans and independents interviewed. Indeed in early February, this previously unheralded figure of modest past achievement had crept into first place in nationwide polls with a 3 percent point lead over Reagan.[20] All was going according to Bush's plan.

Then the New Hampshire primary took place. Bush lost; his support started to drain away, and he never again threatened Reagan.

In New Hampshire where the slide began, it was Bush who was the victim of debate politics. Hoping to get Reagan to debate him one-on-one, Bush was surprised (sandbagged?) when the California governor showed up with the full complement of Republican contenders and demanded equal time for everyone. In the ensuing donnybrook over the debate ground rules, Bush looked like the spoilsport. On election day, Reagan reversed his Iowa loss.

But beyond these tactical blunders that first cost Reagan and then Bush, the same media fascination with the horse race that gave Bush such "momentum" after his upset Iowa win diminished his opportunity to solidify his position in the months of February and March. After Iowa, Bush needed to talk policies and programs to voters, but institutional biases in the mass media made such talk nearly impossible. Immediately after Iowa, Bush himself said that from now on he was going to stop talking strategy and quit discussing "big and little mo," and address the issues. He probably did just that. But the media ignored it, and Bush was never able to create a solid, national consistency. Early on, the Texas Congressman recognized his inability to get his message across. Feeling more and more frustrated as the campaign wore on, he chided the media for its absorption of the horse race. But to no avail. Consequently, the more firmly anchored attitudes about Ronald Reagan bound together a coalition that after New Hampshire never really was challenged.[21] Reagan's nomination was a landslide.

Still Bush's campaign plan was not a total failure. Media attention kept him in the nomination hunt all the way to the Republican Convention. Indeed he was Reagan's only enduring challenger. And ultimately, Bush's successful exploitation of the media's habit to fixate on the winner of the first event in the presidential nomination process resulted in his vice-presidential nomination. Indeed, had Bush not challenged a candidate with Ronald Reagan's traditional organizational strength, his original campaign plan might have garnered him the presidential nomination. In short, Bush understood the patterns and rhythms of the "new politics." He was thwarted by the power of the "old politics." Nevertheless, by exploiting the media, Bush managed to come in second.

Deemphasizing the Incumbent's Record in 1980 and Beyond

The second particular consequence of this new mix of political information was the deemphasis of sustained attention during the 1980 election to the incumbent administration's record. This deemphasis, in turn, played some role in the outcome of the Democratic party nomination and to a lesser (but still important) extent in the outcome of the general election. In both instances, the media's down-playing of the Carter record worked to the disadvantage of the president's challengers.

Both Senator Edward Kennedy and Governor Ronald Reagan sought to make Jimmy Carter's record the focus of the 1980 campaign. The administration's record was the theme of their standard stump speeches and the focus of the most of their special major addresses. Yet both men were frustrated in their attempts to keep Carter's past the topic of national conversation. In both cases, the candidate's success in this attempt ultimately depended on having the media repeat the substance of their arguments. This the media, for journalistic reasons, cannot do.

In Kennedy's case, his failure to control the political agenda and to wrest the nomination from an incumbent President was thwarted by many other factors as well—his own inarticulateness, the ill-advised and damaging television interview with Roger Mudd, President Carter's power as an incumbent to reward his supporters and to punish his detractors, and of course, the hostage crisis in Iran which the media had to cover and Carter used so skillfully to promote his own candidacy. William Crotty, describing the 1980 nominating process, sums up Kennedy's difficulties:

> If Kennedy had articulated the rationale and policy focus of his campaign and his reasons for opposing an incumbent Democratic president early in the campaign as clearly and forcibly as he did before the convention, he might well have unseated an unpopular president with a weak hold on his party's coalition. Kennedy had his opportunities: in November when he announced his candidacy; after the Iowa defeat in his Georgetown University address; or after the crushing defeat in Illinois or the surprise victories in New York and Connecticut. That he was never able to capitalize on these opportunities, that he never communicated to Democrats the fervor and commitment he expressed that night (at the Democratic National Convention) symbolize the failure of his candidacy.[22]

Crotty is correct that Kennedy's failure was partly an inability to communicate a focus for his candidacy. But a partial reason for that failure is that modern mass media elections make such communication far more difficult than it was forty years ago.

The media's treatment of the senator's Georgetown speech is an example. Kennedy and his strategists, sensing the aimlessness of his early campaigning, made a concerted attempt to state his philosophy and to set the tone of his campaign in a major address at Georgetown University. The address was so billed publicly. The speech was good political rhetoric (although not the barnburner his convention speech proved to be). But the media gave its *content* little play; the attack on Carter's record and the call for a renewed commitment to liberal ideas and ideals was old hat. The media emphasized the speech as horse race—a desperate, final attempt to get the broken Kennedy campaign rolling, a carefully orchestrated bit of strategy. In no time, the Georgetown speech was ignored completely; its argument never widely aired.

True, Kennedy did arouse a party and a nation with his speech at the Democratic National Convention. But unlike the Georgetown address, national television and radio broadcast the convention speech in its entirety, uninterrupted, and in their post convention reports, newspapers and magazines paid at least as much attention to the argument as to the style. In short, *part* of the difference in the success of the two communication attempts was the manner in which the information was conveyed. At the convention, voters were exposed more to party-mitigated information and party-communication style; at Georgetown, voters received more media-mitigated information and media-communication style. Voters learn more of value from the former than the latter.[23]

Later in the general election, Reagan faced, to some extent, the same problem Kennedy had faced. To media editors, the governor's stump speech was no longer news, and his attacks on the administration's conduct in office also had grown stale. Therefore, instead of underscoring what Reagan was saying, the media in September and October was emphasizing the more recently introduced (and therefore more newsworthy) war and peace issue raised by the Carter camp and regularly reporting lesser campaign/media created, pseudo issues, such as Carter's "mean streak" and the latest speculation about the ground rules for two-way or three-way presidential debates.

Recall that shortly after Labor Day and throughout the remainder of the campaign, President Carter sought to make Ronald Reagan's lack of foreign affairs experience, his support of increased defense spending and opposition to arms control, and his tendency to speak too glibly, a major election issue.

Repeatedly Carter characterized Reagan as a person prone to be "trigger happy," a man not to be trusted. Again and again, the President told voters that the election was a choice between the greater dangers of war with Reagan and the surer prospects of peace with him. The media, however, transformed Carter's discussion of these important issues into an analysis of a pseudo, campaign issue—Carter's "mean streak."

The "meanness issue" arose out of these attempts and others by Carter to paint a harsh picture of Reagan and his policies. During the fall campaign, Carter, first in Atlanta, charged Reagan with supporting racist policies and catering to racist attitudes, then in Los Angeles asserted the Republican would lead the nation to war, and finally in Chicago saw the California governor dividing "Christian from Jew." The press saw these charges as excessive, strident, vulgar, and pursued Carter about his "mean streak." Finally, in response to a series of questions in a national press conference, Carter admitted that perhaps he had been "overly enthusiastic" in his attacks on Reagan.

The third issue was the partisan intrigue about the likelihood and form of any presidential debates. Reports abounded about the negotiations between the League of Women Voters and three candidates. Indeed, in 1980, the media's natural absorption in debate trivia was heightened by unusual external circumstances. First, Carter's refusal to appear on any platform with John Anderson until he had first debated Ronald Reagan "one-on-one" gave the issue an additional horse race dimension perfectly suited to the biases of the media. And second, the confrontation between Carter and Reagan came so late in the campaign that it was impossible to treat the debates as a thing of the past and move on to other issues.

Emphasis on these issues, whatever its impact on Reagan's fortunes, caused GOP campaign appeals to take a back seat. In particular, from Reagan's point of view, coverage given these issues diverted public attention from the central issue of the campaign—the Carter administration's record.

Shortly before the crucial debate between the two major-party nominees in Cleveland in late October, I received a phone call from a highly-placed Reagan media strategist. The caller was agitated over the Reagan camp's sense that its basic election arguments were not being heard by the voters. The staff had persuasive evidence that what Reagan was saying day after day—his basic campaign appeal—was not being carried by the media. No matter the forum or style he used, the media ignored his message and concentrated on other issues. "What can be done?" my caller asked. "How can you make an election appeal to voters, if you have no way to make the appeal?" As a last resort, the caller looked forward to the Cleveland debate as Reagan's only hope, because in this setting (as Kennedy had done in the convention setting) the California governor could make his arguments directly to the people. No (at least less) media mitigation would be involved.

The point here is not that the war and peace issue in the 1980 election was not significant or that the personal traits of the candidates were unworthy of citizen contemplation. These two issues (the debate-debate issue is another matter) deserved coverage. The point is that modern media-mitigated elections play havoc with fundamental democratic assumptions about elections. Those assumptions encompass the notion that candidates and voters will have access to one another so that the claims and counterclaims of candidates and parties can be understood accurately and evaluated rationally by the electorate. In this process, it must be true that candidates have real control over the appeals they make to the voters. Without control, they cannot be held responsible. In addition, voters, at least in principle, must be able to perceive correctly candidate appeals and therefore able to choose rationally and to hold office-holders accountable for their actions. In media-mitigated elections the assumptions about candidate control and faithful voter understanding are weakened. In media-mitigated elections, candidates have less control over the election dialogue, and voters run a greater risk of misunderstanding the true appeals candidates are making. In particular, media-mitigated elections diminish the challenger's control over a sustained discussion of the incumbent's record, because the incumbent's record is four-year-old history, and therefore it is not so readily viewed as news.

If this deemphasis of the incumbent's record is a trait of media-mitigated campaigns and if V. O. Key and others are correct that voters are most "rational and capable" when they make retrospective judgments about an administration's past performance, then modern elections may pose serious problems for popular control of government.[24] Postelection surveys, however, provide some optimism on this point when they document that the 1980 election (in the final analysis) was a national referendum on, and rejection of, the Carter years.[25] These surveys, then, say something about both the intensity of voter dissatisfaction with Carter and the limits of the media's power to distract voters from more enduring issues and more fundamental considerations. While it is true that candidates and parties have surrendered some control over the election agenda to the mass media, it is also true that the mass media's control is not yet total.

Media Emphasis on Personalities and Crude Ambition

The media environment of modern politics nourishes a second broad trend in the conduct of American elections—the depiction of campaigns not as a clash of partisan armies (as was the case in the late 19th century),[26] not as a clash of alternative ideas and programs (as to some extent is the practice in many contemporary western democracies), but as a cynical struggle between individual personalities. The mass media—particularly television—overly personalizes politics.[27]

Part of this over-personalization of politics can be traced again to the journalist's definition of news and to his style as detached observer.[28] Remember that news is rooted in what is concrete and in what can be documented. Except in the columns of the editorial page, newspapers seldom contain stories about "free-floating" ideas—journalists never *directly* write what they think; they find someone else who will say for attribution what they themselves have been thinking. By some device, all ideas in news stories must be concretely attached to a source.

In this regard, television is even more personality bound. Because usually the person (source) is pictured and because pictures have far more impact on viewers than sound, television naturally forces personality even more to the fore. In addition, abstract, complicated ideas do not picture well; they are best expressed by the printed word. (Capture with a picture the argument of a Supreme Court decision or the intricacies of an energy program.) Even the spoken word—so fleeting—is not well suited to advancing very sophisticated ideas. Add to this the belief within the industry that television news needs to exhibit pace, excitement, and controversy to hold an audience, and there can be little wonder why personal clashes dominate the airwaves.

This tendency to depict the campaign as a test of personal styles, personal ambitions, and personal views helped create and sustain two of the issues that dominated the post-Labor Day period of the 1980 campaign—Reagan the "trigger-happy" person and Carter the "vindictive" person. Without question, many of Carter's campaign speeches indirectly branded Reagan with the "war monger" label, and so the media did not totally contrive this issue. It was, however, "natural" copy for the press, and Carter's success with the issue, the extent of the coverage it received, was in part because the "trigger-happy" Reagan played so readily into media biases. Carter's "mean streak," on the other hand, was to a large extent a press-created issue. Reagan did little to keep the issue alive; he wanted to focus on Carter's record, not on his personal character. Certainly Carter did not clamor for such attention to his character. Focus on this topic, therefore, was media instigated because it nicely served media needs.

This personalization of politics combined with the preoccupation with horse race and strategy leads to an exaggerated emphasis on the candidate's personal campaign style. Patterson found this emphasis in 1976 and pointed up how it affected voter evaluation of the candidates:

> The themes of election news also had an impact on the voters' images of the candidates. News of the candidates concentrated on how well they were running the race, and the impressions that voters acquired correspondingly tended to be stylistic, associated with the candidates' campaign styles and performance. About 65 percent of the impressions that voters gained of the candidates in 1976 were stylistic in nature. Only 35 percent were political— those concerning the candidates' governing capacities and policy proposals.[29]

The 1980 election was a repeat performance.

It is this interest in personal battles, combined with the search for the unusual, combined with the concern for the horse race, that contributed a big boost to John Anderson's candidacy in 1980 and his early surge in public opinion polls.

Consider the factors that favored Anderson in the media. He was unusual, unexpected, and therefore he was news. Anderson's campaign was wholly a personal crusade. His style was vigorous, combative, controversial, and, although he never won a primary, Anderson added zest to the horse race.

Because Anderson ideally suited the media's need, the Illinois congressman received the kind of press—early in the campaign—*that ideally suited his needs.* In their study of the 1980 primary election coverage of CBS *Evening News,* Mike Robinson *et al.* reported that Anderson was treated far more favorably than any of the other candidates. The researchers concluded that in the period January 1 to March 7, Anderson got a "good press" 50 percent of the time, Kennedy and Bush 18 percent of the time, Carter 26 percent of the time, and Reagan 30 percent of the time.[30] In this period, although he didn't receive as much time as the major candidates, Anderson received much more favorable time.

Jimmy Carter was not far off the mark, then, when he charged Anderson with being wholly a creation of the media. Certainly in the beginning, the media boosted the liberal Republican's candidacy. Carter was perhaps a bit too aghast, however, since he catapulted into the limelight in 1976 in precisely the same way. Without media-mitigated elections neither politician would have become the fleeting national figures they both turned out to be.

Media Emphasis on the Negative

The third broad bias of the media in modern elections is to be negative. This negative attitude is not confined to presidential elections alone, but extends to the entire press treatment of the presidency. A recent exhaustive study of the media's coverage of the White House demonstrates that the press is giving far more attention to the presidency than in days past but that coverage also is far more negative and each year it seems to get more negative still.[31] To emphasize again, this tone arises out of the best, not the worst, of motives. It is the unintended, undesirable consequence of the media's goal to be non-partisan and fair and its acceptance of the role of the fourth branch of government. To emphasize again, it is a tone that contrasts with the partisan press of the past where most political figures received regularly at least some very favorable media coverage.

How does the press get from nonpartisan and fair to cynical and negative? To be nonpartisan essentially means to be no political figure's champion. To play the fourth branch role essentially is to accept a defined, institutional responsibility as government critic and ombudsman and to place the press in permanent opposition.

This contrasts with the party's (and party press's) conception of opposition. In democratic theory, parties alternate between power and responsibility and opposition and criticism; the party proposes as well as exposes and opposes. In this conception of things, the party (and its press) has a positive side to its institutional role. The modern press does not; it is a permanent negative.

Taken together, these journalistic responsibilities and canons trap the media in a sustained negative attitude. If it no longer can be a political figure's champion, if it must be evenhanded, if it must live up to the demands of the fourth branch, the media has only one solution—to treat every political figure *equally negatively*. To be critical of all is to meet fully all the demands of modern journalism.

The 1980 election was no exception. In their systematic analysis of the CBS *Evening News* primary coverage, Mike Robinson *et al.* find the overall treatment of the candidates negative, and particularly negative for front-running candidates.[32]

Considering all of the media's habits in the modern era, we can now explain the press's contribution (and it was just one of many) to John Anderson's decline in the 1980 election. First, the media's bias against presenting information about a candidate's programs and record left Anderson's supporters and potential constituency with too many unanchored attitudes and as much adrift as Bush's backers had found themselves. Again, Anderson found what Bush found—the media's emphasis on horse race made it almost impossible to shore up and expand his early support.

Second, while early in the campaign Anderson made good horse-race copy, and therefore, he received a favorable press which resulted for a month or two in the Illinois Republican appearing to be a serious contender, the honeymoon was short-lived. When he emerged as a force to be reckoned with, his media coverage turned negative and cynical. Robinson *et al.* write: "Not surprisingly, as the campaign went on, Anderson's press became less favorable and after the primaries had actually turned somewhat sour. Within a period of 24 hours in mid-June, CBS *Morning News* and *Evening News* carried separate Anderson pieces which made the candidate look silly, inconsistent, or confused."[33]

Beginning in early summer, then, at Anderson's peak in the polls, and throughout the rest of the campaign, the National Unity candidate not only received less coverage, but less favorable coverage, than the two major party candidates. Once Anderson appeared to be a serious contender and the newness of his campaign no longer made news, he too felt the sting of the media's negative tone.

And finally, once Anderson began to decline in the polls, given the media's preoccupation with horse race, the ordinary coverage he got only accentuated his slide from contender to spoiler to footnote. In addition to the media coverage making it extremely difficult for Anderson to talk substance to the electorate, the Anderson campaign was described over and over again as ineffective (see the polls), underfinanced (travel and accommodations not up to presidential-campaign standards), and disorganized (high staff turnover). Regardless of the validity of such reports, by emphasizing the horse race and campaign style, the media insured that the voter would receive a negative view of Anderson. In short, throughout the campaign Anderson was on a media roller coaster. It took him up, and then let him down.

Televised Advertising as an Alternative

If these truly are the modern press's natural biases in elections, then we certainly can understand why candidates *legitimately* turn to such extensive use of paid television advertisements. Only in television ads can the candidates make their substantive and programmatic appeals with the certainty they will be heard by the broad mass of voters as the candidates themselves intend. Political commercials have become a powerful form of election communication because they serve candidates' true political needs and voters' basic information needs. Much like the partisan newspapers of the nineteenth century, televised political ads allow candidates to talk politics, not news, to voters. In any extended democratic system, as the formation of parties showed in America 180 years ago, there needs to be *conduit* for political discussion between leaders and followers. If one does not exist, of necessity one will be invented. In the modern media election, necessity collaborated with technology and invented televised commercials.

Televised ads allow candidates to make clear their own political agendas— to emphasize the issues they, not the press, want to stress. More basic still, commercials give candidates a forum to talk programs and policies—a forum in modern elections that they surprisingly are without. And most importantly, televised commercials allow candidates to repeat their message over and over again until the "party line" gets established.

Again this year as in 1972 when Tom Patterson and I first carefully analyzed the content and impact of televised ads in presidential elections, commercials were informative to voters and useful to candidates.[34] Both Carter and Reagan frequently appeared on camera in their own behalf, both tended to discuss their records as president and governor and their policy commitments on matters of voter concern, and both frequently explicitly challenged the other's record and policies. In both cases, the televised ads of Carter and Reagan in the last month of the campaign were excerpts from, or reliable variations of, their standard stump speeches. The televised ads, therefore, represented to voters the political differences the two candidates sought to emphasize.

For Ronald Reagan, these ads may have been crucial. Not as fully understood by the electorate as Jimmy Carter and having trouble making his appeal through the news media, a heavy advertising budget allowed him to hammer home his themes. His chief technical strategist, Richard Wirthlin, has observed:

> Very early in the campaign, we discovered that Ronald Reagan was
> well known—more than 90 percent of the American electorate
> was familiar with his name—but he was not known well. In early
> September, over 40 percent said they ''knew very little about
> him and what he stood for.'' Our paid media, focusing on Reagan's
> California record, was designed to fill that information gap.
> Campaign 80's ads met that objective well. Through September and
> the first week of October, these ads were run so often that most
> of us grew sick of them. But more and more voters were getting to
> know Ronald Reagan better.[35]

This important—given the mass media's behavior, this absolutely essential—role of television advertising in presidential politics underscores the major blunder in John Anderson's campaign. After hiring one of the nation's best political admen, David Garth, Anderson waited far too long to try to shore up his constituency with a television ad campaign. Had Anderson, early in June, forsaken all attempts at traditional grass roots organization and poured all his funds and whatever he could borrow into television campaign designed to have the Illinois congressman directly state to voters his record, his issue agenda, and his hope for America, he might have remained a contender. Televised commercials were Anderson's only method of giving his constituency and potential constituency the information needed to anchor voter attitudes about him, and they were the only way to counteract the horse-race treatment he was sure to receive in the news media. By mid-August, when no major television ad campaign had been mounted and the negative horse-race press intensified because of a decline in the polls, the Anderson campaign was over.

Media Coverage of Conventions: When Party Comes Through

The only news coverage that rivals television commercials for informing and involving voters is the coverage of the major-party conventions. Voters who watch the national conventions on television show a significant increase in interest about the election and a significant pain in information about the candidates.[36]

Why? Because here again the messages conveyed by the media are controlled more by the candidates and parties than by the journalists. Here again politics is being conveyed, not news. At conventions the candidates and parties present politics, programs, and traditional symbols. As with commercials, the messages are repeated for several nights running. Again, as in the case of commercials, viewers are able to learn the party line.

Consequently, there should be little surprise that both Carter and Reagan showed big gains in strength immediately after their conventions. Media coverage of the conventions, unlike the bulk of its ordinary coverage, is full of the kind of information that anchors opinions, firms up old loyalties, and locks in decisions.

The Presidential Debates

The final media events of 1980 were the presidential debates. The first debate held in Baltimore saw only Anderson and Reagan participate because President Carter declined to appear in a three-way contest. Nevertheless the contest was significant because it marked the recognized end of John Anderson's quest for the presidency. The Anderson camp had long hoped for a national debate as the forum in which the Illinois Republican could speak directly to the American people, contrast himself starkly with the two traditional candidates, and spark life in a center coalition that could win the 1980 election. The debate, however, came too late; his opportunity was long lost. Without Carter's presence, the first debate had a much smaller national audience than the debates in 1960 or 1976, and neither Reagan nor Anderson reaped any political profit from his participation.[37] After the debate, it was clear to everyone that Anderson was finished. Even to Anderson. And without Carter, Reagan too was unable to advance his case. The winner, then, was Jimmy Carter who had staked much on his hunch that a presidential debate without the president would not grab a huge audience or have great electoral impact. Also by not joining the debate, Carter was able to postpone a direct comparison between him and Reagan and the direct attack on his record that came in the second debate, which marked the beginning of the end for the president.

There is no better event than a presidential debate to see clearly the clashing election perspectives of the media and the politician. Indeed presidential debates offer prime examples of all the biases the mass media interjects into the election process whenever it takes a prominent role. To begin with, the media hypes the event and builds great expectations. In this phase the debate is depicted as critical to each candidate's fortunes (to the horse race), and the strategies, tactics, and techniques are examined in detail. As soon as the debate is over, the expectations inevitably are dashed because the candidates seldom say anything that is newsworthy, i.e., they repeat their campaign themes. In the aftermath of the debate, the media emphasizes who won and lost, not who said what, and reports all the polls on voter reaction to the candidates.

In 1980, the fixation of the media with polls, technology, and horse race reached new heights with the ABC emphasis after the second debate on results from a nationwide poll rigged up by the telephone company. Viewers were asked to call one of two telephone numbers to indicate whether they believed Reagan or Carter had won the debate. A computer kept track of the tally that resulted from approximately 700,000 calls.

The poll, however, was worthless. It was representative of no known voting population, and it was heavily biased in favor of Reagan—it favored the candidate with the wealthier coalition, supporters who had access to a phone and the fifty cents the call cost; it favored the candidate whose supporters had the higher level of intensity to make the effort to place the call, and it favored the candidate whose support was concentrated in the West where it was nine o'clock when the call had to be made, not the East Coast where it was midnight. Little wonder the poll showed Reagan a two to one winner.

ABC nevertheless emphasized the tally produced by this technological trick even though the network acknowledged the result had no meaning. While it is true that during the week following the poll, ABC was criticized heavily for this stunt by almost every segment of the industry, this treatment of the debate was a glaring example of the mass media's underlying instincts.

The media's view of presidential debates was best summarized, however, by the second question asked the candidates in the first debate in Baltimore. Reporter Daniel Greenberg asked:

> Gentlemen, what I'd like to say first is I think the panel and the audience would appreciate responsiveness to the questions rather than repetitions of your campaign addresses.
>
> My question for the Governor is:
>
> Every serious examination of the future supply of energy and other essential resources, including air, land and water, find that we face shortages and skyrocketing prices, and that in many ways we are pushing the environment to dangerous limits. I'd like to know specifically what changes you would encourage and require in American lifestyles—in automobile use, housing, land use and general consumption—to meet problems the aren't going to respond to campaign lullabies about minor conservation efforts and more production.[38]

Quite clearly Greenberg's question shows the natural conflict between the press and party and between journalist and candidate. The reporter asks the candidates to make *news,* not politics. He says, "Don't repeat what you've been saying all these years. Say something different." As journalist, Greenberg is disgusted by the candidates using a national debate to build a national coalition. In this quintessential political event, Greenberg wants preeminent political figures to play no politics. Without hesitation, the reporter even goes further and asks the politicians to say something that will damage their electability. Quite predictably, both candidates ignored Greenberg's goading and spoke their "campaign lullabies."

In late October in the second debate in Cleveland, both candidates approached the event as if it were a national tent meeting, a forum to rally the faithful for the final crusade. Both saw the debate as an opportunity to make their appeal to the voters with minimal media interference. In this second debate, watched by at least twice as many viewers as the first, the audience approximated the proportions reached in 1960 and 1976.[39]

Carter reiterated the dangers of Reagan's foreign policy ideas, the shallowness of his international experience and understanding, and the risk in his opposition to arms control and the SALT II treaty. At every opportunity, real or imagined, Carter made a direct appeal to the traditional elements of the Democratic party coalition—labor, blacks, the urban Northeast, the rural South, etc.—to stand by him for the sake of traditional Democratic party values. It was good politics, but Carter's style was cold and stiff, and his attacks on Reagan fell flat.

It was Reagan who succeeded. By his low-key, relaxed performance, by his statements in support of the principle of arms control (if still not the SALT II treaty itself) and by his promise to continue dialogue with the Soviets, Reagan was able to dampen the impact of the "mad-bomber issue." In a direct comparison, on the same platform, Reagan appeared just as presidential, just as competent, as Carter. And most importantly, Reagan was able at last to focus the American public's attention on the Carter administration record. At every opportunity, real or imagined, Reagan attacked the Carter record. Reagan's debate theme was summarized succinctly by these two sentences from his closing statement: "When you go to the polls, you will make a decision. I think when you make that decision, it might be well if you ask yourself, 'Are you better off now than you were four years ago?'"[40]

On election day, voters appeared to do just that, and Reagan won a solid victory. Thus the second debate, coming late in the campaign, set the tone and the agenda for the final week before the election. It, along with Reagan's effective paid media, superior grassroots organization, and the strong instinct of voters to judge the past rather than mandate the future was a key element in returning a Republican to the White House in 1980.

The Impact of Mass Media Elections

In the final analysis, mass media elections not only result in less well-informed, more volatile, and disorganized electorates, but also lead to a more cynical and alienated electorate. It is this that is the cause for the greatest concern.

The picture of politics painted by the mass media is a picture without redeeming social value. In the media, politics is practiced without principle or public purpose solely by manipulation and entirely for personal gain and ambition. By ignoring a politician's record, down-playing his programmatic statements, side-stepping his principles and ideology, the modern press constructs a one-dimensional political man. Think back to the last time the media explained a political figure's action on the basis of personal principle or public purpose. Now recall all those juicy stories where a political figure's actions were explained on the basis of pressure from this or that group or to advance this or that ambition. In the media, only the crassest motives prompt people to political action.

There are three great dangers to such a picture of politics. First, it simply does not represent reality. Political figures operate out of a complex set of motives. Sometimes they act out of principle and conviction rather than solely out of political expediency. Second, this inaccurate and jaundiced view of the political process over the long run corrupts the sense of trust and public-mindedness that is essential to the conduct of healthy democratic government. Finally, this view of politics—at least by implication—also demeans the electorate by depicting voters as too foolish and so without judgment and conviction that politicians are able to bribe and bamboozle them at every turn.

The press coverage of the Kennedy-Carter primary race illustrates the point. The press tended to view Kennedy's decline solely as a failure of political technique—he lacked a tested organization, his ads were hastily conceived—or of personal circumstance—the rumors about his private life, the memory of Chappaquiddick. In the same vein, Carter's resurrection was seen as evidence once again of the magic of his manipulative skills—Carter's televised ads vigorously exploited Kennedy's personal weaknesses, his Rose Garden strategy made political profit out of the Iranian crisis.

Certainly it was not a theme of the press treatment of the race that Kennedy was committed deeply to the liberal values, philosophy, and programs of America's past and present and that Carter was an equally committed centrist who had significant disagreements with the Democratic party's liberal wing.[41] In this explanation of things, Kennedy does badly because even inside the electoral base of the Democratic party, his liberal views are not held widely enough to produce electoral victory in a sufficient number of the states. This explanation, however, was not offered. Instead of principle and political philosophy dividing the senator and the president, it was ambition and politics.

In the end, then, the most alarming danger of mass media elections is that they have little sensitivity to the reality of principle and moral purpose that forms the soul of a people's politics.

Chapter 9 The Election of 1980 and Its Consequences

Paul T. David

The 1980 election was clearly a rejection of President Jimmy Carter. It was also to a large extent a rejection of the Democratic party. Conversely, it was not only a personal victory for Governor Ronald Reagan, it was also a partisan victory for the Republican party.

The Reagan sweep extended to most states and all regions of the country. It was accompanied by the first Republican takeover of the United States Senate since the Eisenhower victory of 1952. Republican gains in the House of Representatives were substantial—enough to gain working control of much legislation whenever as many as thirty conservative Democrats decide to vote with the Republican minority. The immediate outlook is for a government almost as much under Republican dominance during 1981–82 as it was during the first two Eisenhower years, 1953–54.

All of this requires more than the usual effort to interpret what happened in the election of 1980, the object of this chapter.

The Election Returns

First, a look at the returns for President, Senate, and House of Representatives.

The Vote for President

In the popular vote for president, Governor Reagan was the winner by 51 percent to Carter's 41 and John Anderson's 7. As table 9.1 shows, there were significant differences in the regional split of the vote.

Table 9.1

Regional Divisions of the Vote for President, 1980 (in Percentages)

Region	Carter	Reagan	Anderson	Other	Reagan's Plurality
Northeast	42.7	47.0	8.8	1.5	4.3
Middle West	40.9	50.9	6.7	1.5	10.0
South	44.6	51.8	2.9	1.1	7.2
West	34.4	54.0	8.8	2.8	19.6
United States	41.0	50.7	6.6	1.7	9.7

SOURCE: Computed from final official election returns as reported by *Congressional Quarterly Weekly Report*, vol. 39, January 17, 1981, p. 138.

Carter ran best in the South and almost as well in the Northeast, without coming close to a majority of the votes in either region. Reagan ran best in the West and carried majorities of the vote in both the South and Middle West. Reagan's plurality was extraordinary in the West, with almost a twenty-point lead in that region. His lead was 10 percent in the Middle West, about 7 in the South, and only 4 percent in the Northeast, where the contest was most closely fought. In their original strategies, Carter had assumed that his base in the South would hold, that he would run well in the Northeast, and that the contest would be decided in the big industrial states from New York to Illinois. Reagan conversely had assumed that his base in the West would hold, that he could make inroads in the South, and that he would win or lose in the industrial states of the Northeast and Middle West. The results were obviously related to these expectations, but not very closely.

Reagan's majority was spread so completely across the country that he was the winner of 489 electoral votes in 44 states. Carter carried only 6 states and the District of Columbia for a total of 49 electoral votes. The states carried by Carter were Rhode Island, Maryland, and West Virginia in the Northeast, Vice President Mondale's Minnesota in the Middle West, Carter's native Georgia in the South, and Hawaii in the West. Carter probably could have carried several more Eastern states, including New York and Massachusetts, if Anderson had not been on the ballot, but Reagan would have been the clear winner nation-wide even if all of Anderson's votes had gone to Carter. Anderson's popular vote was markedly less than his showing in preelection polls, but was sufficient to qualify him for post-election federal financing by exceeding the 5 percent threshold.

Turnout was down in the presidential election for the fifth time consecutively, another factor that at least to a minor extent was probably detrimental to the Carter showing. In 1976, the turnout was 54.4 percent of the voting age population; in 1980 it was calculated on the final returns at 53.95 percent.[1] Turnout was up in the South, continuing a trend that has been running for some time and that undoubtedly reflects increasing black participation in voting in that region.[2] But in New York State, for example, turnout was down by about half a million votes. Carter lost the state by about 160,000 votes, and it appears likely that much of the turnout decline was among groups most critical to Carter's success—Jews, blacks, and blue-collar workers.[3]

The Senate Outcome

Before the election, Republicans had hoped to gain four or five seats in the Senate. *Congressional Quarterly Weekly Report* had predicted that they might gain two or three.[4] In the actual outcome they gained twelve seats, for a Senate majority of fifty-three Republicans to forty-six Democrats and independent Harry Byrd of Virginia. This was a larger Republican majority in the Senate than the party had enjoyed at any time since the days of Herbert Hoover.[5] Eighteen new Senators were elected, of whom sixteen were Republicans. As the result of elections in both 1978 and 1980, over half of the Republicans in the Senate—twenty-seven— were elected in those two years and are of correspondingly short service.

Liberal Democratic Senators, several of them senior committee chairmen, were especially decimated by the Republican sweep. The National Conservative Political Action Committee, NCPAC, had targeted six of them for strenuous opposition: Birch Bayh of Indiana, John C. Culver of Iowa, George McGovern of South Dakota, Thomas F. Eagleton of Missouri, Frank Church of Idaho, and Alan Cranston of California. Bayh, Culver, McGovern, and Church were all defeated, all except Church by substantial margins. Eagleton and Cranston were the survivors. Others who were defeated included Warren Magnuson of Washington, chairman of the Senate Appropriations Committee; Gaylord Nelson of Wisconsin; and John Durkin of New Hampshire.

In the South, the Republicans gained four Senate seats, considerably changing the representation from that region. In Georgia, long-term incumbent Herman Talmadge was defeated by Mack Mattingly, a former Republican state party chairman. In North Carolina, incumbent Democrat Robert Morgan was narrowly defeated by John P. East, a conservative political science professor who was helped by the supporters of Republican Senator Jesse Helms. In Alabama, incumbent Democrat Donald Stewart had been defeated in the primary by Jim Folsom, Jr., son of a popular former governor. Folsom in turn was defeated in the general election by retired Admiral Jeremiah Denton, a former Vietnam prisoner of war and a favorite of the Moral Majority. In Florida, incumbent Democrat Richard Stone had been defeated in the primary by Bill Gunter, leader of an opposing-party faction. Gunter in turn was defeated by Paula Hawkins, bringing to two the number of Republican women in the Senate, Nancy Landon Kassebaum of Kansas being the other.

Not all of the new Republican Senators are conservatives. Arlen Specter of Pennsylvania, Warren Rudman of New Hampshire, and Slade Gorton of Washington are said to be from the moderate wing of the party.[6]

But the tone of the new Senate is undoubtedly much more conservative than it has been for many years. The Republicans not only have their majority, but have become more conservative as they gained in numbers, while the Democrats who remain are on the whole more conservative than those who have departed. President Ronald Reagan can expect strong support for his budget-cutting and legislative programs in the Senate, as well as for his appointments needing confirmation.

The Changes in the House of Representatives

The Republicans gained a net total of 33 seats in the House of Representatives, leaving the Democrats with a majority of 243 to 192. It was the best Republican showing in the House since 1956, when 201 Republicans were elected.[7] Most of the Republican gains, moreover, came at the expense of incumbent Democrats, of whom 27 were defeated, an unusually large number.

The substantial Democratic majority assured control in organizing the House and in retaining control of committee chairmanships and staff positions. But the number of conservative Democrats who can be expected to vote with the Republicans much of the time has been estimated by *Congressional Quarterly Weekly Report* as at least 30.[8] Allowing for the fact that a few liberal Republicans may defect on some party-line votes, there still seems likely to be a working conservative majority for much of the Reagan program in the House. Many close votes and protracted delays can be expected in the House in the 97th Congress.

The Republicans had mounted an unusually intense media campaign to defeat senior Democrats and increase Republican representation in Congress. They spent something like nine million dollars in an effort to persuade voters to "Vote Republican, For a Change."[9] Eight senior Democrats, each with over eighteen years of service, were defeated. The most conspicuous losers were John Brademas of Indiana, the Majority Whip, and Al Ullman of Oregon, the Chairman of the Ways and Means Committee. Others who lost included James C. Corman, Chairman of the Democratic Congressional Campaign Committee, and Harold T. Johnson of California, Chairman of the Public Works and Transportation Committee. Two senior Democrats who had been involved in the Abscam scandal, Frank Thompson, Jr., of New Jersey, and John M. Murphy of New York, were defeated. The most prominent Democrats who survived were the Speaker, Thomas P. O'Neill, Jr., of Massachusetts, the Majority Leader, Jim Wright of Texas, and the Chairman of the Interior Committee, Morris K. Udall of Arizona. But the elections of new committee chairmen and the realignment of power relationships in the House were extensive.

The Republicans were allowed to increase their representation on most House committees in line with their increased membership of the House. But this process was not automatic and was dependent on the will of the majority Democrats. House Speaker O'Neill announced in November that he would seek to retain disproportionate Democratic majorities on three key committees, Rules, Ways and Means, and Appropriations.[10] In January he succeeded in doing so.[11]

How the Voters Split

Polling of voters by the television networks as they left the polls has provided a rich supply of data on how different groups of voters divided their votes. Tables 9.2 through 9.6 report results that were obtained by the CBS/*New York Times* polling.

Among the self-identified Democrats, 26 percent voted for Reagan, as against 11 percent of the smaller number of Republicans who voted for Carter. Independents were nearly two to one for Reagan, but also gave Anderson one of his highest showings with 12 percent.

Self-identified liberals, a much smaller group than the Democrats, gave 27 percent of their votes to Reagan, while 71 percent of the conservatives voted for him.

Men voted more heavily for Reagan than women, by 54 percent of the men to 46 percent of the women. Women who favored the equal rights amendment (ERA) voted heavily for Carter, while those who opposed it, a smaller group, voted heavily for Reagan.

Blacks voted for Carter by 82 percent to 14 percent for Reagan, almost the same as their split between Carter and Ford in 1976. Blacks were almost the only identifiable group whose support for Carter was as strong in 1980 as it had been in 1976. Whites, who had divided almost evenly between the candidates in 1976, were for Reagan in 1980 by 55 percent to 36 for Carter.

Among the identified religious groups, the born-again white Protestants voted more heavily for Reagan than any other group, giving him 61 percent of their votes. Catholics gave 51 percent of their votes to Reagan, which may be compared with the 44 percent they gave President Gerald Ford in 1976. Jews, who had voted two to one for Carter in 1976, gave him only 45 percent of their votes in 1980, with 39 percent for Reagan and 14 percent for Anderson—one of Anderson's highest scores. Protestants were heavily for Reagan, 56 percent to Carter's 37.

Table 9.2

Patterns of the Vote for President (1980) According to Partisanship and Ideology (in Percentages)

	Carter	Reagan	Anderson	Carter-Ford in 1976
Democrats 43	66	26	6	77–22
Independents 23	30	54	12	43–54
Republicans 28	11	84	4	9–90
Liberals 17	57	27	11	70–26
Moderates 46	42	48	8	51–48
Conservatives 28	23	71	4	29–70
Liberal Democrats 9	70	14	13	86–12
Moderate Democrats 22	66	28	6	77–22
Conservative Democrats 8	53	41	4	64–35
Politically active Democrats 3	72	19	8	. . .
Democrats favoring Kennedy in primaries 13	66	24	8	. . .
Liberal Independents 4	50	29	15	64–29
Moderate Independents 12	31	53	13	45–53
Conservative Independents 7	22	69	6	26–72
Liberal Republicans 2	25	66	9	17–82
Moderate Republicans 11	13	81	5	11–88
Conservative Republicans 12	6	91	2	6–93
Politically active Republicans 2	5	89	6	. . .

Young people were the only age group that favored Carter; those under thirty either split their votes evenly or gave a slight majority to Carter. Voters over thirty gave a substantial majority of their votes to Reagan.

Voters with family income below approximately the $15,000 level, 27 percent of the voters, gave Carter a plurality of their votes. Voters above the $15,000 level, 59 percent of the total, gave Reagan heavy majorities of their votes. (Apparently 14 percent of those polled did not reveal their income level.)

Blue-collar workers, about one-sixth of the voters, went for Reagan by a slight plurality, 47 percent to 46 for Carter. Labor union households, however, were for Carter by a small plurality, 47 to 44 percent. The much larger group of nonunion households were heavily for Reagan, as were professional, managerial, and white-collar workers when taken separately.

Table 9.3

Patterns of the Vote for President According to Groups (in Percentages)

	Carter	Reagan	Anderson	Carter-Ford in 1976
East 32	43	47	8	51–47
South 27	44	51	3	54–45
Midwest 20	41	51	6	48–50
West 11	35	52	10	46–51
Blacks 10	82	14	3	82–16
Hispanics 2	54	36	7	75–24
Whites 88	36	55	8	47–52
Female 49	45	46	7	50–48
Male 51	37	54	7	50–48
Female, favors equal rights amendment 22	54	32	11	. . .
Female, opposes equal rights amendment 15	29	66	4	. . .
Catholic 25	40	51	7	54–44
Jewish 5	45	39	14	64–34
Protestant 46	37	56	6	44–55
Born-again white Protestant 17	34	61	4	. . .
18–21 years old 6	44	43	11	48–50
22–29 years old 17	43	43	11	51–46
30–44 years old 31	37	54	7	49–49
45–59 years old 23	39	55	6	47–52
60 years or older 18	40	54	4	47–52
Family Income				
Less than $10,000 13	50	41	6	58–40
$10,000–$14,999 14	47	42	8	55–43
$15,000–$24,999 30	38	53	7	48–50
$25,000–$50,000 24	32	58	8	36–62
Over $50,000 5	25	65	8	. . .
Professional or manager 40	33	56	9	41–57

Table 9.3—cont'd

Patterns of the Vote for President According to Groups (in Percentages)

	Carter	Reagan	Anderson	Carter-Ford in 1976
Clerical, sales or other				
white-collar 11	42	48	8	46–53
Blue-collar worker 17	46	47	5	57–41
Agriculture 3	29	66	3	. . .
Looking for work 3	55	35	7	65–34
Education				
High school or less 39	46	48	4	57–43
Some College 28	35	55	8	51–49
College graduate 27	35	51	11	45–55
Labor union household 26	47	44	7	59–39
No member of household				
in union 62	35	55	8	43–55

Voters who thought they were better off than a year previously, only one-sixth of the voters, were heavily for Carter. Those who thought their family finances were about the same, 40 percent of the voters, split evenly between Carter and Reagan. Those who thought they were worse off than a year ago, about a third of all the voters, were heavily for Reagan, by 64 percent to Carter's 25.

Voters who thought that unemployment was the more important problem were mainly for Carter, but the larger group who thought that inflation was the more important problem were for Reagan two to one.

Voters who thought the United States should be more forceful in dealing with the Soviet Union even if it increased the danger of war were for Reagan two to one; those who disagreed were for Carter two to one.

It was during the last week before the election that 23 percent of the voters decided how they would vote; this group split their votes 46 percent for Reagan, 38 for Carter, and 13 for Anderson.

Ever since the New Deal days of Franklin Delano Roosevelt, the Democratic party has depended heavily on a coalition of union labor, other blue-collar workers, ethnic groups, Jews, Catholics, blacks, and Southerners. The white South broke away in the Harry Truman election of 1948 and has been missing most of the time since then. Carter carried the South in 1976 as a native son, but would have had trouble in doing so without the black vote in the South. Otherwise, the Carter coalition of 1976 looked very much like the one that had elected Franklin

Table 9.4
Patterns of the Vote for the President According to Economic Conditions (in Percentages)

	Carter	Reagan	Anderson	Carter-Ford in 1976
Family finances				
Better off than a year ago				
16	53	37	8	30–70
Same 40	46	46	7	51–49
Worse off than a year ago				
34	25	64	8	77–23
Family finances and political party				
Democrats, better off				
than a year ago 7	77	16	6	69–31
Democrats, worse off				
than a year ago 13	47	39	10	94–6
Independents, better off 3	45	36	12	. . .
Independents, worse off 9	21	65	11	. . .
Republicans, better off 4	18	77	5	3–97
Republicans, worse off				
11	6	89	4	24–76

Roosevelt four times, as many commentators hastened to point out. One major dissenter was Everett Carll Ladd of the University of Connecticut, who has argued repeatedly that most elements of the Democratic coalition had weakened considerably years ago in their support for the Democrats. He thought that this was still true in 1976, with Carter's election in spite of defections in the coalition.[12] In 1980, Carter still had support by small pluralities from the lowest income groups, from union labor, from Jews, and from young people, and he had heavy support from blacks. He has lost his majority support from the South, from Catholics, and from the working class other than union members. It no longer seems possible to argue that the old-time New Deal coalition still exists in Democratic presidential politics.

What the Voters Thought of the Candidates

There is every reason to believe that how the voters voted was largely determined by what they thought of the candidates, particularly Carter and Reagan. In An-

Table 9.5

Patterns of the Vote for the President According to Issues
(in Percentages)

	Carter	Reagan	Anderson	Carter-Ford in 1976
More important problem				
Unemployment 39	51	40	7	75–25
Inflation 44	30	60	9	35–65
Feel that U.S. should be more forceful in dealing with Soviet Union even if it would increase the risk of war 54	28	64	6	. . .
Disagree 31	56	32	10	. . .
Favor equal rights amendment 46	49	38	11	. . .
Oppose equal rights amendment 35	26	68	4	. . .

derson's case, about half of his total vote came from people who said they were mainly voting against the other candidates. This was true for only a quarter of the Carter voters and one-sixth of the Reagan voters.[13]

When voters were asked about the leadership capabilities of the candidates, 62 percent considered Reagan a strong leader; only 32 percent thought so of Carter.[14]

When asked whether each candidate offered a vision of where he wants to lead the country, 67 percent credited Reagan with such a vision, while 48 percent so credited Carter.[15]

On the other hand, when asked whether the candidates understand the complicated problems a president has to deal with, 70 percent thought that Carter understood the problems, against 51 percent who thought so of Reagan.[16]

When asked if one of the candidates says too many things carelessly, without considering the consequences, 66 percent of the voters had this opinion of Reagan, 46 percent of Carter.[17]

When asked which candidate would do the best job in solving the nation's economic problems, 41 percent of the voters favored Reagan, 22 percent Carter, 11 percent Anderson, and 26 percent saw no difference among the candidates.[18] On a closely related question, 43 percent of the voters thought the economy would

Table 9.6

Patterns of the Vote for the President According to Time of Decision (in Percentages)

	Carter	Reagan	Anderson	Carter-Ford in 1976
When decided about choice				
Knew all along 41	47	50	2	44–55
During the primaries 13	30	60	8	57–42
During conventions 8	36	55	7	51–48
Since Labor Day 8	30	54	13	49–49
In week before election 23	38	46	13	49–47

SOURCE: 1976 and 1980 election day surveys by the *New York Times*/CBS News Poll and 1976 election day survey by NBC News.

Tables 9.2–9.6 based on 12,782 interviews with voters at their polling places. Shown is how each group divided its vote for President and the percentage of the electorate belonging to each group.

get better if Reagan were elected, while only 21 percent thought so if Carter were elected.[19] In repeated polling over the year before the election, there were never more than 20 percent of the voters who thought that Carter was doing an excellent or good job in handling the economy, while 80 to 85 percent of the voters thought he was doing a poor job or one that was only fair.[20]

On the war issue, when asked in October 1980 which candidate would be best able to keep us out of war, 52 percent of the voters favored Carter, while only 23 percent favored Reagan.[21] But on the more general issue of whether Carter had done a good job in his handling of foreign affairs, in repeated polling from March to September 1980, fewer than 30 percent of the voters thought that Carter had done a good or excellent job, while 70 percent or more thought he had done a poor job or one that was only fair.[22] On the specific question of Carter's handling of the situation resulting from the holding of the hostages in Iran, over 60 percent of the voters were in disapproval from May to October, 1980.[23]

Why the Polls Went Wrong

On the eve of the election, most commentators and public opinion pollsters were predicting that the election would be close, in fact too uncertain in its outcome to be called in advance. Actually, most of the published polls were closer to the outcome than the people interpreting them, but estimates of the electoral college outcome that focussed on particular states were all such as to inspire caution. *Newsweek,* for example, in its November 3, 1980, issue credited Reagan with 220 electoral votes to Carter's 133, with 185 electoral votes too close to call. Big industrial states such as Pennsylvania, Ohio, and Illinois were among those considered too close to call.[25]

Among the regularly published public opinion polls, the NBC/Associated Press poll came closest to predicting the actual outcome. They had been giving Reagan a substantial lead during September and October. Just before the debate between Carter and Reagan on October 28, they were crediting Reagan with 48 percent of the vote, Carter with 41, and Anderson with 11. The ABC/Louis Harris poll was crediting Reagan with 48 percent of the vote to Carter's 45 and Anderson's 8 as of October 30 to November 1.[26]

Among the pollsters themselves, the favorite explanation of why the polls were not more clearly for Reagan was the supposition that public opinion began shifting in Reagan's direction in the aftermath of the debate between Carter and Reagan, which occurred exactly a week before the election. The shifting continued throughout the weekend before the election and up to the moment when voters went to the polls. According to Daniel Yankelovich, the pollster for *Time* magazine, "The dissatisfaction with Carter was there all along, but people couldn't bring themselves to vote for Reagan. The debate changed that."[27] Apparently it was mainly Reagan's hawkish views that had scared people, and his disclaimers and general attitude in the debate relieved their previous worries. In one poll of likely voters after the debate, it was found that 41 percent thought that Reagan had won, while only 26 percent thought Carter had won, with 27 percent believing the debate was a tie and 6 percent with no opinion.[28]

The timing of events suggests that the hostage issue was a factor in triggering final dissatisfaction with Carter. It was on the Sunday before the election on Tuesday that the conditions set by the Iranian Majlis for the release of the hostages became known. According to Patrick Caddell, who was doing private polling for Carter, on that Sunday 31 percent of the voters thought the Iranian terms were unreasonable; by Monday the percentage had increased to 47 who thought so. Caddell found in spot polling that Carter was slipping rapidly on that Sunday and Monday—five points below Reagan on Sunday and ten points below on Monday.[29]

Reagan's own pollster, Richard Wirthlin, had different unpublished findings that gave Reagan a substantial lead even before the debate, and had him gaining further thereafter. Wirthlin tended to discount the effects of the hostage issue while emphasizing the effects of the debate. He was quoted as saying "The debate was successful in conditioning the environment for the takeoff."[30]

The problems of the published polls "touched off the most skeptical examination of public opinion polling since 1948, when the surveyors made Thomas

Dewey a sure winner over Harry Truman."[31] In retrospect, it seems evident that the pollsters for the candidates, Caddell and Wirthlin, were much more nearly clear on the outcome in advance than the public pollsters. The main reason was the fact that the candidate pollsters continued their polling day by day right up to the moment of the election, regardless of expense. During the whole campaign, Caddell is said to have run up bills of some $2 million, while Wirthlin's operation was credited with spending $1.3 million.[32] As profit-making enterprises, the published polls could not afford to do as much polling or to continue it as long.

Whatever the details, it seems certain that late-crystallizing sentiment favored Reagan beyond what the public polls were measuring. Those who were previously undecided split preponderantly for Reagan. Voters drifted away from Anderson and back to the candidates of the two major parties at the moment of decision. And undoubtedly a considerable number of Democrats who has assumed that they would vote for Carter finally voted for Reagan.

How Influential Were the Religious Groups?

During the campaign, the press and the mass media gave considerable attention to religious groups of white Protestants who were newly active in politics. Most conspicuous was the Moral Majority, but there was also the Christian Voice and the Religious Roundtable, all led by fundamentalist ministers with large television audiences.[33] The total population influenced by these groups has been estimated as high as forty million people.

The issues of concern to these groups include support for prayer in the schools, opposition to the equal rights amendment (ERA), support for a constitutional amendment outlawing abortion, opposition to rights for homosexuals, and other moral or family issues that have been neglected in this sectarian age. In the 1980 presidential year, the effort was to mobilize these religious groups for activity in politics, with the leaders of the groups actively favoring Ronald Reagan. The groups also concentrated on a number of campaigns for the Senate and House of Representatives, particularly in the South and West.

Despite large claims, the results of all this effort seem to be questionable. As already noted, the born again white Protestants voted two to one for Reagan, but the probability seems to be that they would have done so anyhow. In some parts of the South, there may have been some increase in white turnout as the result of special efforts. The Moral Majority and similar groups may have been effective in defeating four or five members of the House of Representatives. They have been given substantial credit for the Republican Senate victories in Oklahoma and Alabama.[34]

Lance Tarrance, a Houston pollster who has done surveys for the Moral Majority, has called it "one of a number of short-term forces" in the Republican victory, but seems doubtful that these religious groups will become an enduring political force.[35] It is, of course, true that the Republican party has historically found most of its strength among white Protestants outside the South. Aside from the Carter election in 1976, the white Protestants of the South have been moving into the Republican party in presidential elections at least since 1948. It seems likely that they will continue to do so, whatever the efforts of the Moral Majority and similar organizations.

Alternative Agendas for President Reagan

One choice faced early by President Reagan as he took office could be formulated as follows: Should he give primary emphasis to his program for curing the ills of the economy? Or should he give priority to the issues favored by the Moral Majority and similar groups? And could he persist in his intention to give only minimal attention to foreign affairs?

The economic issues of inflation, unemployment, and excessive governmental regulation have undoubtedly aroused the greatest amount of voter concern. They probably account for more than a majority of those voters who switched from Carter or Anderson to Reagan late in the campaign. These are the groups that are probably most critical to the building of a continuing Republican position as the dominant political party in the country.

By contrast, the issues that concern the Moral Majority—ERA, prayer in the schools, an amendment outlawing abortion, putting down the homosexuals—are issues that appeal to a smaller but highly vocal group in the electorate. This group has shown every tendency to put pressure on President Reagan and the Republicans in Congress to proceed with their programs. The support of the religious groups has been useful to the Republican party, and it is support that will not lightly be cast aside.

A relevant factor in the decision, however, is how far the Republican party and President Reagan are willing to go in an effort to gain and retain the support of younger voters under thirty-five years of age. This group is largely uninterested or opposed on the issues favored by the Moral Majority. It is very much concerned about economic issues. Where it goes in future years may be decisive for the future of the Republican party.

What Kind of a Mandate for President Reagan?

It is traditional in American politics for the winner in a presidential election to claim a mandate from the voters to carry out his proposed programs. These claims grow stronger when a striking victory is obtained as the result of an upset. President Reagan himself has been modest about making mandate claims, but has been vigorous in pressing the programs he promised before the election. His supporters in Congress and the public, however, have not only been ecstatic over his victory but sweeping in their claims for what it portends.

Reagan has proposed to roll back inflation, cut the federal budget, reduce taxes, build up the national defenses, restore American prestige abroad, and reduce the burden of federal regulations on business. All of these aims are strongly supported by the hard core of his most faithful followers. They also undoubtedly have considerable support as general objectives among the general public.

Voters leaving the polls were asked by the CBS/*New York Times* polling operation "Which issues were most important in deciding how you voted?" Some voters made more than one choice, but their answers can be summarized in table 9.7.

When asked a related question on what their main reason was for voting as they did, 38 percent of the Reagan voters simply said that "It's time for a change." This was almost twice the number who gave any other reason, and far more than the 11 percent who said they voted for Reagan because "He's a real conservative." Among the 38 percent who declared "It's time for a change," about one-third considered themselves conservatives, while 27 percent of them were Democrats. The change group differed from Reagan on many specifics and were obviously not completely committed to his proposals. They were more discontented with Carter than favorable to Reagan, but they formed an important part of his majority and presumably favor giving him a chance to show what he can do.[36]

Table 9.7

Most Important Issues for Reagan and Carter Voters (in Percentages)

	Reagan Voters	Carter Voters
Inflation and the economy	40	23
Balanced budget	26	14
Unemployment	20	29
U.S. prestige around the world	19	12
Reducing federal income tax	13	7
Crisis in Iran	9	21
Equal rights amendment and abortion	5	8
Needs of big cities	1	4

SOURCE: *U.S. News and World Report*, 89, November 17, 1980, p. 39.

It seems clear that the Reagan mandate should be read mainly as an opportunity. He has a mandate to turn the country around if he can do so. But the mass of the voters is still reserving judgment, and will still be doing so until time and events have demonstrated that the Reagan programs can be successful.

Was It a Realigning Election?

For the first time in many years, it is appropriate to ask whether the recent election was a realigning election, one marking a long-term change in the balance of the party system. The question arises only when there is a general overturn of party control of the government. It did not arise in 1968, when Richard Nixon won the presidency, because the Democratic party retained control of both houses of Congress. It did arise in 1952, when Eisenhower won the presidency and the Republicans took both houses of Congress. But the Democrats returned to power in Congress in 1954 and retained control in 1956 and 1958. The Eisenhower victories of 1952 and 1956 looked much more personal than partisan in retrospect.

One must go back to 1932 and the Democratic sweep with Franklin Roosevelt to find the basis for comparison with the recent election. This time, as in 1932, there has been a partisan victory giving broad control of the government, and doing so after many years in which the new majority party had been in the wilderness. The election returns also seem to show a broad shift in the views of the electorate—at least a shift from the tenets of a moderate liberalism in the direction of a more conservative posture for the electorate and the government. The old Democratic coalition has been gravely weakened if not shattered completely. The white South has been gone for years, Catholics are voting Republican by substantial majorities, blue-collar workers are deeply divided. Only blacks and the lowest-income groups have stayed solidly Democratic.

Against all this, it may be noted that Reagan's victory was based on just 51 percent of the voting population, which in turn was not much more than half of the total population. Reagan's true support may not exceed a quarter of the whole population by very much. Unlike 1932, there was no outpouring of new voters who had not bothered to vote in previous years; total turnout was down rather than up. Turnout was especially low among the youngest voters, those under thirty years of age, and those who voted were as much for Carter as for Reagan. The Republicans failed to take the House of Representatives, supposedly the more popular branch of the legislature, although also the one where incumbency is most important. The electorate as a whole is clearly dissatisfied with the Democratic party's handling of the problems of the economy and probably also with its posture on national defense. But not much of the electorate is ideological at any time.

There may have been some increase in the number of voters who consider themselves conservatives, but their number is still far short of a majority.[37]

The net of the situation seems to be that the Republican party has been given an opportunity to prove itself as a governing party—an opportunity that it has not had since 1952–54, when it rapidly lost it. If President Reagan is able to succeed with a substantial portion of his better promises, starting with reducing inflation, and does so with party support in Congress, then the Republican party may be able to look forward to victories again in 1982 and 1984. Otherwise, it seems probable that there will be renewed Democratic strength in 1982 and 1984.

What may be more truly the case is that there is no longer a partisan majority for either party in presidential politics. Every presidential election may be at the mercy of short-term forces and there may be continuing discontent with leadership at all levels. In that case, this may be the beginning of a period of some length in which one-term presidencies are the rule and strong leadership is more often missing than present. It is not a pleasant long-term outlook.

Chapter 10 Illinois and the Presidential Election of 1980

Peter W. Colby and Paul M. Green

On November 4, 1980, over 5 million Illinois residents (85 percent of the state's registered voters) cast ballots to decide the future direction of their country. In the presidential contest Republican Ronald Reagan easily outdistanced Democrat Jimmy Carter and Independent John Anderson to capture Illinois' 26 electoral votes. In this chapter we will analzye how Reagan took the state; what parts of Illinois gave him the most support; where this election fits in the overall pattern of previous Illinois presidential contests; whether Reagan's triumph had an impact on other important elections throughout the state; and how the Illinois returns compare with results in other states around the country.

As a highly competitive two-party state, Illinois has one of the best records of voting with the winner, being one of thirteen states to vote the same way as the nation in at least 85 percent of this century's presidential contests. In 1980, the candidates all put a major effort into Illinois, one of the handful of states seen as crucial for Reagan, Carter, and even Anderson. The final preelection polls were divided, the Associated Press and *Time* and *U.S. News and World Report* calling Illinois too close to predict. And when the election was over, Illinois was within one percent of mirroring the nationwide distribution of the vote.

Overall Campaign Strategy

American presidents are elected via the electoral-college method. Each of the 50 states and the District of Columbia is assigned a number of electoral votes equal to its representation in Congress, ranging from 3 in Alaska and other low-population states to 45 for California. Whichever candidate receives the most popular votes in a particular state generally receives all of that state's electoral votes. Winning the election requires capturing 270 of the 538 electoral votes.

Thus, even in these days when campaigns are based on national public opinion polling and the national media, especially network television, the central focus of presidential election strategy remains the assembling of victories in enough states to acquire 270 electoral votes. Jimmy Carter, as in 1976, sought to win the South and add to it enough states in the Northeast and the Midwest to reach 270. Ronald Reagan intended to sweep most of the West, cut into Carter's base in the South, and win enough of the large midwestern and eastern states to achieve the magic 270. In short, as is often the case, the two candidates concentrated their efforts in several large states which both felt they could and must win in order to be elected president.

One of those states was, of course, Illinois. With twenty-six electoral votes and a highly competitive balance between the Democrats and Republicans, Illinois made an inviting target for both candidates. Moreover, as the home state of John Anderson, Illinois was a significant state in the independent campaign.

Jimmy Carter, having lost Illinois by a little over 100,000 votes in 1976 to Gerald Ford, came into the Fall 1980 campaign with a rather difficult situation in the state. On the positive side, he had won both the 1976 and 1980 Democratic primary elections in impressive fashion, and had showed substantial strength in southern Illinois in his narrow defeat by Ford. Carter had never had good relations, however, with the leaders of the Democratic party in Chicago. He had challenged the late Mayor Daley's slate in several suburban and downstate districts in the 1976 primary, he had feuded throughout his first term with Cook County Democratic Chairman George Dunne, and finally he wound up on the outs with Mayor Jane Byrne, a strong Ted Kennedy supporter. In addition, the Jane Byrne struggle against Mayor Daley's eldest son seemed to have tied what was left of the Machine in knots.

Downstate, Carter's problems with farmers and the Moral Majority coupled with Reagan's appeal dimmed Carter hopes for a repeat of his strong showing there in 1976.

Finally, the long-term population trends seemed to be moving slowly but inexorably against Democratic candidates. The Democratic city of Chicago and downstate St. Clair and Madison counties were declining in population, the Republican suburbs in the 5½ counties around Chicago were growing. (The 5½ are Cook, outside of Chicago, Lake, McHenry, DuPage, Will, and Kane counties. The latter 5 are often called the "collar counties.") Generally, though to a much lesser extent, this pattern was repeated throughout the 96 downstate counties, with Democratic areas in decline or stagnant and Republican cities and counties growing, at least slowly.

As November 1980 neared, many experts argued that Carter's plurality in the city of Chicago would decline drastically from 1976 and that his downstate vote would at best equal his showing in 1976 when he lost the 96 counties by a total of 112,000 votes, almost exactly the margin of his statewide defeat. It was felt that Carter could still win Illinois, however, by cutting into the Republican margin in suburban Cook and the collar counties.[1]

Our own past studies of Illinois elections have indicated that such predictions and strategies are less than well-founded.[2] We have pointed out that despite the decline in the size of the total vote in Chicago, the Democratic portion of electorate has been steadily increasing, enough so to off-set the decline. Similarly, we have argued that the power of the Democratic Machine has been generally over-rated and that the changing socioeconomic composition of the city's population has more than counterbalanced the loss of party organizational strength. Thus, we would have expected Carter's Chicago margin in 1980 to be similar to that of 1976.

As for the suburbs, we have argued that reports of a Democratic breakthrough transforming the previously Republican stronghold into a two-party battleground have been greatly exaggerated.[3] GOP victory percentages there have remained quite stable as the population and total vote have grown rapidly, resulting in increasing voting margins for most Republican candidates. In fact, our data have shown that Republican pluralities in the suburbs are now sufficient to match Democratic pluralities in the city, which leaves elections to be won and lost among the other ninety-six counties of the state. Taken as a unit, vote totals downstate fluctuate considerably more than in either the city or the suburbs, and final results are generally quite close to state totals.

The 1980 Outcome in Illinois—General Observations

Ronald Reagan crushed Jimmy Carter and John Anderson in Illinois. Reagan's percentage margin nearly duplicated the national percentage margins between the major candidates. The five minor presidential candidates on the ballot received only 1.3 percent of the vote—thus making their totals almost irrelevant in any analysis of the Illinois vote (see table 10.1).

Carter's victory margin in the city actually increased despite the turmoil within the Democratic party there; Reagan's margin in the suburbs was higher than Ford's in 1976; the Republican suburban margin was just 18,000 votes less than the Democrats' city margin; and the difference between the narrow Republican win in 1976 and the sweep in 1980 was the 282,000 increase in their downstate plurality, which built the statewide margin by 264,000 votes. As time goes by, it seems ever clearer that John Kennedy's 1960 victory was in fact the last time that Chicago will ever outvote the rest of the state. By 1968, Nixon's showing in the suburbs was sufficient to balance enough of the Chicago plurality of Hubert Hum-

Table 10.1

Percentage Breakdown Illinois 1980 Presidential Vote

	Carter	Reagan	Anderson	Total Vote Cast for President	% of Presidential Votes Cast
All Candidates					
8-way	41.72%	49.65%	7.30%	4,749,162	
3-way	42.28	50.32	7.40	4,686,261	98.6
2-way	45.66	54.34		4,339,507	91.37

SOURCE: All Illinois returns taken from Illinois Board of Elections Official Abstract of Votes, November 4, 1980.

Table 10.2

Percentage Breakdown Illinois 1980 Presidential Vote—by Region (in Percentages)

	Carter	Reagan	Anderson
Chicago	68.48	26.43	5.09
Suburban 5½ (Cook County townships plus the counties of Lake, McHenry, Kane, DuPage, and Will)	31.71	58.83	9.46
Other 96	35.74	57.34	6.92

phrey that the Republican margin downstate meant statewide victory. In 1976 the suburb-city balance was exact, and in 1980 nearly so, thus confirming the importance of downstate in Illinois presidential contests. Those looking for reinvigorated competition in the city saw a Democratic margin that was the highest for a presidential candidate since 1940, excepting the Lyndon Johnson sweep of 1964. Others expecting Democratic gains in the suburbs found instead the second-biggest victory margin for a Republican presidential contender ever, surpassed only by Nixon's reelection in 1972.

Tables 10.2 and 10.3 show where Reagan pieced together his landslide in Illinois. The Republican candidate was unable to stem the growing Democratic presidential strength in Chicago. Carter received 68.5 percent of Chicago's vote which measured out to a 482,221 vote city plurality over Reagan. As we have said in our previous writings, however, Chicago can no longer dominate statewide races in Illinois. Carter, despite the fact that he upped his 1976 city percentage

Table 10.3

Vote Total Breakdown Illinois 1980 Presidential Vote—by Region

	Carter	Reagan	Anderson	Plurality
Chicago	785,262	303,041	58,413	C–482,221
Suburban 5½	542,130	1,005,652	161,740	R–463,522
Other 96	654,021	1,049,401	126,601	R–395,380
Total	1,981,413	2,358,094	346,754	R–376,681

almost 1 percent and increased his Chicago plurality by almost 57,000 votes—lost the state to Reagan.

The Republican candidate's suburban 5½ strength nearly matched Carter's Chicago power. Political pundits' preelection warnings about a possible Anderson factor eroding GOP suburban presidential vote margins never materialized. To be sure it could be argued that Anderson hurt Reagan more in the suburban 5½ than he damaged Carter in the city but in real vote terms Anderson made little or no difference to the Illinois outcome. In fact if every Anderson Illinois voter had switched to Carter, Reagan still would have carried the state.

Reagan's 5½ plurality fell just 18,699 votes short of Carter's Chicago total, thus nearly neutralizing the Democrat's city plurality. In sum, vote totals in the heavily populated six-county area cancelled out each other and as we have said before this fact "made downstate the key to victory."[4]

Downstate rejected Jimmy Carter's candidacy. The other 96 gave Reagan a staggering 395,380 plurality. The 1980 GOP presidential candidate more than tripled Jerry Ford's 1976 downstate margins against Carter. Thus, when downstaters flocked to Reagan's banner their votes combined with their suburban allies to overwhelm Carter in Illinois. In effect the 1980 Illinois presidential race was a story of three landslides—Carter received one in Chicago—Reagan gained the other two in the 5½ and other 96 regions.

A Regional Analysis of the 1980 Presidential Vote in Illinois

Chicago

Tables 10.4 and 10.5 reflect Chicago's continuing decline as a determinant force in Illinois elections. In 1980 the state's largest city cast less than ¼ of the Illinois presidential vote. Chicago's 1980 total vote was over a half million less than the total city turnout in the 1960 John Kennedy-Richard Nixon contest. As table 10.4

Table 10.4

Total Vote Cast for President by Region

Chicago	5½	Other 96	Total Vote
1960 1,680 (35%)	1,235 (26%)	1,843 (39%)	4,757
1976 1,227 (26%)	1,656 (35%)	1,836 (39%)	4,719
1980 1,166 (24.50%)	1,733 (36.50%)	1,851 (39%)	4,750

Total Change −514 (−10.50%)	+498 (+10.50%)	+8	−7

NOTE: Totals expressed in thousands of votes.

Table 10.5

Percentage Breakdown—What Each Region Contributed to Each Major Candidate's Total Vote in Illinois (in Percentages)

	Carter	Reagan	Anderson
Chicago	39.63	12.85	16.85
Suburban 5½	27.36	42.65	46.64
Other 96	33.01	44.50	36.51
Total	100	100	100

reveals, most of the city's voter loss was picked up by the surrounding suburban 5½—while the downstate turnout remained pretty much the same. Moreover, table 10.5 clearly shows that of Reagan's total statewide vote less than 13 percent of it came from Chicago. In fact if every Reagan voter in Chicago had stayed home on election day—the former California governor would have still carried Illinois.

Inside Chicago Democrat Carter ran roughshod over Reagan and Anderson. The former president captured 47 of the city's 50 wards and chalked up a 482,221 plurality over his Republican foe. Reagan was only able to capture the all white, upper-middle class far northwest side 38th, 41st and 45th wards. Moreover, the Republican challenger won at least 40 percent of the vote in only 10 other wards and was *unable* to win a paltry 5 percent of the vote in 15 wards.

The Democratic landslide in Chicago was not unexpected. In 1976 Carter beat Ford in the city by 425,000 votes with a 67.7 percent plurality. In 1960 Kennedy had defeated Nixon in Chicago with a 63 percent plurality and a 456,000 vote margin. What is remarkable about recent Chicago presidential-voting trends is that despite a decreasing city population and subsequent lower total voter turnout—Democratic presidential candidates have increased their pluralities in the city. For example, in 1980 Carter's city vote was down a little less than 30,000 from his 1976 Chicago total. Yet his plurality over his 1980 Republican foe increased by almost 57,000 votes. The reason for this seeming inconsistency is that Chicago Republicans are quickly becoming an endangered species.

In 1980 a little over 300,000 Chicagoans voted for Reagan. Granted the Anderson candidacy does complicate any direct comparison to 1976, but even if one adds all of Anderson's 58,413 voters to the Republican column (obviously not all Anderson voters were Republican—in fact, our guess is that a comfortable majority of them were Democrats and Independents) the 1980 GOP Chicago vote would be down almost 28,000 from 1976. The main factor causing this GOP Chicago decline is the growing number of black voters in the city.

Black voter loyalty to the Democratic party is unquestionable. *In the fifteen predominantly black wards in the city Reagan's combined vote did not equal Carter's lowest single black ward plurality.* None of these fifteen black wards gave Carter less then 93 percent of their vote in a one-on-one match-up with Reagan.

The rhythm of demographic change in Chicago finds the city gaining or retaining more staunch black Democratic voters while at the same time it is losing a greater number of potential white Republican voters. A large chunk of the remaining nonblack Chicagoans, both white and Hispanic, also support Democratic presidential candidates though not to the same degree as their black counterparts. Thus, in 1980 Reagan was able to better Ford's 1976 spread against Carter in only one city ward—the heavily Jewish far north-side 50th ward. Even Chicago's Democratic Mayor Jane Byrne's major ticket-splitting effort to reelect Republican States Attorney Bernard Carey in his race against her archenemy Democrat Richard Daley did not shrink or alter Carter's city totals.

Suburban 5½

Reagan demolished Carter and Anderson in the vote rich suburban 5–½-county area surrounding Chicago (see table 10.6). He whipped Carter in suburban Cook by the same percentage margin as Ford beat the Georgian 4 years earlier. In the 5 collar counties Reagan upped the GOP percentage to an impressive 69 percent. Once again the Anderson "no difference" is apparent in these results. Anderson made his best statewide showing in the 5½ area, but as table 10.7 reveals, in suburban Cook he took votes away from both major candidates in equal portions and in the collar counties his candidacy may have slightly hurt Carter not Reagan.

A closer look at suburban Cook reveals that Carter carried two of thirty townships, Evanston and Calumet. In 1976 Evanston had been the Democratic candidate's only township triumph. A two-man comparison of 1976 and 1980 pres-

Table 10.6

5¹/₂ Breakdown of 1980 Illinois Presidential Vote

	Carter	Reagan	Anderson	Total
Suburban Cook	339,322	553,533	91,299	984,154
DuPage	68,991	182,308	29,810	281,109
Kane	29,015	64,106	9,179	102,300
Lake	48,287	96,350	17,726	162,363
McHenry	14,540	40,045	5,871	60,456
Will	41,975	69,310	7,855	119,140
Total	542,130	1,005,652	161,740	1,709,522
	(31.71%)	(58.83%)	(9.46%)	

Table 10.7

5¹/₂ Total Vote of Illinois Presidential Contests, 1976 and 1980

	Carter	Ford-Reagan
Suburban Cook		
1976	365,715 (38%)	597,950 (62%)
1980	339,322 (38%)	553,533 (62%)
Difference	− 26,393	− 44,417
Total Vote % Drop-off	− 7%	− 7%
Collar Counties		
1976	231,837 (35%)	425,460 (65%)
1980	202,808 (31%)	452,119 (69%)
Difference	− 29,029	+ 26,659
Total Vote % Drop-off	− 12.5%	+ 6%

NOTE: Leaving Anderson out of 1980 analysis, one sees in 1980 an equal percentage dropoff in the suburban Cook vote for Carter and Reagan compared to 1976. In the collar counties Reagan outdid Ford's totals by 26,659 votes while Carter dropped by over 29,000 from his 1976 performance.

idential elections in suburban Cook (leaving out Anderson) shows Carter's percentage of the vote going up in fourteen townships while his vote percentage dropped in the other sixteen. His greatest percentage increases were in Evanston, Calumet, and Oak Park and his biggest decreases took place in River Forest, Orland and Lemont.

An analysis of Carter's 1980 and Kennedy's 1960 suburban Cook vote reveals some remarkable comparisons. Most startling is the similarity between each man's vote percentage in individual townships. Many townships vary only a few percentage points in the votes given to both Democratic presidential candidates.

These townships tend to be in the north and northwestern part of Cook County and they have remained stalwart Republican in their political preference. On the other hand a few townships like Evanston and Oak Park, perhaps due to an influx of new black residents, have become decidedly more Democratic in their presidential preference.

Interestingly some townships which have received a large number of white, Catholic former Chicagoans have become more erratic in their voting behavior. One such township is Worth, located southwest of the city where one sees Carter losing in 1980 by the same percentage and plurality that he lost Worth in 1976. Democratic-states-attorney candidate Richard M. Daley, however, made remarkable vote gains in Worth compared to the 1976 democratic-states-attorney candidate. While Worth's ethnic voters spurned Carter's candidacy, enough latched onto Daley's bid to chop over 13,000 votes off the traditionally large Republican majority. And perhaps the most ominous of all facts concerning Daley's Worth township's results was that 56 more people cast ballots for states attorney than voted for president! Thus, it can be argued that certain Democratic candidates, Carter not being one, can cut into normal Republican pluralities in heavily ethnic Cook County townships.

Reagan beat Ford's spread against Carter in each of the 5 collar counties with the Republican's biggest jump coming in Will County. GOP presidential vote power has become awesome in the collar counties during the last 20 years. DuPage, the biggest and most Republican of all the collar counties, has become the Orange County, California, of Illinois. DuPage, like Orange, has grown so rapidly in recent years that it can now produce large enough GOP vote margins to cut significantly into the Democratic big city vote. Moreover, in Illinois when DuPage's Republican muscle is combined with the rest of the suburban 5½ GOP pluralities, Democratic strength in Chicago in statewide elections is nearly neutralized. This growing raw political power can be best illustrated by the following fact. In 1960 the suburban 5½ gave Nixon a 212,756 vote margin while two decades later it gave Reagan a 463,522 vote plurality.

The Other Ninety-six—Downstate Illinois

In every corner and section of the state Reagan smashed his major opponents. Besides Cook County Carter was able to win only two other Illinois counties— St. Clair and Alexander, both of which are in the deep southern part of the state. Traditionally southern Illinois has been very hospitable to Democratic presidential candidates. The region's farmers, miners, and union workers loyalty to the Democratic party stretches far back into the nineteenth century, but in 1980 they too bought into the Reagan landslide. According to the *Southern Illinoisian*, "southern Illinois voters overwhelmingly cast their lot with Republican Ronald Reagan . . . [giving] the former California Governor more than 55% of [their] votes."[5]

In the western part of the state, the *Rock Island Argus* talked about an unexpected Reagan romp and its impact on local races. In central Illinois the *Champaign-Urbana News-Gazette* called the election "an epic victory for the Republican party and an incredible rejection of the Democratic philosophy."[6] And in the northern part of the state, the *Rockford Register Star* wrote "Illinois voters feeling the pinch of inflation and resentment toward big government, sent a testy give me no excuses message to their political leaders in this election."[7]

The political attitudes expressed in the press were reflected in the downstate vote returns. Except for Whiteside County, Reagan beat Ford's spread against Carter in every Illinois county in the other 96. The successful 1980 Republican candidate received 77,873 more total votes than Ford won in 1976. Meanwhile Carter's total downstate numbers dropped 204,623 votes from 1976 to 1980.

The Democratic downstate debacle can be best described by looking at the vote margins given to Carter and Reagan. An examination of other 96 returns reveals some remarkable vote turnarounds throughout the state. In southwestern Illinois, St. Clair county Carter support dropped from a 18,844 plurality in 1976 to a 3,983 margin in 1980. In neighboring Madison County an even more amazing vote shift took place. In 1960 and 1976 Madison gave the Democratic presidential candidate approximately 12,000 vote pluralities in each election. In 1980 Reagan beat Carter in Madison County by 7,300 votes.

The central part of the state saw perhaps the most dramatic presidential vote flip-flop. As table 10.8 reveals, heartland and Illinois voters leaped aboard their native son's bandwagon. The astonishing GOP increases in these four central Illinois counties more than doubled Ford's 1976 margin and more than quadrupled Nixon's 1960 plurality.

In the past we have argued that in Illinois "there are many different downstates."[8] Historically, not all of the other 96 counties have similar voting patterns,

Table 10.8
Republican Pluralities in 4 Central Illinois Counties

	1960	1976	1980
LaSalle	20	2,009	10,505
Peoria	6,468	11,920	19,539
Sangamon	5,690	5,292	20,018
Tazewell	3,446	6,130	18,557
Total	15,624	25,351	68,619

and in presidential elections downstaters can significantly differ in their political choice. In 1980, however, President Carter's reelection bid was rejected almost throughout the other 96. In a postelection day editorial the *Quincy Herald-Whig* summed up downstate feelings about the campaign and the defeated incumbent president. "For the White House," it wrote, "Americans most of all yearn for leadership and competence. They want a president to at least act like he understands the system and knows what he is doing. Jimmy Carter's instincts may have been good . . . but he could not communicate, even as he attempted to manipulate images, that he was a leader."[9]

Illinois and the National Presidential Campaign

In understanding elections, it is also useful to examine the images and issue positions of the candidates as perceived by the voters. Most political scientists believe that an ever-increasing portion of those citizens who do vote make their choices during the campaign based on their reaction to the personal qualities or policy positions of the candidates.[10]

As Illinoisans are demographically quite representative of the nation's population, we can expect that they will respond to candidates and issues in much the same fashion as the nation as a whole. Support for this assumption comes from the work of the comparative state politics project[11] and Daniel Elazar's theory that American political culture can be separated into three streams, traditionalistic, moralistic, and individualistic, all of which are represented at once only in Illinois and Ohio.[12]

Direct evidence of the similar attitudes in Illinois and the nation towards the 1980 presidential election are presented in Table 10.9.[13] Given these similarities, we can with some confidence examine the results of national "exit" polls and apply them to Illinois to get a general idea of how responses to candidates and issues shaped the election results.

Jimmy Carter sought to convince the voters to focus on the candidates and to choose the most capable. He argued that many of the problems the nation faced were difficult, but that he had the intelligence, patience, and experience to cope with them as well as anyone, and certainly better than Ronald Reagan. He portrayed his opponent as a man inexperienced in national affairs and as one who tended to offer simplistic, extremist, and often dangerous responses to terribly complex issues. In postelection comments, Carter's advisors candidly admitted that they knew that if the election turned on the Carter record, they would lose.[14]

Ronald Reagan, in contrast, attempted to keep attention centered on the issues.

Table 10.9

The New York Times/CBS News Poll—October 14, 1980

Illinois and the Nation	Percentage of Probable Electorate	
	In Illinois	In Rest of Nation
Political Party		
Democrat	40	46
Independent	32	26
Republican	23	25
Political Philosophy		
Liberal	17	17
Moderate	49	45
Conservative	27	32
Family Finances		
Better off than year ago	24	22
Worse off than year ago	29	30
Labor Union Household	31	28
Issues		
Believe it possible to balance budget and cut taxes at same time	36	34
Believe inflation is more important problem than unemployment	57	61
Favor United States seeking military superiority over Soviet Union, not parity	56	60
Favor constitutional ban on abortion	29	31
Favor equal rights amendment	44	55
Concerns About Candidates		
Fear Reagan would get nation into war	34	34
Fear a worsened economy if Carter is reelected	27	33

Polls conducted in Illinois October 5–10, nationally September 10–14 and September 19–25.

Early in the campaign, Reagan put a major emphasis on promoting his record as Governor of California. Then, having "conditioned the environment," he moved into "an attack mode."[15] His theme of the final stretch of the campaign, "are you better off than you were four years ago?'' served to remind voters of the Carter record and particularly the problems of the economy.

In the final analysis, Carter's effort to put attention onto the candidates was a two-edged sword. While he did create some doubts about Reagan, he was also simultaneously reminding people of himself and the polls showed consistently that he was perceived as a poor leader and ineffective president. The Gallup Poll reported by the *New York Times* just four days before the election, showed Reagan with a highly favorable rating of only 23 percent, but Carter's score of 30 percent was little better.[16] When Johnny Carson asked his television studio audience "should John Anderson withdraw?" there was much applause. But when he added "should Carter and Reagan withdraw?" there was even more.

In 1976, one of three voters cited "honesty in government" as the most important issue and most of them went to Carter.[17] But in 1980, honesty was no longer a major concern. Instead, leadership was named by one-fourth of his voters as a key reason for backing Reagan. The voters' perceptions of Carter's personal qualities, his greatest asset in 1976, had become a liability in 1980 as attention shifted from simply being a good man to being an effective president.[18]

The cornerstone of Carter's anti-Reagan attack, that his election would run the risk of nuclear war (a major fear of presidential advisor and foreign policy specialist, Amy Carter), did not produce the hoped-for results, as shown by the *New York Times-CBS News* election-day surveys. Not only did a very substantial majority of those responding favor more forceful dealing with Russia even if it risked war, but Reagan did better with the minority who opposed such a policy than Carter did with the majority who supported it (see table 10.10).[19]

But the major issue was the economy. In 1976, about 56 percent of the voters cited inflation, high taxes, or unemployment as their most important concern, but by 1980, two-thirds listed one of these economic issues. How voters concerned with the economy divided among the candidates is best illustrated by the issue of family finances (see table 10.11).[20]

How badly this hurt Carter is illustrated by a comparison of 1976 and 1980 (see table 10.12).[21]

Table 10.10
U.S.–Soviet Policy

	Carter	Reagan	Anderson
Feeling that U.S. should be more forceful in dealing with Soviet Union even if it would increase the risk of war (45%)	28	64	6
Disagree (31%)	56	32	10

SOURCE: *The New York Times*/CBS Polls

Table 10.11

Family Finances

	Carter	Reagan	Anderson
Family Finances			
Better off than a year ago (16%)	53	37	8
Same (40%)	46	46	7
Worse off than a year ago (34%)	25	64	8

Source: *The New York Times*/CBS Poll

Table 10.12

Family Finances and Political Party

	1980			1976	
	Carter	Reagan	Ander-son	Carter	Ford
Family Finances and Political Party					
Democrats, better off than a year ago (7%)	77	16	6	69	31
Democrats, worse off than a year ago (13%)	47	39	10	94	6
Independents, better off (3%)	45	36	12	. . .	. . .
Independents, worse off (9%)	21	65	11	. . .	. . .
Republicans, better off (4%)	18	77	5	3	97
Republicans, worse off (11%)	6	89	4	24	76

Source: *The New York Times*/CBS Poll

Impact of the 1980 Illinois Presidential Race on Other State Contests

U.S. Senate

If there was a ray of sunshine for Illinois Democrats in the 1980 election, it emanated from the smiling face of Secretary of State Alan Dixon. Dixon easily trounced his Republican opponent and downstate Belleville, Illinois, neighbor Lieutenant-Governor Dave O'Neal, to capture the United States Senate seat vacated by Adlai Stevenson. Dixon's slogan "A senator from Illinois for Illinois" capsulized his strategy of stressing the importance of state and not national issues. On the other hand, O'Neal's "Matt Dillon style" of political commercials (he has been St. Clair County Sheriff), though appealing at first, did not ultimately catch on with the voters. Moreover, at the end of the campaign the lieutenant governor was forced to spend most of his time giving fumbling explanations about his use of state airplanes for political trips, thus placing him totally on the defensive and dooming him to defeat.

Alan Dixon's victory in light of the Reagan landslide is impressive but not remarkable given the Belleville Democrat's previous track record. Dixon in Illinois politics is simply an "election machine." He has never lost a political contest in thirty years and has served in the general assembly, as Illinois state treasurer and Illinois secretary of state.

In his 1978 secretary of state reelection bid, Dixon won every county in the state, every township in Cook County, and every ward in Chicago—in baseball jargon, he pitched a "perfect game." Thus any comparison between the GOP presidential triumph and the Democratic United States senate victory must be tempered by the astounding statewide popularity of Dixon.

As table 10.13 reveals, Dixon beat O'Neal in all three statewide regions. He squeaked by in the suburban 5-½, narrowly won downstate and annihilated O'Neal in Chicago. The growing trend of voters splitting their tickets is quite obvious in Dixon's 5-½ and other 96 returns. Many thousands of Illinois voters in these two regions cast a Reagan-Dixon ballot. Dixon won a majority of downstate counties, a majority of Cook County townships and carried one of the five collar counties (Will). If future Democratic candidates in Illinois wish to win statewide, Dixon's election gives them the blueprint—stay close in the 101-½ counties of Illinois and then wipe the GOP out in Chicago. Beating the GOP downstate was the key because it should be noted that though Dixon received over 100,000 more votes in Chicago than did Carter, O'Neal and not Dixon would

Table 10.13
Regional Breakdown—U.S. Senate Race in Illinois

	Dixon	O'Neal	Plurality
Chicago	814,776	223,804	D–590,972
5½	842,187	839,539	D–2,648
Other 96	909,339	882,953	D–25,386
Total	2,565,302	1,946,296	D–619,006

be the new Illinois junior United States Senator if the Democrat Dixon had run as poorly as the Democrat Carter did in the rest of the state.

University of Illinois Trustee Contests

If Dixon's victory was sunshine to Illinois Democrats, the University of Illinois trustee race was the darkest cloud. To political professionals the results of these rather inconspicuous contests involving three candidates from each party are the truest indicators of party power. A comparison of 1960 and 1980 University of Illinois contests, even more than Reagan's triumph, portends hard times ahead for Illinois Democrats.

In 1960, Democratic University of Illinois trustee candidates won 30 of the state's 102 counties on their way to an impressive 167,000 average vote victory. To be sure, Cook County with its bedrock Chicago machine vote keyed a Democratic clean sweep but, moreover, these University of Illinois trustee candidates were able to stay relatively close downstate. In 1980, however, Democratic University of Illinois trustee candidates won only ten counties, and because of the personal popularity of candidate Nina Shepard, they were able to win one of the three University of Illinois slots. The average Republican vote statewide was 37,774 greater than the Democratic totals; and this was accomplished despite the fact that Cook County's Democratic University of Illinois vote increased over 15,000 from 1960.

Similar to the presidential contest, Illinois Republicans gained windfall vote increases in the collar counties. From 1960 to 1980 the GOP University of Illinois trustee votes grew by almost 100,000 votes in this region. Downstate, especially in previously solid Democratic bailiwicks like Madison and St. Clair counties, Democratic University of Illinois trustee strength dropped dramatically. The question that arises is whether the Democratic drop-off is due to a shifting of political fortunes in Illinois or is it simply a byproduct of Carter's unpopularity.

A county-by-county comparison of Reagan's and Carter's vote with their respective party's University of Illinois vote reveals a partial answer. Reagan ran ahead of his GOP University of Illinois trustee running mates in every Illinois county. Carter on the other hand outpolled the Democratic University of Illinois trustees candidates in only 61 of the state's 102 counties. Carter's inability to run ahead of his party's trustee candidates is quite remarkable given the enormous fall-off in votes cast between the presidential and University of Illinois trustee races. In fact, 1980 saw over 20 percent of Illinois residents who went to the polls not bother to vote in the University of Illinois trustee race (this was a considerable percentage fall-off drop compared to 1960). Thus it appears that a substantial group of Democratic voters rebelled against Carter's candidacy but that a number of them came back for other races. Nevertheless, the same demographic trends which aided Reagan's landslide are working against Democratic fortunes in the state.

General Assembly Races

Reagan's Illinois victory had an impact on a few crucial state senate and state representative contests. Not surprisingly all these districts were located in the more politically competitive downstate region. In the state senate, Democrats lost two seats (the thirty-sixth and forty-ninth), both of which are located in the western part of Illinois. The GOP candidates in these races barely squeaked by their Democratic foes and the local press in both districts claimed Reagan's strength carried the day for the winners. Except for two other relatively close state senate contests in Will County (the forty-second) and another tight one for downstate (the fifty-fourth), every senate victor in both parties won by landslides. Thus, the Democrats held onto control of the state senate by a razor-thin thirty–twenty-nine margin.

In the Illinois house contests, Republicans gained control picking up three seats, all of which were located downstate. Except for a few isolated examples, the 96 downstate counties provided the only politically competitive areas in Illinois. Reagan's popularity in this region provided enough coattails for challenging GOP house candidates to give the Republicans a house majority. It must be stated that despite the Reagan win, however, enough ticketsplitting took place downstate to give several local Democratic candidates narrow victories. In sum, the general assembly contests pretty much resembled the presidential election in Chicago and the suburban 5½—Democratic landslide wins in the former; a GOP crushing triumph in the latter. Only downstate proved to be competitive and here, because Reagan gave many GOP candidates an extra boost, the Republicans made significant gains.

Conclusion

In November, 1978, we wrote in *Illinois Issues* "Suburbanization of American life has weakened big city Democratic bailiwicks in state politics. Detroit in Wayne County and Chicago in Cook can no longer produce large enough vote margins to allow Democratic presidential candidates to carry their states."[22] We believe this prediction was affirmed in the 1980 Illinois presidential contest and to a similar degree in other northern and eastern states. Carter was unable to find an issue which could break the demographic chain of events which finds big cities like Chicago losing their political muscle to the suburban areas. The Democratic candidate's effort to make "war and peace" the campaign's main issue was a realization on the part of his strategists that this was the only issue on which they could bridge the gap between their urban base and the new suburban power.

Reagan, on the other hand, merely had to look and sound presidential and avoid making irrational and controversial statements. His advisors, horrified by Reagan's early campaign blunders dealing with Taiwan, evolution, and the Vietnam War, ended the chance for future goofs by putting the California governor under wraps. Reagan was packaged, prepared, and programmed during the final two months of the campaign. Crucial issues like the economy, presidential leadership, and Iran broke his way, thus setting the stage of his near total blitz of Carter on election day. The West and much of the South were Reagan country from the outset but the Middlewest and Northeast were supposed to be battlegrounds. Once Reagan convinced GOP suburbanites of his credibility, however, the Republican candidate rode demographic trends in states like Illinois to easy victories.

As for John Anderson, he turned out to be a spoiler for neither candidate and in fact, his candidacy affected the eventual outcome very little.

In 1932, the Democrats put together a coalition of the poor, blacks, Catholics, union members, big city dwellers, and the "Solid South," which survived at least until 1964 in sufficient strength to enable the Democrats to win seven of nine presidential elections during this period, losing only in 1952 and 1956 to Dwight Eisenhower. Signs of strain were very evident, however, among Catholics and union members in the North and in the white South generally. By 1972, it was generally agreed that the Democratic coalition was pretty well dead in presidential politics, killed by the new politics, the new South, and the inherent conflicts between the values and interests of the coalition.[23]

Jimmy Carter, however, patched the coalition together in 1976. Although he had considerable difficulty with the white ethnics in the major metropolitan areas of the Midwest and Northeast, Carter held enough of their votes to capture a slim victory over Gerald Ford because of his showing in the South. As Scammon and Wattenberg have clearly demonstrated, the key element in Carter's election from a social group standpoint was the southern white protestant. Examining the eleven states of the old confederacy, they have demonstrated the steady desertion of these voters from the Democrats after 1940 and the decline of electoral votes after 1960 when the desertion reached a level in presidential voting below 50 percent (see tables 10.14 and 10.15).[24]

It is argued convincingly by Scammon and Wattenberg that Carter was supported simply because of regional pride, the same kind of "finally one of our own can win" feeling that benefitted John Kennedy among Catholics in 1960. By adding the white South to what he could hold together of the rest of the Democratic party's normal support groups, Carter could just barely eke out a victory. In Illinois, Al Monroe has demonstrated that Carter support in the primaries of 1976 and 1980 as well as the general election of 1976 correlates with the amount of

Table 10.14
Southern White Protestants from National Democratic Party
Vote Deviation

1936	+ 19%
1940	− 26%
1944	+ 19%
1948	+ 5%
1952	+ 6%
1956	+ 9%
1960	− 4%
1964	− 14%
1968	− 18%
1972	− 19%
1976	− 5%

SOURCE: *The New York Times*/CBS Poll

Table 10.15
Democratic Percentage of Southern Vote (11 states of confederacy)

	Democratic Percent	Democratic Electoral Votes
1960	50.5	81
1964	49.5	81
1968	30.9	25
1972	28.9	0
1976	54.1	118

settlers from the South in a county.[25] Thus Carter's downstate support in Illinois is probably attributable to the same factors as his support throughout the South. From the perspective of 1980, Carter's 1976 victory looks like a fluke—a deviation from long-term trends running against the Democrats.

Democratic prospects in future presidential elections in Illinois and for that matter upcoming 1982 statewide contests do not look very promising. The Democratic party needs to break out of its urban stranglehold with new ideas, new programs, and new people. Its strength is more and more being isolated in Chicago, which has a diminishing population and problems peculiar only to itself. No matter who wins in the current battle for political control in Chicago, the Democratic party in one form or another, will dominate. As the city turns out less and less of the statewide vote, however, candidates locked into this single constituency will find it impossible to win statewide races.

The 1980 presidential election in Illinois should lift the hearts of the Republican party. Political momentum is definitely on their side and as long as the Democrats are unwilling or unable to break out of their Chicago roots, Republicans will have a relatively free ride in state contests. To be sure, popular Democrats like a Dixon or an Adlai Stevenson can still win statewide, but these Democrats are the exception rather than the rule. Reagan won Illinois without Chicago. His bedrock GOP support in the 5-½ suburban counties cancelled out Carter's Chicago margin and it was once again downstate that proved to be the key to victory. Thus the crucial issue in upcoming Illinois statewide elections may well be whether downstate returns to a more balanced political region or whether Reagan's immense personal popularity has tipped downstate permanently Republican.

Chapter 11 The Transition: From Nomination to Inauguration

Laurin L. Henry

The 1980 election led to a presidential transition, the fifteenth in this century and of these the eighth of the type involving a change of party control at the White House.[1] In recent times transitions have come with increasing frequency. We had eight new presidents in the first half of this century, but we have already had seven since 1950. Of the latter seven, five led party turnovers. Under the Constitution we must have at least three new presidents, and are likely by some combination of election and death to have four or five, in the less than twenty years remaining before 2000.

The nation has always vaguely understood the risk of a letdown of effective government when a change of administrations coincides with a national crisis—1860–61 and 1932–33 provided experiences in point.[2] For a long time that risk was simply accepted as inevitable and a tolerable price to pay for the blessing of regular, free elections. But nowadays the stakes are higher, escalated by nuclear missile arms, large social and economic expectations, and complexities of government that make the presidency harder to grasp. At the same time, as Richard Neustadt points out, frequent turnover makes newness and inexperience a chronic condition of the presidency, increasing the possibility of error that will leave the incumbent with a permanent political handicap and start the cycle to another early transition, perhaps seriously endangering the nation in the process.[3] Thus the problems of transition become a contributing cause as well as a consequence of the instability that seems to afflict the parties and the presidency in our time.

Recognition of the dangers of transition has led to measures to buffer the shock of change and achieve an effective assumption of power by the new administration. Beginning with Truman and continuing through Carter, outgoing presidents have tried to arrange a safe and orderly transfer of responsibility to their successors. From Eisenhower onward, not only have presidents-elect intensified their efforts to be ready on January 20, but, as suggested by the title of this chapter, planning for a possible transition has begun long before election day, at least by nonincumbent candidates. Experience at managing transitions has produced a considerable institutionalization of the transition process—a generally understood series of tasks to be done, deadlines to be met, procedures to be followed.[4] Some of the institutionalization is only informal, based on precedent and the obvious interest of the participants. Some of it is embedded in the statutes—indirectly, as in modern laws governing the budget process, and quite directly, as in the Presidential Transition Act.[5] Although this amalgam of law, precedent, and experience guides all those involved in many important respects, there remains substantial room for variation. The 1980–81 transition from Jimmy Carter to Ronald Reagan displayed examples of continuity and learning from the past, as well as some deliberate innovations and useful lessons for the future.

As a piece of political history, the transition of 1980–81 was more interesting than the campaign that preceded it. Reagan's decisive victory, coupled with Republican gains in Congress that produced a GOP majority in the Senate and the probability of strong Reagan influence in the House, excited the political community with the possibility of a major shift toward conservative policies. Groups frustrated since the Goldwater candidacy of 1964 now claimed a mandate to govern, while Republicans of all stripes jockeyed for position and moderate and liberal Democrats were left demoralized. In the weeks after election, President-elect Reagan and his associates conducted their side of the transition in a way that revealed effective planning and more finesse than had been expected, at least in Washington. Although the Reagan performance was not flawless, the transition served its essential purposes of consolidating the Reagan victory, advancing public acceptance of Reagan as the new national leader, laying the foundation for postinaugural initiatives, and maintaining the necessary continuity in national security and delicate diplomatic negotiations. On the Carter side the routines of turning the government over to a successor administration were carried out in a way that adequately fulfilled expectations but with a lack of enthusiasm that was natural in view of the president's recent rejection by the voters. Carter's last weeks were dominated, of course, by his negotiations to free the American embassy hostages in Iran. The countdown as Inauguration Day approached, climaxing in the release of the hostages at the very hour transfer of power was occurring in Washington, was drama that almost upstaged the new president and his inauguration. This chapter deals with preelection through Inauguration day.

Before Election

As usual when an incumbent president is running for reelection, the Carter White House made no visible preelection preparations for a possible surrender of power.

The president and his associates were preoccupied with the campaign and Iran. Carter treated his opponent with disdain and tried to avoid statements or acts that might lend credibility to the thought of Reagan as a successor. One exception was the televised debates. Another was Carter's compliance with the tradition of offering intelligence briefings on the international situation to the opposition candidate, which had been done in every campaign since 1944. This offer was made somewhat belatedly and at first rejected by Reagan; later Reagan did accept briefings, but the whole business seemed to be carried out in minimal fashion.[6] We must await the Carter memoirs to find out if he gave any thought to how he would regenerate an administration for the second term if he won.

In contrast to little or no preparation on the Carter side, Reagan began early in the campaign to plan for a transition. His approach seemed so deliberately chosen to avoid what were widely considered mistakes by Carter four years earlier that a retrospective look at the Carter effort is in order.

In 1976, Carter had begun to think about transition even before the convention, and as soon as the nomination was secured he established a transition planning office in Atlanta. This staff was unprecedented, both in its size and visibility and the fact that it was financed with campaign funds accountable under the federal election laws. It was dominated by issue-oriented persons recruited for this purpose, many of them new to the Carter movement. Its leader, Jack Watson, although an Atlantan, was not of the Carter inner circle. The transition planners had no role in the campaign, but as election day approached they received a considerable amount of press attention as the prospective source of advice on Carter appointments and policy. After election a power struggle ensued in which Hamilton Jordan and other Carter insiders, perceiving the planning effort as politically unrealistic and a threat to their positions, succeeded in reasserting control. Watson and his key associates were relegated to second- and third-level roles, and the personnel operation was reorganized. Parts of the planning group evolved into a series of agency-transition teams that were active in Washington for a few weeks but essentially on the fringes of early Carter decisions. The confusion of all this hurt the reputation of the emerging administration, led to a ragged and fairly slow appointment process, and contributed to a loss of unity and control as several of the Cabinet designees were able to avoid Carter staff guidance and act independently in choosing key subordinates and assuming power in their spheres. The success of the original campaign staff in dominating the transition and organizing the White House seemed to harden the Carter "outsider" posture vis-à-vis Congress and the Washington community—a self-imposed limitation that may have permanently damaged Carter's presidency.[7]

Ronald Reagan, like Jimmy Carter in 1976, emerged early as a front-runner for the nomination and, once nominated, seemed a likely winner. Throughout the election year, he encouraged his advisers and supporters to consider what was to be done when the presidency was secured. As early as April 18, at a meeting in

Washington with a group of defense- and foreign-policy advisers, Reagan asked them to think beyond campaign strategy to policy and budget recommendations for the first 100 days of a new administration. As the campaign went on, this group, under the coordination of Richard Allen, was expanded to 132 members, divided into 25 working groups in the foreign and defense field. After the convention a similar network of economic and domestic policy advisers was started under the leadership of Martin Anderson, assisted by Darrell Trent. This eventually included 329 persons in 23 issue-area groups.[8] These policy task forces, a familiar phenomenon in all recent presidential campaigns, included many prominent persons and were mainly for the purposes of providing suggestions—and endorsements—for the campaign, but as victory came in sight their several hundred members thought increasingly of advising the president-elect.

Transition planning in a more specific sense, however, revolved around Reagan's trusted aide, Edwin Meese III, who had served him in the California governorship and other capacities and was now campaign chief of staff with particular responsibility for issues and strategy. Reagan established no transition-planning office, as Carter had done, but beginning in midsummer Meese gave part of his time to directing several people who were working, separately and quietly, on various aspects of a postelection plan. Ronald Frankum, a California lawyer, sketched a transition organization. Pendleton James, an executive recruiting consultant who served in the Nixon White House personnel office, planned a personnel operation. Peter McPherson, a Washington attorney, performed confidential missions in the capital, including, as the election approached, scouting for space and contacting the General Services Administration about a transition headquarters. These activities attracted no public attention until September, when James and Helene Von Damm, Reagan's private secretary as governor, moved from California to set up an advance base in Alexandria, Virginia; this was done quietly and produced only brief notices in the press. Also about this time a Presidential Transition Trust was established to receive contributions to finance such activities without being counted as campaign contributions.[9]

Beyond the closely guarded activities under his direct control, Meese gave encouragement to several other transition planning enterprises that were self-starting and self-financed. Even before the convention, Caspar Weinberger, one of the few members of the Reagan inner circle with major Washington experience, encouraged a former associate, Robert Freer, to develop a network of volunteers to gather information about the departments and agencies. Freer's contacts were mostly persons who had served at middle levels in the Nixon and Ford administrations and were now placed in Washington offices of law firms and business corporations. From July to October, Freer coordinated preparation of a series of papers, each sketching the responsibilities and organization of an agency, identifying the key offices and their occupants, and summarizing policy issues, particularly those that might present problems or opportunities in the transition period or early in the new term. These papers were fed to Reagan headquarters through Weinberger, although Meese was well informed about the activity and had direct contact with Freer on occasion. As election day approached and the initial round of agency papers was completed, Freer's group proposed to expand itself into a series of agency transition teams that would be prepared to feed information to Reagan right after election and to "envelop" the new agency heads as they were designated.[10] There was no response to the latter suggestion to assign guides to incoming agency personnel.

Also active in Washington during the summer was the Heritage Foundation, an organization sponsored by some of the more conservative elements of Congress and with connections to right-wing circles throughout the country. The Heritage Foundation developed a 3,000-page study of government agencies, programs, and personnel with intent to provide the blueprint for Reagan policies.[11] This enterprise, too, was encouraged by Meese.

As usual in an election year when change is in the air, organizations and groups of all kinds ranging from scholarly and professional through special interest, partisan, and ideological made plans, undertook studies, and put out feelers toward the possible new administration. Considering his mainstream responsibilities in the campaign, Meese was remarkably accessible and receptive, fostering widespread hopes of participation in the launching of a Reagan administration.[12]

Postelection Organizing

On election night President Carter telephoned President-elect Reagan to offer his congratulations and set the transition process in motion along lines well sanctioned by precedent and the Presidential Transition Act.[13] The next day Carter designated Jack Watson (now serving as White House chief of staff) to be the administration's coordinator of transition arrangements and principal point of contact with the Reagan staff. Watson in turn delegated responsibility for oversight of the detailed arrangements to the Office of Management and Budget, where Associate Director Harrison Wellford coordinated the designation of a transition liaison officer in each executive agency and the preparation of agency briefing books to be turned over to Reagan representatives.[14]

On the day after election Reagan made no public appearances; we may presume that he was briefed on the transition plans and the most urgent preliminary decisions were made. The second day, November 6, Reagan met the press in California and announced that William J. Casey, who had been his campaign director, would be chairman of a transition executive committee, and that Meese would be transition director.[15] In the next few days Meese lined up the principals to staff the transition organization and completed arrangements with GSA for offices in Washington.

Meese and a small advance guard arrived in Washington on the evening of November 11. The next day they met with Watson and his staff (with whom they had been conferring daily by telephone) to review the transition plans and confirm arrangements for a meeting between Carter and Reagan the following week. These discussions were cordial and the Carter people stated that they would defer initiatives on various matters and make no unnecessary policy decisions, athough the administration would not abandon support for certain important proposals still before Congress. Later in the day, Casey, Meese, and several of their key associates met the press in the offices that the GSA had provided for the Reagan transition at 1726 M. Street, NW.[16]

Reagan's Preparations

The Transition Organization

In the next several days the preelection plans were transformed into a bustling, complex transition organization. The planners obviously had sought to avoid the conflict between the campaign organization and the transition group that had plagued Carter in 1976. The organizational scheme started with an elaborate superstructure with a designated place for all of the existing major advisers and staff. Thus the executive committee, chaired by former campaign director Casey, included his campaign codirector, Anne Armstrong, Senator Paul Laxalt, Meese, Weinberger, and several other friends and advisers of long standing. Meese, as transition director in charge of the newly created operational parts of the organization, was flanked by three senior advisers, all from the campaign organization: Richard Allen for foreign affairs and national security, Martin Anderson for domestic and economic policy, and Weinberger for budget and management. There were also seven deputy directors, including James A. Baker, Michael K. Deaver (Reagan's personal aide for many years), Lyn Nofziger, (Reagan's former press aide and political adviser), and others from the campaign organization such as Verne Orr, Drew Lewis, William Timmons, and Richard B. Wirthlin, (Reagan's top pollster). As matters developed, some of these senior appointees turned out to be essentially honorific, others definitely functional; some were to remain California-based to serve Reagan personally and travel with him in the interim, others were to help manage the transition organization in Washington.[17]

Meese's staff in Washington was assembled from many sources: his preelection transition planners, former campaign staff, the issue advisory committees, academics from universities and the conservative-leaning think tanks, friendly business organizations and law firms, participants in the Freer, Heritage, and other voluntary studies, and veterans of the Nixon and Ford administrations. Thus recognition was given to many elements of the Reagan coalition and to the importance of expertise and Washington experience while reserving the key positions for insiders of long standing with the president-elect.

Several main parts of the transition staff can be identified. Most numerous and visible was the operations group headed by William Timmons, a Reagan campaigner with both White House and congressional staff experience. Operations consisted of a large number of separate teams responsible for making contact with and gathering information about each executive department and agency, including the independent agencies, both major and minor, and the regulatory commissions. Altogether there were almost a hundred teams, varying in size according to the importance of the agency, with the average about five members.

To protect everyone against unauthorized persons claiming to represent the president-elect—a problem in every transition—it was agreed with Watson that transition team members must be nominated by Timmons and cleared through Wellford at OMB before gaining access to their agencies and official materials. This process helped the Carter people to clarify the status of a few persons who appeared with missions from other parts of the Reagan organization. Questions were raised about some members of Congress who were initially proposed for transition teams. OMB took exception to this on the ground that it would blur executive and legislative status and provide congressional access to materials that the executive might consider privileged; the Reagan organization accepted this position and withdrew the congressional names.[18]

Perhaps more serious questions were raised by the inclusion on some of the transition teams of individuals with contractual or regulatory relationships or a history of conflict, including in a few cases litigation pending, with the agencies to which they were designated. When the agencies objected to some of these people, Wellford relayed their concerns to the Reagan office. The Carter position was that composition of the teams was a Reagan responsibility, although the administration had the right to decide what information was to be made available—which presumably might depend on the nature of the team. A few individuals with the most obvious conflicts were withdrawn or shifted to other teams, but most of the nominees stayed, and in the end the administration cooperated with a number of persons about whom it had distinct reservations. A little later, when there began to be press comment about possible conflicts of interest by transition-team members, the Reagan office pointed out that although transition-staff members were exempt from the general statutes and regulations concerning conflict of interest, all had been required to file statements disclosing their financial and other interests (not available to the press); the attorneys advising on conflict of interest for presidential appointees had reviewed the transition-team cases also, and individuals on the teams were avoiding personal involvement in any particular areas where there might be a question of conflict.[19] Despite this defensiveness, it was clear that the Reagan organization was not inclined to be ultrasensitive about such matters, considering all this a natural consequence of the political process by which agency critics and formerly losing policy advocates had become winners.

Efforts were made to discipline the agency teams in other ways. There was a hierarchical structure, each team leader reporting to one of five cluster directors, who in turn reported to Timmons. The teams were given a series of deadlines. Each was to submit a "first look" report by mid-November to identify issues or problems that might have to be dealt with before inauguration. They were to be prepared by early December to provide comprehensive briefings about their agencies, their personnel, their policy issues, and their pending decisions to the new department and agency heads as they were announced. Final reports, with policy recommendations, were due in early January.[20] As each team was organized it was given the briefing materials previously accumulated, including the Freer project papers, the Heritage Foundation studies, and other sources. On first contact with their agencies, teams received the official briefing books prepared under administration auspices. Then the teams fanned out in the agencies to interview officials and gather additional information, including in many cases special reports prepared at their request.

The second large part of the Reagan transition staff was James' personnel group. The preelection planning had produced a computer-based system for classifying and recording the resumes that were now pouring in. Organized in functional groups parallel to the agency teams, the personnel activity included personnel experts and generally knowledgeable persons in various policy fields and an increasing number of lawyers to scan resumes and advise prospective appointees on the restrictions and requirements concerning conflict of interest, which had been tightened under new legislation passed in 1978. Personnel stood ready to provide information on possible cabinet appointees but recognized that these would be special decisions taken by the president-elect and his personal advisers on considerations transcending the computer. Personnel's special target was 87 positions at the deputy and undersecretary rank, for which they hoped to have lists of 5 to 10 names each to present to the cabinet members when designated. After that came a list of 100 more positions at the assistant-secretary level. The goal was to have these approximately 200 appointees chosen by inauguration day. There was an outspoken intention to insure effective participation by the president-elect's staff in the subcabinet appointments, to avoid the independent choices that some of the Carter cabinet designees had been able to make in 1976.[21]

Third was the office for policy coordination, headed by Darrell Trent. This group had responsibility for pulling together policy information, providing top-level briefings to the cabinet appointees, and developing briefing and policy options papers for Reagan and his immediate advisers. It gathered material from various sources, including the agency teams and the campaign-period issue advisory network. This was apparently more of a supporting than a policy recommending activity, since Allen and Anderson, the key foreign and domestic policy advisers, were outside this structure at a higher level and maintained elite advisory groups of their own.[22]

In addition to the three main operating parts of the transition organization there were various staff units, including a press office headed by James Brady, and a business and accounting office headed by Verne Orr.

Outside of the formal structure of the transition organization there were other groups, some important and some not. One was a set of long-standing personal friends and backers of Reagan, mostly Californians, including his personal attorney, William French Smith, Justin Dart, Holmes Tuttle, Alfred Bloomingdale, Charles Wick, and Henry Salvatori. This constituted a senior review group particularly to advise on cabinet and other high appointments. Although this "kitchen cabinet" met mostly in California, some of its members were in Washington at times, and a small staff on its behalf later emerged under the special sponsorship of Nofziger, mainly as a watchdog against subcabinet appointments of insufficiently conservative faith.[23]

Another group, which apparently remained mostly on paper, was a congressional advisory group headed by Laxalt, who was very active personally in this period as a bridge to the Republican congressional leaders.

As the weeks passed the transition organization evolved, some units and persons in the original plan faded away and new ones appeared. It also grew far beyond initial expectations or any previous president-elect's staff. Because there were so many volunteers, the size of the organization was hard to establish, but estimates ranged from 1,000 to 1,200, of which perhaps 500 were on the payroll. The $2 million in federal funds available under the Transition Act to cover travel, communications, and other services as well as salaries, were soon exhausted, as apparently had been anticipated, and were supplemented by about $1 million in private funds through the presidential trust. This rampant bureaucracy was a source of some amusement in Washington, after all the Republican rhetoric, and Carter officials enjoyed recalling that they had done the job with about 350 people and returned a fourth of the Transition Act funds to the Treasury.[24]

The Reagan Style

As the Reagan people arrived in Washington they seemed determined to avoid the political and public relations mistakes of previous incoming administrations, which often had been characterized by suspicion, protectiveness, and arrogance. Meese and his associates were friendly and communicative. They not only made contact with their opposite numbers in the Carter administration and their prior political allies but they made special efforts to establish relations with Congress, the press, and various professional and interest groups. Antibureaucracy rhetoric was toned down. They almost courted the Washington establishment.

The effort to gain acceptance and confidence peaked when Reagan himself arrived in Washington on November 17. Blair House being committed to previously scheduled foreign visitors, the Reagans occupied the house on Jackson Place maintained for former Presidents. Reagan began his week with a trip to Capitol Hill for calls on both the Republican and Democratic legislative leaders. The first evening the Reagans dramatized their desire for friendship by giving a large dinner at a private club for a cross-section of leading local citizens—including many prominent Democrats—representing government, the arts, business, the press, religion and the professions. Reagan followed this gesture to the Washington community by further congressional visits, including one to Senator Edward Kennedy; he had a conference with former-President Gerald Ford, called on the justices of the Supreme Court, and gave a dinner for all the Republican senators and their wives. He also visited the headquarters of the Teamsters, who had been his principal supporters from labor, and attended a private dinner at the home of the columnist George Will, who assembled some influential members of the press and conservative intellectuals.

The ostensible purpose of Reagan's visit to Washington, of course, was to meet with President Carter and receive high-level briefings. He did have two briefings from the CIA, sandwiched among his other activities, and on November 20 Reagan went to the White House, where he met with President Carter for 85 minutes. No details of their talk were available, except that they had discussed transition arrangements and certain issues likely to be on the presidential desk after January 20. While the principals were meeting, Rosalyn Carter and Nancy Reagan toured the mansion, and senior aides on the two sides reviewed White House organization. All these talks apparently were cordial, and the day ended with statements of mutual appreciation, pledges of future cooperation, Reagan's intent not to interfere with the responsibilities of the outgoing administration, and everyone's determination to maintain unity in negotiations over the hostages in Iran.

On November 21, Reagan made a visit to transition headquarters on M Street, where he encouraged the troops and had a session on foreign policy with a group of notables assembled by Allen, which included Henry Kissinger, Alexander Haig, and Democratic Senator Henry Jackson. Then after a week that had charmed the political community, produced many favorable comparisons with the aloofness of his predecessor, and augured well for his influence with Congress, the president-elect returned to California to make decisions about the Cabinet.[25]

Appointments

In making the key appointments in his administration, Reagan started with the top White House positions, apparently feeling that it was important to settle the futures of some individuals on whom he was already heavily relying and to get his own staff in place before commissioning department heads. He made two announcements on November 14, before his Washington trip.[26] Somewhat surprisingly, the top-ranking post of chief of staff went to James Baker, a Texan of Washington experience who had worked himself into the Reagan organization after managing George Bush's campaign for the presidential nomination. Meese would be Counselor to the president, with responsibility for policy. Further decisions were made and announcements filtered out through late November and December. Michael Deaver, who had hardly left Reagan's side for years, would be deputy chief of staff, with responsibility for appointments and scheduling, completing a top triumvirate with Baker and Meese. Under Baker, Max Friedersdorf, a Washington lawyer with much congressional and White House experience, would handle congressional relations; James would continue in charge of personnel, and James Brady, a relatively newcomer who earned his spurs as the transition office spokesman, was somewhat belatedly named to handle the press. Richard Allen as national security adviser, and Martin Anderson as his counterpart for domestic policy, would operate under Meese—an innovation intended to solve an old White House problem of keeping incumbents of those positions under control and in proper relationship to cabinet secretaries.

Speculation about the Cabinet of course had been going on since election, and during Reagan's Washington meetings, especially those with Republican congressional leaders, numerous individuals were assessed. The staff meanwhile had been busy, and when Reagan returned to California he reportedly carried seventy dossiers on prospective appointees worked up by James' office.

The decision-making on Cabinet and top White House appointments was a relatively open process, both in widespread participation of advisers and information reaching the public about who was under consideration. The process began with meetings of the kitchen cabinet. Under the chairmanship of William French Smith, twenty-one senior advisers met on November 21 to assemble recommendations. The following day this group met with Reagan himself for three hours. To the public, this marked a slight change in the tone of Reagan's transition. The reports—and pictures—of this group of mostly elderly, very conservative gentlemen advising the president-elect on the cabinet were in some contrast to the moderation and low partisanship displayed on Reagan's Washington visit. Although some kitchen cabinet members remained involved in discussions about appointments, as the meetings continued over several days the balance of participation seemed gradually to shift to top staff and advisers who clearly would have direct responsibilities in the new administration—Vice-President-elect Bush, Meese, Baker, Deaver, Senator Laxalt, Casey, and a few others. Also as the time passed, leaks and trial balloons arising from the early discussions put some of the early candidates, apparently favorites of the kitchen cabinet, under intense scrutiny by the press and political circles. After several days a few persons prominent in the early speculation either took themselves out or faded from consideration.

Deciding on the top appointments took longer and involved more conflict and negotiation than expected, as Reagan and his top staff tried to listen to everyone and balance all the considerations of faction and party, regions, experience, and anticipated compatability. The personnel planning apparently had not fully anticipated the time-consuming processes required after a presumptive appointee was identified. This involved both an FBI check and a review and discussion with the candidate of possible conflicts of interest. The new requirements of financial disclosure, coupled with government salaries that had not kept pace with private sector earnings, caused some persons to withdraw late in the process.

While his staff was checking and negotiating, Reagan himself had a leisurely Thanksgiving holiday at his ranch. For several days in early December there was little visible activity around the president-elect. Each day Reagan met briefly with aides and made a few phone calls, but he found time to attend to personal matters such as visits to his dentist and his barber. On December 8 he and Mrs. Reagan went to New York, where they spent two days. He met with various notables, including Cardinal Terence Cooke and a delegation of black leaders, while she selected clothing.[27] On December 10 they arrived for their second post-election visit to Washington, this time staying at Blair House.

The following day the first group of Cabinet choices was announced: Donald Regan for Treasury, Caspar Weinberger for Defense, William French Smith for Justice, Malcolm Baldrige for Commerce, Richard Schweiker for Health and Human Services, David Stockman for OMB, and William Casey for CIA. The appointees were presented to the press by staff; Reagan himself did not attend, reportedly because he did not wish to distract attention from those chosen.[28]

The second set of Cabinet choices was announced on December 16. This consisted of Alexander Haig for Secretary of State and Raymond Donovan for Labor. After another week of negotiations and rumors several more choices were announced on December 23: James Watt for Interior, John Block for Agriculture, Samuel Pierce for Housing and Urban Development, James Edwards for Energy, and Jeane Kirkpatrick to be Ambassador to the United Nations. This completed the Cabinet except for the choices of Terrell Bell for Secretary of Education, an office which was expected to be soon abolished, and William Brock for Special Trade Representatives; these announcements were not made until early January.

Thus despite advance planning and staff work, the Cabinet was named two to three weeks later than in other recent transitions. The Cabinet was well received and generally judged to be balanced with persons from various regions and wings of the party, including Californians of Reagan's personal choice and Easterners that he hardly knew. There was executive experience in such persons as Haig, Weinberger, and Casey, congressional experience in Schweiker and Stockman, and a gesture toward Reagan-supporting Democrats in Kirkpatrick. The designation of only one black, one woman, and no Hispanic disappointed those interests, but perhaps the most vocally critical were Reagan's supporters in the Moral

Majority and other strongly conservative groups; only Edwards, a former governor of South Carolina sponsored by Senator Strom Thurmond, came with that endorsement.

Government by Transition

From mid-November to mid-January, the transition headquarters in Washington was a focal point of political attention. Reagan was in California most of the time and not making much news. The Cabinet announcements were delayed. Perhaps in compensation, Meese and the other transition leaders were highly available to the media. The papers were full of background stories, leaks, speculation about imminent decisions, policy ideas being tried out, and contests for appointment, so that official announcements and actual events contained few surprises. In this period, 1726 M Street seemed to have a life of its own; Washingtonians referred to "the transition" as an institution like the White House or the Congress.

Much of the news, probably more than justified, came from the agency transition teams. After the exhilaration of entering the agencies, collecting materials, and quizzing the Carter officials wore off, the teams tended to feel isolated out in the agencies. Their reports went through channels to operations headquarters on M Street, which presumably shared them with the personnel and the policy groups. Urgent matters were taken up at the early-morning meetings of the top leaders, but agency team members seldom penetrated this level, and often they could see little use being made of their recommendations: personnel had its own system and sources, and policy concentrated on Reagan's own need and a few priorities declared by the top staff. Naturally, ambitious and frustrated team members began sharing their policy ideas and their assessments of people and situations with the press.

The leading consumers of the products of the agency teams were supposed to be the designated agency heads, but these were slow to appear, and for some of the noncabinet agencies the teams had turned in their work and gone home before the new heads were announced. In a few instances there was welcome acceptance and good use made of the transition team products, especially by cabinet members with limited Washington experience. Other cabinet nominees followed the pattern of Alexander Haig, who moved quickly to pull together former associates and develop his own sources of information without much reference to either his agency team or the transition policy group. Weinberger, angered by trial balloons that had been floated from the defense team before his arrival, including efforts to block appointment of the person of his choice for deputy secretary, sent the group packing after one meeting.[29] Incidents of this sort, well reported, contributed to an increasing impression of disarray in the Reagan organization.

There was considerable public speculation, and apparently some argument among Reagan's advisers, about setting up policy-making processes that would be effective and compatible with Reagan's preferred work habits. As governor, he had established a "chairman of the board" style, tending to stay aloof from details and concentrate on choices among alternatives worked out by department heads and advisers. Could this be the basis for some form of "cabinet government" that would place greater responsibility on the department heads and restrain the power of White House staff? The Washington establishment, accustomed to hearing such talk at the onset of every new administration, tended to be skeptical, as Weinberger and other Reaganites brought forth their visions of cabinet government.[30] Meanwhile Meese and Baker moved ahead filling out the While House table of organization along traditional lines except for the innovation of placing the domestic policy and national security advisers under a single top policy adviser. Eventually there was announced a plan for a series of "Cabinet councils" chaired by department heads which would hammer out policy recommendations and present them to the president in Cabinet.[31] Reagan met with his Cabinet fairly frequently in the weeks after January 20, as most new presidents tend to do. Whether the Cabinet councils could compete with such activists as Meese and Stockman and escape the fate of most previous Cabinet committees seemed doubtful.

Buried somewhere in the transition staff, a small group headed by former college professor Richard Beal developed for Meese an "Initial Actions Project" to identify the most strategic presidential-level objectives and a desirable sequence and timing of events to be unfolded in the early weeks and months of the new administration.[32]

While the Cabinet announcements were late, the subcabinet choices were correspondingly later, as these decisions had to be negotiated between the prospective agency heads and the Reagan staff. Government salary levels and conflict of interest requirements proved complicating factors for many prospective appointees at this level whose fortunes were not yet made. There was also increasing political pressure to take care of campaign activists, contributors, congressional proteges, and ideologues on the right. As inauguration approached, Pendleton James came under increasing criticism from all sides for the slowness of the appointment decisions, and especially from "original Reaganites" disappointed because so many posts were going to Nixon and Ford "holdovers" and other traditional Republican establishment types.[33]

Policy Development

Policy making in the highest-priority areas largely escaped the hurly-burly around transition headquarters. This was especially so in the field of economics, where deteriorating conditions, coupled with Reagan's commitments and the strong voices of well-placed advisers, pushed this problem into top-level attention ahead of the work of the agency transition teams and the decisions on key executive appointees. In mid-November, as one set of Reagan aides was assembling the transition teams, including several for economic agencies, another group was assembling an economic policy coordinating committee headed by George P. Schultz, former secretary of the treasury. This committee was built around the chairmen of eight of the policy task forces organized during the campaign, including such personages as Arthur F. Burns, Alan Greenspan, Caspar Weinberger, Paul McCracken, and Charles Walker, plus a few others such as Milton Friedman, former Treasury Secretary William Simon, and Representative Jack Kemp of New York, whose proposal for a 30 percent income tax cut over three years had been supported by Reagan during the campaign. This group met in California for three days in mid-November and had some time with Reagan himself before his first postelection trip to Washington.[34]

The economic advisers agreed that quick moves were imperative, including some combination of spending reductions, tax cuts, controlling the money supply, and stimulation of the economy through deregulation. There was apparently considerable disagreement about the priorities, however, and in the days following the meetings most of the participants continued the argument through statements to the press. Weinberger, who had headed the task force on government spending, urged a quick attack to reduce disbursements in the current fiscal year, by about $30 billion. Kemp and others believed that short-run expenditure cuts of that size would be very difficult, politically and otherwise, and put their faith in immediate tax cuts and deregulation, believing that these measures plus curtailment of growth of expenditures and assurance of a favorable climate for business over the next few years would stimulate the economy and soon lead to a balanced budget—a view that the nation was learning to call "supply-side" economics. Other old heads, such as McCracken, said that the economy was like a great ship that could be turned only gradually and warned against expectations of a quick fix.[35] Monetarists, although apparently a minority among the advisers, continued to put their main faith in controlling the money supply.

Among the papers before the group was a hard-hitting memorandum entitled "Avoiding A GOP Economic Dunkirk," sponsored by Kemp but written mostly by his colleague David Stockman, a young congressman from Michigan.[36] This paper, which was widely circulated around Washington in the latter part of November, emphasized supply-side doctrine and served as the main platform of the eventually successful campaign to have Stockman chosen for director of the Office of Management and Budget. Stockman got an early start on his task, digging into budgetary data immediately after his designation on December 1, while the other leading economic appointees were slower to appear; Donald Regan, future Secretary of the Treasury, was new to Washington and took some time to assemble a staff, and Murray Weidenbaum was not nominated chairman of the Council of Economic Advisers until a few days after inauguration.

The discussions went on through December and early January, with somewhat less talk about the billions that could be saved by curtailing fraud and waste—with which Meese had been entertaining the public—or what could be slashed out of current year spending, and correspondingly greater emphasis on tax reduction and controlled expenditure over a two- or three-year period. At any rate, the debate kept public attention on the issue, and in early January the Reagan advisers made a decision-forcing commitment by announcing a target date of February 3 for the unveiling of the Reagan economic program—a date on which there would eventually be a little slippage but not much as such things go. As the Reaganites began to consult legislators about the timing and process by which Reagan's measures might be handled in Congress, members of the congressional budget committees pointed out the potentiality of the relatively new procedures created by the Congressional Budget Act of 1974. This act, about which many Republicans had never been enthusiastic, called for a vote early in the session on a "reconciliation" of anticipated revenues and proposed expenditures by fields, thus constituting a powerful device for focusing both congressional and public attention and securing a commitment through a single vote on a coherent package of spending and tax proposals.[37]

As compared to economic policy, development of Reagan foreign and national security policy in the transition period was slower, more discordant, and less conclusive. On many fundamentals, of course, Reagan's positions were clear: firmness toward the Soviet Union, strengthened defense, free trade, and opposition to communist subversion and expansion everywhere. But exactly how these would be translated into specific commitments and actions with respect to the Middle East, defense of Europe, arms limitation negotiations, Japanese imports, civil war in El Salvador, and a hundred other spheres remained to be seen.

In his first postelection press conference, Reagan made the customary American unity statement: "I want the world to know that there is no political division that affects our foreign policy." In the same meeting, however, he identified two areas where his approach would differ from Carter's. He would not negotiate arms control divorced from other issues with the Soviet Union—a reassertion of Kissinger-era "linkage"—and he wanted a consistent policy on human rights—a code statement suggesting diminished concern about the internal policies of anticommunist but authoritarian regimes.[38] After that, Reagan made few direct foreign policy statements and tended to speak in generalities when he did, such as on the occasion of a meeting on the border with the president of Mexico. The main exceptions concerned Iran, on which, as inauguration day approached, he made a number of statements seeming to back away from his earlier expressions of solidarity with Carter, expressing personal outrage at the "criminal" conduct of the revolutionary regime in holding our hostages.

There was no lack of activity. Reagan himself discussed pressing issues with Carter, received State Department and CIA briefings, had get-acquainted visits with foreign leaders and emissaries, and met with various advisory groups. His top staff members and advisers received briefings from Carter officials, met other foreign representatives, and studied recommendations of their own task forces. Notables purporting to know Reagan's mind visited foreign capitals. From transition teams and advisers of varying degrees of authenticity issued a stream of public and private recommendations, predictions, and opinions that were frequently conflicting and occasionally descended to the level of guerrilla warfare against Carter officials or each other.

Sensing the rising confusion, Richard Allen on November 29 sent a memorandum to all 120 members of Reagan's Foreign Policy Advisory Board and all transition teams in the national security area directing them to curtail their public comments on international affairs.[39] It was also announced that a special unit was being set up in the transition office to keep track of all the contacts between Reagan advisers and representatives of foreign governments, and the CIA followed up a few days later with a warning about penetration of the transition group by Soviet agents.[40] It was not clear whether these cautions were aimed at transition-team members or at higher-level figures such as Henry Kissinger who in recent days had ventured public remarks about Carter's handling of the Iran negotiations, or Charles Percy, newly ascendant chairman of the Senate Foreign Relations Committee, who was in Moscow conferring with Soviet leaders. At any rate, the warning did not stop the leakage or the controversies. Within a few days there were leaks of diplomatic cables, apparently through the transition team, which had got them from the State Department, reporting on boat-rocking statements Percy had made to the Soviets about the Middle East, China, and other delicate subjects.[41] Then there were comments from other Reagan advisers attacking Percy. Also in early December there were several leaks from a Reagan transition team on Latin America criticizing Carter policy in that area, particularly El Salvador. The epitome of this was a report of a trip by an unofficial emissary with close ties to hawkish Reagan advisers to El Salvador to advise rightist elements there not to take seriously the "official" Reagan lines's disapproving talk of a right-wing coup against the center government. About this time the Carter ambassador in El Salvador, Robert White, went public with an angry protest that all this talk had undercut American policy and made his position untenable.[42]

Despite the infighting, a number of constructive steps were taken, some of them evidence of effective collaboration by Reagan advisers, especially Allen, with outgoing Carter officials. In late November, "a senior Reagan aide" communicated to high South Korean officials visiting Washington the president-elect's strong support for the administration's low-keyed efforts to deter the execution of Korea's leading opposition politician on charges of sedition. Later, when these efforts apparently had proven successful, it came out that the Reagan pressure had been baited with suggestions that the new administration would reexamine Carter's plan to withdraw American troops from Korea, and that the South Korean president would be welcomed for an early official visit.[43] In early December, as the threat of Soviet military intervention in Poland seemed acute, White House aide Jody Powell announced that there had been consultation with Reagan advisers and warned against any government getting the mistaken impression that the transition would affect the American government's will or ability to respond appropriately. Richard Allen went on nationwide television to echo the warning, indicating that "the consequences of an invasion would be severe and long-lasting."[44] On his first visit to Washington Reagan dodged a meeting with Prime Minister Begin, but Allen conveyed a message both directly to Egypt and Israel and through Carter's special ambassador to the Middle East, Sol Linowitz, that President-elect Reagan strongly supported continuing negotiations pursuant to the Camp David agreements.[45]

Although issuing warnings about aggressive Soviet behavior, the president-elect's approach to overall relations with the Soviet Union was cautious. After Senator Percy had told the Russians that the president-elect would give high priority to resuming arms control negotiations, Meese said in a television interview that opening talks in a few weeks was "certainly possible," but stressed that Percy was speaking for himself and noted that early talks could only be "discussions that could lead to negotiations."[46] Reagan himself left little doubt where his priorities were. In an interview with *Time* magazine shortly after election, he said that "The first job is to let the Soviets see the course we are going to follow domestically."[47] Now, despite various warnings by pundits that the world would not wait while he organized the United States to his liking, Reagan reiterated: "I think for the first few months anyone in this position ought to concentrate on our economic problems and getting started on that."[48]

Carter Grits It Out

From election day onward, Jimmy Carter suffered the frustrations of a lame duck. Disappointment over his political rejection must have been sharpened by the sight of Reagan making one public relations coup after another, and by the outpouring of newspaper feature stories analyzing what had gone wrong with the Carter administration. His main hope for a graceful exit was to get our hostages out of Iran on terms the American public would consider reasonable, but this depended on the cooperation of people over whom he had little leverage—some of whom, indeed, actively desired to see him further humiliated—and the negotiations dragged on and on. Despite his troubles, Carter displayed courtesy to all and a dignity that almost hid his bitterness.

Among Carter's duties were to deliver the principal messages that traditionally start the political year. His final state of the union message, as customary with outgoing presidents, was addressed more to the public and history than to Congress. It was a thoughtful exploration of major world issues—prevention of nuclear war, expansion of freedom and human dignity, and preservation of natural resources and the environment—which deserved more attention than it received.[49] Carter's final budget leaned toward Reagan policies, calling for restraint in domestic spending, more for defense, and smaller deficits, but it was promptly criticized by Republicans as a "political" document.[50]

Down in the executive departments and agencies the exodus of Carter officials began early and increased toward inauguration day as the Reagan team made it clear that they wanted the Carterites out and were not interested in any holdovers. In any transition it is a problem for outgoing officials to know what matters to try to bring to a conclusion and what to leave to their successors. Generally they tend to defer difficult and controversial issues, particularly if they anticipate a different approach by the new administration. This time the Carter officials seemed more inclined to push to the end and get their ideas embedded in policy even in some areas of direct policy conflict with Reagan positions. This was particularly so in the general sphere of regulation, and in the last weeks of the administration the Federal Register was swollen with an outpouring of new regulations concerning energy, labor, health, and environmental matters.[51] There was acute controversy over the Department of Justice's action in a long-pending court case in which the PACE—the widely used civil-service examination for recruiting college graduates—had been challenged for racial bias; the Reagan transition team thought it had an understanding that the matter would be held over, but a higher-level official at Justice went back to the court with a proposed consent decree calling for changes in examining practices that, the Reaganites thought, would establish a racial quota system.[52] There was also an embarrassment over an order extending a program of aid to minority business enterprises. After the agency inspector general challenged the extension as illegal, the administration sought to cancel the extension, but the necessary paper failed to reach Carter's desk in the confusing final days of the administration, and the subject was left for Reagan to handle.[53] These late-hour decisions were defended by the Carter people as falling within their period of responsibility, which was certainly correct from a legal point of view, but it did seem that in some cases they were motivated by a desire to get on the record and put the onus of changing policy in controversial areas onto the Reaganites. It is not entirely clear whether there were more decisions of this kind than in previous transitions, or whether it was the existence of more Reagan transition team watchdogs that brought attention to them.

One area where there was distinctly less cooperation between outgoing and incoming groups was in the budget. In the Truman-Eisenhower and the Eisenhower-Kennedy transitions, representatives of the president-elect had access to most of the analyses and preliminary decisions, in effect getting an inside view of the budget being put to bed in the closing weeks of the old administration. This time, officials of the Office of Management and Budget held the Reagan representatives at arms length until the budget was essentially locked up. When criticized, they said they were following the precedents of the Ford administration as it had dealt with them in 1976. Even so, this represents a deterioration in transition practices from earlier times, and one of considerable importance to an incoming administration placing a high priority on budgetary revision.[54]

Carter's main preoccupation during the transition, as it had been for the past year, was the hostages in Iran. From the low point after the failed attempt at military rescue in April, communications had gradually been built up during the summer and fall through a variety of secret, unofficial, and third party channels. While the American campaign was going on, the death of the Shah, internal political developments in Iran, and the outbreak of war with Iraq began to push the Iranians toward settlement. By November the Iranian demands were still extravagant but beginning to be concrete enough to be discussed through the Algerians who were emerging as the principal third-party negotiating channel. It began to appear that the makings of a deal were present: return of the hostages in exchange for financial considerations including release of Iranian assets frozen in American banks and perhaps some concessions with respect to American citizen claims against Iran and assets of the Shah held in the United States. Shortly before election the Iranians aroused hope with talk of early release, but their demands were so complex it was not possible to deal with them quickly. This, however, provided opportunity for Deputy Secretary of State Warren Christopher, head of the negotiating group, to go to Algiers with a counter offer, which produced a "final" offer from Iran on December 19. The price tag was high—$24 billion in round numbers—which created real doubt whether enough money could be found over which the president had any control. Although Christopher and the experts thought something could be worked out, Carter's mood at year's end, widely reported in the press, was one of discouragement and fear that the issue would have to be turned over to Reagan.[55]

After his late November meeting and statement of solidarity with Carter on the hostage issue, Reagan was quiet on the subject for some weeks, clearly intending to leave the problem in Carter's lap as long as he could. In early January, James Reston reported that Carter officials had tried through Haig, Weinberger, and Meese to get Reagan or someone on his behalf to review the terms of the proposal they were about to send through the Algerians, since Reagan might have to deal with its consequences, but the Reaganites declined to get involved.[56] The same day that this story appeared, Reagan's responses to reporters' questions began to equivocate about his solidarity with Carter: although he supported Carter and expected that any agreement Carter made would be one he could support, he could issue no "blank checks." He also noted that if agreement was not reached by the time Carter left office, he would feel free to review the terms of the American offer.[57] A few days later, Reagan, in an apparently angry outburst, denounced the Iranians as "kidnappers," "criminals," and "barbarians." This produced howls of outrage in Tehran, and some fear in Washington that it had killed chances for agreement, but in fact it may have helped convince the Khomeini-dominated government that it could expect harder terms from Reagan and was better off dealing with Carter.[58]

As the days to inauguration slipped away, the negotiations moved slowly. To the Iranian "final" demand for $24 billion, the United States made a counteroffer of $7 billion, with a January 16 deadline. This brought a new final demand for $9.5 billion. Feeling the agreement might be possible but calculating that the complex transactions to free the money could not be completed before January 20, the administration again approached the Reagan camp for support and again was denied unequivocal commitment to follow through on any deals incomplete as of January 20. With its position thus hardened, the administration offered $7.8 billion to be released by inauguration day, and negotiations proceeded from there. Several more days were required to work out the details involving the Treasury, the Federal Reserve, American banks both at home and their branches abroad, the Bank of England, and Iranian financial institutions. There were long days and sleepless nights as the communications flew back and forth between Christopher and his team in Algiers and the president and his staff at the White House. Finally, believing that all was settled, Carter announced early on January 19 that agreement had been reached and the hostages would be released shortly. Then additional obstacles appeared, first an Iranian protest over a technical arrangement demanded by the American bankers, and then objections by the Federal Reserve representative in Algiers. These were not worked out until the early morning hours of January 20. At 6:50 A.M. on inauguration day Carter telephoned across to Blair House to tell Reagan's staff—the President-elect was still asleep and did not come to the phone—that the deal was complete and the hostages would soon be on the Algerian planes that had been standing by. Even then there was another delay until after 8:00, Washington time, before the Bank of England completed its review of the documents and transferred funds to the credit of Iran.

This supposedly completed the transaction, and the president waited anxiously through the morning for the report that would enable him to make a public announcement that the hostages has been turned over to the Algerians and were airborne out of Iran. But, as Reagan appeared at the White House, he and the president made the traditional journey to the Capitol, and the inaugural ceremony started, the word still did not come. Not until Carter the ex-President arrived at Andrews Field to board the plane to return him to

Georgia was the word flashed that the hostages were airborne. On his arrival in Atlanta, Carter made the public announcement he had so desperately wanted to make from the White House. Later in the day it was announced from the White House that Reagan had asked Carter to go to Germany as his representative to greet the hostages. It was both an appropriate gesture of consideration for his predecessor and consistent with Reagan's position for the past year that the hostages were Carter's issue, for better or for worse.[59]

Some Comparative Notes

In closing we may venture some comments on the evolution of transition practices.

In the first modern attempts to "manage" transitions, great importance was placed on early designation of the Cabinet. Accepting this view, Eisenhower in 1952 completed the job on December 1. Since then, Cabinet choices have come progressively later in every transition. Reagan finished the main job on December 23, with a couple of lesser decisions deferred until after the holidays.

Why the slippage? Obviously the job is becoming more complex in terms of expectations about professionalism in executive recruiting, technological capacity making it possible to consider more data about more people, and the increased sensitivities and requirements for dealing with problems of conflict of interest. In broader terms, this may be another manifestation of White House-centered as compared to department-centered government. The growth of preelection planning prepares the president-elect and his immediate associates to deal with matters that formerly would have had to be left untended until they could be turned over to future agency heads. The numerous and prestigious White House staff positions receive priority in the president-elect's decision processes, as he seeks to assure his key staff members from the campaign of the future places and builds his administration outward from himself.

Delay on the Cabinet appointments is also perhaps one of the unanticipated consequences of the Presidential Transition Act. That act undoubtedly has succeeded in its main objectives by providing a statutory obligation of cooperation between incoming and outgoing administrations, by legitimating access by representatives of the president-elect, by providing public funds for their support. But setting up the transition staff to some degree delays consideration of the Cabinet, and once in place the existence of the transition staff diminishes the urgency of getting agency heads on the job. The act has led to transition staffs vastly greater than anything contemplated in the early 1960s, including the ubiquitous agency transition teams. This growth of staff stems directly, of course, from amendments to the act which have authorized larger sums for the president-elect's use. But it also seems to reflect something of a snowballing phenomenon, as the existence of more paid staff and large headquarters facilities have provided capacity to absorb more and more volunteers. Distinctions between official and unofficial, public and private, have been largely lost, both respecting the status of individuals and the use of funds. Reagan's friends who contributed large sums to help support the transition staff may have felt no self-serving motive in giving them, and he presumably felt no inappropriate obligation as a result of accepting them, but the transaction certainly can be interpreted as insuring the continued access of the kitchen cabinet to decisions which the president-elect should be making in light of his new responsibility to all the people.

Nineteenth-century presidents-elect felt that their ambiguous status put them under an obligation of silence and reclusive behavior; they particularly avoided any actions that might be regarded as presumptuous or intruding on the responsibilities of the president in the area of foreign relations. Contemporary presidents-elect are becoming foreign-policy activists. Reagan made the customary declarations of intention not to intrude. He then apparently found it not inconsistent to have well-publicized meetings with the president of Mexico and the chancellor of West Germany, to have members of his staff meeting with numerous other representatives of foreign governments, and to permit other individuals purporting to represent his views or speak on his behalf to speak freely at home and to travel abroad on both quiet and well-publicized missions. This activity had beneficial results in some cases, such as Korea. In other areas, such as El Salvador, uninhibited behavior by Reaganites may have seriously damaged the capacity of the Carter administration to pursue its policies.

Like most other outgoing presidents, Jimmy Carter declared his intention to bear full responsibility until inauguration day. And, like most of them, he found himself impelled to seek the concurrence or support of his successor as he carried on delicate negotiations in the closing weeks of his administration. The record here was mixed. There appears to have been good cooperation in laying down a policy line on Korea and on Poland. Regarding Iran, as the pressures mounted Carter seems to have found his designated successor evasive and noncommittal. Or did he? Although the Reagan staff rebuffed White House attempts to get Reagan to review the details of proposed offers to Iran, it should be noted that the most important instance of Reagan himself speaking out concerned Iran. In this instance, his forthrightness seems to have contributed to a successful outcome. Was this accidental, or could it have been arranged with Carter?

The Iranian issue, although of high visibility and importance to American prestige and self-respect, was not in the short run a war-or-peace matter. Throughout the transition period there loomed the threat of Soviet force to quell the unrest in Poland. Reagan's limited statements on the subject during the transition supported administration warnings to the Soviets. But if the Russians had moved into Poland, or if—to take another example—there had been a new Middle East war involving Israel, could Carter and Reagan have reached an understanding about what to do? The relations between president and president-elect on matters of state remain ambiguous, contingent, and risky for the nation.

Chapter 12 American Parties in the Eighties: Declining or Resurging?

James W. Ceaser

Before the presidential election of 1980, the conventional wisdom among analysts of American politics was that political parties in America were in a state of decline and perhaps on the road to extinction. This decline, it was said, could be seen in virtually every respect in which party strength is measured—in the loss of influence of party organizations in the nominations of presidential candidates, in the diminishing percentages of citizens identifying themselves as party adherents, in the declining impact of presidential election voting on congressional contests, and in the inability of parties to function effectively as instruments of coordinating policy-making between the president and the Congress. For a brief moment during the 1980 campaign, the decline of parties even reached the point where it seemed that a nomination by a major party, a prerequisite for election to the presidency since 1828, might no longer be necessary. An obscure congressman from Illinois, John Anderson, challenged the entire system of political parties by simply nominating himself as an "independent" candidate, a strategy he believed fit the nonpartisan tenor of the times. Anderson rose remarkably in the polls from the status of a virtual unknown early in 1980 to the pinnacle of being favored by 26 percent of the American electorate in June.[1]

Since the 1980 election, little has been heard of the "decline of parties." On the contrary, more and more analyses have been commenting on the surprising strength of American parties, or at any rate, of the Republican party. With a landslide victory for Ronald Reagan, an impressive gain of thirty-three seats in the House, and a dramatic and quite unexpected increase of twelve seats in the Senate, the Republican party emerged from the election of 1980 looking anything but in a state of decline. It was not just the size of the Republican victory, however, that impressed most observers, but the *way* in which Republicans conducted the 1980 campaign. In recent American politics, the tendency has been for candidates for Congress and the presidency to run as individuals, deemphasizing their party connection. But in 1980, most Republicans ran *as Republicans,* stressing their party affiliation and asking voters to change the *party* that held power in Washington; and since the inauguration of President Reagan—admittedly not a very long time—the Republicans in Congress have worked together quite well and have shown a surprising willingness to follow the lead of their president. Both Republicans and Democrats alike now seem to be operating on the assumption that the future of the Republican party, and for that matter the future of the Democratic party as well, rests with how Americans judge the success of the Republican economic program.

The apparent reversal in the strength of American parties has left many wondering what happened in the 1980 election. Was it the case that America's political analysts were wrong before the 1980 election and that American parties were stronger than they appeared? Or is it the case that analysts are wrong today and that parties are weaker than they appear? Or is it the case, finally, that these analysts have been correct all along, and that parties were in fact declining in strength before the 1980 election but have since miraculously managed to revive themselves?

As tempting as it might be to deal with this issue in terms of one of these alternatives, none of them can adequately account for the recent developments affecting American political parties. What we are confronted with in the entire debate over the decline of political parties is a conceptual problem that requires first an analytical discussion that distinguishes among the possible causes of party strength. Thereafter, we can return to the immediate political context and address the question of the current status of American parties in a way that can make sense of recent developments.

The Causes of Party Strength

Four basic causes can be said to determine the strength of American political parties. The first cause is found in the ideas or doctrines toward political parties, by which I mean the prevailing views, held either by elites or the public, about the role parties should play in the American political system. All institutions vary in their strength and character according to what people think their functions should be. Doctrines are particularly important in establishing the strength of political parties, as distinct from the presidency or the Congress, because parties have no status in the Constitution which guarantees them certain powers or functions.

As an example of a doctrinal explanation of party strength, one can cite a passage from a recent work by Austin Ranney, one of America's leading scholars of political parties: "Americans . . . deal uneasily with the necessities of partisan political organization because of their widespread belief that political parties are, at best, unavoidable evils whose propensities for divisiveness, oligarchy and corruption must be closely watched and sternly controlled."[2] In addition to looking at mass attitudes toward political parties, Ranney traces elite opinions and finds that after 1968 a doctrine known as "reform" gained widespread support among political leaders. The reform view, which is generally hostile to the prerogatives of parties, helped to activate popular suspicions against parties and created a climate of opinion in which legislators and party officials were virtually compelled to take steps to reduce the parties' power.

The second cause of party strength derives from legal and structural factors, meaning party rules and federal and state law, including court decisions, that bear directly on the powers and arrangements of the parties. Included in this category, for example, are the national party rules governing delegate selection for the conventions adopted by the national Democratic party since 1968; state laws that provide for primaries in the nomination of congressional candidates and the selection of delegates to the national party conventions; federal laws governing campaign financing; and court decisions respecting the extent of permissable patronage employment and the rights of voter participation in primaries.

Legal and structural factors are often linked closely to doctrines concerning parties for the obvious reason that legislators and party officials usually write laws and rules to reflect their conception of the role that parties should play. Because of this connection, it is often possible to speak of these two causes at the same time without distinguishing between them. Yet the two causes are different, frequently, as they operate, causing tension with each other. These differences result, among other reasons, because legal changes are adopted without regard to doctrines about parties by institutions like the courts or state legislatures, which may have other priorities; and because legal rules often have consequences quite different and even contrary to those which legislators intend.

As an example of a legal (and doctrinal) explanation of party strength, one can cite a passage from a recent essay by Jeanne Kirkpatrick, currently America's ambassador to the United Nations and a respected analyst of American political parties:

> The most important sources of party decomposition are the *decisions* taken by persons attempting to reform the parties. Some of these efforts at party reform have aimed to weaken one or both parties . . . others [were] undertaken to perfect the political process but have had the unintended effect of hastening party deinstitutionalization. . . . Of all of (the) reasons for the continuing decline in the parties' ability to perform their traditional functions, I have stressed reform. Whether undertaken by the parties, the Congress, or the courts, reform, along with its

intended and unintended consequences, is, I believe, the most important cause of this decline.[3]

The third cause of party strenth derives from what, for want of a better term, can be called *environmental* factors, by which is meant developments affecting parties that arise from changes in the social structure or in the state of communications technology. In this category, for example, I would place the rise of the "New Class" in modern postindustrial societies and the vast changes in electioneering that have resulted from the advent of television, campaign polling, and the use of computer technology.

For illustrative purposes, one can again refer to the works of contemporary scholars employing this explanation, this time citing two different authorities. Everett Ladd, a well-known electoral analyst, accounts for the decline of parties by emphasizing the impact of the New Class and the associated rise in educational levels:

> A large segment of the [American] electorate now describes itself as
> independent. . . . Higher levels of information bearing on political issues
> and hence a higher measure of issue orientation, and a general feeling
> of confidence in one's ability to judge candidates and their programs apart
> from party links, are promoted by the experience of higher educa-
> tion. . . . An electorate which is highly educated . . . will be bound
> less by partisan identification in its electoral behavior. This cause of party
> irregularity is unlikely to recede.[4]

Arthur Schlesinger, Jr., the famous historian, stresses the communications revolution: "Some political scientists blame the decline of parties on the reform movement of the last decade. But party reform was a response, not a cause. . . . The reason for the deep and perhaps incurable crisis of the system lies . . . above all in the organic change wrought in the political environment by the electronic revolution."[5]

The fourth cause that determines party strength derives from the political context, by which is meant changes in the salience of issues that confront the nation, the way in which statesmen present these issues, and the degree to which party members share a common public philosophy and act together as participants in a genuine association having a political purpose. Scholars of critical realignments in American electoral history have emphasized this idea of a periodic surge and decline of partisan commitment. At certain moments when the political climate is charged with heated debate over profound issues, members of one or both of the parties (or perhaps a third party) become firm advocates of a political cause; at other moments, when the issues presented are of less perceptible importance, one finds less commitment and enthusiasm, and members may remain with their party more from habit or interest than from principle.

Alexis de Tocqueville was the first analyst of American politics to identify the significance of the political context for influencing the character and strength of political parties. In making his classic distinction between "great parties" and "small parties," Tocqueville observed:

> There are times when nations are tormented by such great ills that the
> idea of a total change in their political constitution comes into
> mind. . . . That is the time of . . . great parties. . . . There are times
> when the human spirit believes itself firmly settled on certain fundamen-
> tals and does not seek to look beyond a fixed horizon. That is a time
> for . . . small parties. . . . Great political parties are those more attached
> to principles than to consequences [while] . . . small parties are gener-
> ally without political faith.[6]

Modern realignment theorists have adapted this distinction to fit the milder pulse of conflict within American history. As James Sundquist has written:

> When a community goes through a realignment period, it is in the grip
> of an issue of transcendent power. The voters who have polarized on
> the issue have experienced deep emotions . . . these emotions are trans-
> ferred to the parties. [After the crisis] the parties lose the sense of
> moral purpose that energized them in the crisis. They become cautious.
> Participation in party affairs slackens. . . . People are again heard to
> say "The parties don't stand for anything" and "there's no difference
> between the parties."[7]

Long-term vs. Short-term Effects

These four causes of party strength—the doctrinal, the legal, the environmental, and the political—are *analytic* categories; in the real world, they are not pure and separable causes but rather continually interact with each other in a complex cause-and-effect relationship. For analytic purposes, however, these four causes will be treated as discrete variables, and for the moment it will be assumed that none of them is a simple function of any other.

Each cause has certain general properties or characteristics. Doctrinal and legal factors, which can be discussed together, tend to exert a steady influence over a long period of time. Prevailing consensuses about the role of parties and basic legal configurations do not change very often. Over the course of American history there have been only five major identifiable "systems" of presidential nomination, which is the central task performed by American national political parties. These are roughly parallel shifting views about the role of parties.

1. Nonpartisan elections (1789–1796). In this period, there were no party nominations, and the presidential selection process was handled entirely by the electoral-college system outlined in the Constitution. This system was designed by the Founding Fathers, who were hostile to political parties and who consciously sought to exclude them from American national politics.

2. The congressional caucus system (1800-1820). Political parties developed and nominated presidential candidates in meetings of their members from Congress.[8] At this point, many still shared the Founding Fathers' hostility toward parties, but thought that parties were necessary temporary instruments to promote vital purposes.

3. The "pure" convention system (1832-1908). Presidential candidates were nominated by conventions composed of delegates chosen under rules established by the parties acting as self-governing, private associations. The delegates tended to reflect the interests of the state-party organizations. During the 1920s and 1930s Martin Van Buren and his followers conducted a sustained defense of the idea of stable party competition in American, and parties subsequently became accepted as the legitimate instruments for nominating presidential candidates.

4. The "mixed" system (1912-1968). Presidential candidates were nominated by conventions composed mostly of delegates selected in the same manner as under the pure convention system; a significant minority of delegates, however, were chosen in state-run primary elections, and some of these were bound by state laws to vote for the national candidates to whom they were pledged on the ballot. The doctrinal attitude towards parties during this period was ambivalent, reflecting in part the favorable view that developed during the period of the pure convention system and in part the hostility that had been engendered by the attack of the Progressive Movement during the period from 1908–1920.

5. Direct democratic system (1972–1980). Presidential candidates are still nominated in party conventions, but the conventions are now composed mostly of delegates selected in primaries and bound in their votes to national candidates. The conventions therefore perform no independent discretionary function, but merely record the decisions of the voters. The doctrine toward parties in this period, or at any rate throughout most of the 1970s, reflected the "reform" view of mistrust for party organizations and a belief in direct democracy in candidate selection.[9]

Although doctrines and basic structural configurations do not change very often, it is essential to keep in mind that they can be changed through deliberate and conscious intervention. Opinion leaders and legislators are in a position to influence attitudes towards parties, and party officials and legislators have the legal authority to change party structures.[10] Political scientists tend to focus a great deal of attention on these legal structures, not because they are the only cause of the strength and character of an institution, but rather because they constitute the element over which political actors have the most direct control. Through their authority to devise rules and pass laws, party leaders and legislators can attempt to build a party structure that will exert certain influences and that will endure for a relatively long time. These legal structures, of course, may be able to produce their intended results only if certain environmental factors prevail; intelligent legislative efforts therefore must attempt to take into account the way in which legal factors interact with the environment.

The third cause that influences party strength, environmental factors, also produces long-term effects. Although environmental influences can change unexpectedly in response to new socio-economic and technological developments, for the most part basic environmental influences such as class or a communications sytem endure for an entire era. They are "constants" that continually shape the operation of the political system.

Unlike doctrine and legal causes, environmental factors are largely beyond the control of political actors. This does not mean that legislators are unable to regulate certain aspects of their influence as they impinge on the political system. In France, for example, election polls are banned from being published during the week prior to the election in an effort to limit the impact of this technological development on election results.[11] Yet such legislative measures, though not unimportant, remain limited in their impact on the influences exerted by basic environmental factors. Ultimately these influences are beyond legislative control, especially in free societies. Legislators cannot simply control basic socioeconomic forces such as immigration or education levels; nor can they do more than adjust the context within which technological change influences political life.

The fourth cause of party strength, the political context, is characterized by the absence of any qualitative change, by which is meant simply that there is always a variation in the intensity of commitment to political action. Although Karl Marx prophesized an end to politics under certain conditions, and Daniel Bell predicted an end to ideological strife, neither circumstance seems to have materialized. Perhaps we simply have not reached the proper conditions. Nevertheless, there remain—and most likely will remain—episodic surges and declines in the intensity with which people view political affairs.

The political context, accordingly, presents the nation and its party system with an ever-changing series of stimuli. At certain moments, as already observed, issues are perceived as more important than usual, and people come together either in new parties or under the umbrella of an existing party label and form genuine associations committed to pursuing a common public philosophy. When the intensity of commitment is especially strong, a party will probably find some way to work temporarily in unison even if the legal arrangement under which the party operates works against strong parties. At other moments, when the intensity is absent or when the party members share no common public philosophy, effective coordination—at least in the American system of separated powers—may be difficult to achieve, even where legal factors promote strong parties by American standards.

In emphasizing that the political context presents the nation with ceaseless variation, one should not conclude that politics is governed by forces completely beyond rational human control. Along with changing environmental conditions and new circumstances of domestic and international politics, deliberate attempts by political thinkers and statesmen to mold new public philosophies lead to the rise and decline of the intensity of issues. The point, however, is that the efforts of reasoned thought to change the political system never cease. Some issues, of course, may be "permanently" settled by the intervention of thought in politics, as, for example, the form of the political system itself. Yet ideas continually generate new agendas. Indeed, in democratic societies, it is *not* the purpose of institutional arrangements to attempt to end political controversy, but to create a setting in which controversies are moderated and settled in ways that do not destroy the society.

Party Strength and the Current Status of American Parties

With this analysis of the causes of party strength in mind, we can return to the question of what it means to say that American political parties have undergone a change in strength. A change could conceivably refer to a strengthening or weakening of parties that results from any one of these four factors. Yet most analysts when they speak of a change probably have in mind not a temporary cyclical downturn or upturn, but rather a long-term trend that results in stronger or weaker parties across an entire cycle of political variation. Party strength, in other words, should be understood as a function of long-term institutional properties, meaning the influences exerted by doctrinal, legal and environmental causes, but *not* political causes. To the extent that parties change in strength because of the political context, one would want to specify clearly that this is the reason, for everything we know about this political cause leads to the conclusion that periodic "ups" and "downs" are not unusual, but on the contrary constitute the normal pattern of affairs.

During the 1970s, when political analysts began to remark on the phenomenon of party decline, it was especially difficult to distinguish among these four causes because all of them were impelling parties in the same direction. Parties grew weaker because of the doctrinal attack of reform; because of the adoption of party rules and laws which, intentionally or inadvertently, took powers and functions away from the party organizations; because of socioeconomic and technological changes that made it more difficult for parties to operate effectively; and finally because the dominant party of the era, the Democratic party, lost its sense of public purpose and had no program or approach for dealing with the issues of the day. Indeed, because all of these causes were leading toward the same result, some analysts failed to keep clear in their own minds the different sources of the change; everything was lumped together into a single, undifferentiated phenomenon—the decline of parties—which was used frequently as an explanatory factor in its own right, independent of the factors that caused it.

If we keep the different causes of party strength in mind, however, it should be possible to formulate a comprehensive interpretation of what has happened to American parties in the past decade. Their status can be summarized and analyzed by stating four theses:

1. Political parties have become much weaker over the past decade. In the very recent past (1979–81), this condition has changed only marginally, with some factors leading to further decline and others promoting a slight strengthening.
2. The weakness of parties before the 1980 election, however, frequently was exaggerated. Political factors contributing in the short-term to the decline of parties were not always carefully identified, with the result that many overstated the extent of the decline and underestimated the potential of parties to serve as vehicles for political realignments.
3. The strength of our parties in 1981 (such as it is now sometimes perceived) may be exaggerated. Just as political factors contributed to the weakness of parties during the last decade, so they may be contributing "artificially" to their strength today, temporarily masking their real weaknesses.
4. The situation today, however, presents a new opportunity for genuine party revitalization through structural changes. The doctrine of "reform" that contributed to the decline is out of favor. This change in the climate of opinion has increased the freedom of party officials and legislators to take conscious steps to strengthen the parties.

Thesis #1: Political parties have become weaker over the past decade, and this condition has changed only marginally in the last year.

The visible and measurable indices of party decline, such as partisan identification and party-line voting in Congress, have been catalogued by numerous scholars in the past decade and need no review here.[12] Of greater interest may be the broad consequences of party decline on the operation of the American political system. Defenders of strong political parties from Martin Van Buren in the nineteenth century to contemporary political scientists like Nelson Polsby have argued their case on the grounds that effective parties perform certain beneficial functions.[13] Parties serve as mechanisms for building and maintaining relatively broad and stable coalitions; they channel and moderate the ambitions of presidential aspirants by "forcing" candidates to become consensual leaders; they discipline factions and interest groups by making them partake in the give and take of coalitional politics; and they provide a supplementary extra-constitutional instrument for facilitating cooperation between the president and Congress in a separation of powers system.

A system of party competition dominated by two relatively strong parties can accordingly be viewed as a kind of political institution, meaning a structure of arrangements that promotes certain fixed tendencies or patterns of behavior. As parties decline and no similar structures take their place, a process of deinstitutionalization occurs, meaning a situation in which there are fewer (or no) predictable tendencies or patterns of behavior. The result of deinstitutionalization is disaggregation and volatility, a condition in which political activity moves now one way and now another in response to short-term and contingent factors. To use a nautical analogy, a deinstitutionalized system is characterized by all sail and no ballast. It is precisely this kind of volatile politics that has become more characteristic of American politics as parties have grown weaker.

The effects of the recent deinstitutionalization of the party system are most evident in the selection of presidential candidates. The previous tendency of parties to select steady consensual leaders no longer operates, and the character of current nominees is left, so to speak, to chance. Today, presidential nominations in America are decided in primary elections, which is to say by public opinion. Decisions made by public opinion in this context, where there are often many candidates and no party labels to structure voter choice, are characterized by a great deal of volatility; they are subject to the influence of such seemingly irrelevant factors as minor campaign mistakes and rapid shifts in momentum. Public "moods" change, and candidates, following the polls closely, may pose as "nonpoliticians" in one election year and "professionals" in the next. Furthermore, to the extent that the news media play a role in shaping public opinion, public opinion becomes even more volatile. News in America, and especially television news, constantly emphasizes the new and dramatic development; its standard of newsworthiness is the deviation of an event from prevailing expectations. By virtue of this emphasis, news has the effect of stimulating interest in the new and random development, thus producing results contrary to the steady influence of institutional structures.

With the elimination of party control over the nomination of presidential candidates, American politics has also lost an important link that connected the presidential nominee to other elected officials in the party, including members of

hese leaders no longer have any direct power over the choice
y have less obligation to support him once he is elected.
ent case of President Carter, a candidate may be nominated
' his own party, a circumstance that hardly inspires cooper-
ty's elected officials. With less assurance of support from
n party in Congress, presidents tend to turn more to public
of their authority. Public opinion, however, has proven a
reed on which to lean, and presidents have suffered a loss in
in the policymaking process. By its very nature as a system
the American regime imposes formidable obstacles to as-
ower to implement a coordinated political program. The
made this task even more difficult to achieve.

itself, the centralizing influence of parties has also di-
st decade. Of course, parties in Congress in the 1960s
veak instruments, and one would have to go all the way
Speaker Cannon at the turn of this century to find truly
al parties. By its nature as a local representative system,
does not promote party government in Congress. Nev-
0s congressional party leaders could at least attempt to
forming alliances among a few highly powerful com-
e reforms in Congress in the 1970s, especially in the
entralize authority from the committees to the subcom-
er around 139 in the House alone. Coordination under
olicy-making subcommittees has been schizophrenic,
luggishness (as in energy legislation in the 1970s) and
ironmental legislation early in the decade).[14] Under a
angement, such unpredictable and dramatically different
at one might expect.

ampaign finance legislation passed in the 1970s has
ding even further from the parties and has stimulated
l action committees, which in effect are rivals to political
s area, it can be said that rather than seeing a process
on, we are witnessing the beginning of an institution-
orks to the detriment of political parties. Again, as in
Congress a decade ago, parties in the 1960s were *not*
es of fundraising. Most funds for political campaigns
dividual candidates for office, with the largest source
om individual citizens. The campaign finance legislation
ibutions of individuals and groups, as well as providing
esidential campaigns. It has evolved in such a way,
e distinct advantages for groups. Political action com-
e money to campaigns that individuals ($5,000 per

campaign for groups compared to $1,000 for individuals.) Much
portant, however, is the fact that the law allows independent expend
campaigns without limit as long as the money spent is not coordinate
by the candidates' official campaign organization. While both indivi
groups can make these expenditures, in practice it has been the politi
committees that have spent most of the independent money, since the
the organization and political sophistication to mount campaign
The law therefore has created an incentive for the formation of thes
and in recent years there has been a tremendous increase in their nu
activity. Many of these groups promote specialized interests or io
viewpoints, and the campaign finance legislation has therefore
increase the influence of factional groups at the expense of the m
effect of political parties.

During the last two years, changes in party structure have only m
affected the strength of American parties. Confirming the trend of
presidential nominees were again chosen by a *de facto* system of
mocracy, with the national Democratic Convention even going so
adopt a rule allowing national candidates to replace delegates who th
to break their pledges. In addition, in the 1978 and 1980 congressio
paigns and in the 1980 presidential campaign, independent expend
political action committees rose dramatically over earlier years.

There were, however, two changes that promoted the strength o
In the Republican party, the national chairman, William Brock, und
remarkable effort to enhance the capacities of the national organiz
succeeded in substantially augmenting the assistance, both financial
nical, that the national party provided to congressional candidates,
ties, and even candidates for state offices. Because of the succe
Republican party, Democrats are now trying to emulate Brock's ef
it appears that stronger national staffs are likely to become a perma
of American party organization.

The second change, seemingly very technical, nonetheless had a si
impact on party organizational activity in the 1980 presidential ca
Under the campaign finance legislation in 1976, state and local orga
were limited in the amount of money they could raise and spend
of their presidential nominee, which depressed participation in loca
zational activities. In 1979, an amendment to the campaign—finan
lation lifted most of these restrictions and permitted the state and loc
to spend as much as they could raise for certain campaign activities, i
voter registration, volunteer assistance, and efforts to bring voters to
This change enabled the Republican state and local parties to spend $1
on behalf of Ronald Reagan. (The Democrats spent only $5 millio
important than the sums spent was the increase in citizen involvemen

affairs. Indeed, the law demonstrated the significance of legal factors in accounting for party strength.

Thesis #2: The weakness of American parties before the 1980 election was exaggerated because of the failure to recognize the short-term impact of political factors.

Although the decline of parties as institutions over the last decade has been significant, the extent of this decline was probably exaggerated before the 1980 election. The political context, with its cyclical "ups" and "downs," worked in the last decade to depress still further the effectiveness of the parties. Specifically, the Democratic party, which had been the majority party in America ever since the election of Roosevelt in 1932, lost any clear sense of unity and purpose. This loss was symbolized during the 1976 Democratic nomination campaign when none of the leading presidential aspirants chose to designate himself as a "liberal." *Liberalism* had been the term that Franklin Roosevelt introduced into American politics in the 1930s to describe the Democratic party's public philosophy of the positive or welfare state. Thereafter, liberalism had served as the core that defined the party's program. But by the 1980s Democratic politicians either rejected liberalism or chose not to identify openly with that label. Indeed, the last Democratic president, Jimmy Carter, was anything but a liberal in the classic American sense.

The extent of the Democrats' loss of a common public philosophy can be appreciated by contrasting the performance of the Democratic party from 1976 to 1980 with the high expectations that many had for the party just after the 1976 election. James Sundquist, one of America's most astute electoral analysts, argued in an article in 1976 that the Democratic party was now prepared to assume control and provide a coordinated program. Sundquist based his position on the argument that the old Southern wing of the party, which had been preoccupied with stopping the civil rights revolution, was now dead. With Southern Democrats now more like their Northern and Western colleagues, there would be no impediment to the Democrats' enacting their liberal programs. In Sundquist's words:

> On the Democratic side, the old anti-New Deal "bourbon" wing
> that thwarted and frustrated Democratic presidents from Franklin
> Roosevelt to John Kennedy has been dwindling rapidly . . . There
> is at least solid reason to believe that the prospect for an effective,
> lasting partnership between the president and Congress has never
> been better than it will be during the era that the inauguration of
> President Carter has ushered in. The long season of hostility and
> stalemate between the branches should have passed. The American
> government should begin to work again.[15]

Sundquist would certainly be the first to admit that this cooperation among Democrats failed to materialize during the Carter administration. This failure did not result from the opposition of "bourbon" Southern Democrats—Sundquist was correct on this point—but from the fact that the entire party had lost its sense of direction. The old conservatives were gone, but the new party was not committed to a liberal program and indeed was no longer certain what liberalism meant.

The reasons for the decline of liberalism are too complex to treat in detail here. One factor, however, was that by the end of the 1960s liberals had completed action on many of their most important programs for social welfare and civil rights; and the new agenda of liberalism since the mid and late 1960s has not been popular with many traditional Democrats. It consists on the one hand of programs to enforce greater equality, including the busing of school children to achieve racial balance, affirmative action and quotas for minorities, and schemes for income redistribution. On the other hand, it consists of liberalism on "social" and cultural issues, including advocacy of more freedom of expression, more protection for the rights of the accused and criminals, women's rights, right to abortion, and environmentalism. On these social issues, American public opinion was highly divided, and even many former liberals split with the new liberalism.

Finally, liberalism, understood as big government, was perceived by the American people in the late 1970s not to be working. Whereas from the period of the New Deal until the 1970s the expansion of the welfare state seemed compatible with a healthy and growing economy, by the mid-1970s this no longer was true. During the 1970s the American economy entered a period of low growth, high inflation, and high taxes. Whether or not the growing size of the public sector and the large deficits were the main causes for these economic problems, the public began increasingly to think that this might be the case. Between 1976 and 1980, the Democrats either bore the responsibility for this economic situation or else had the "bad luck" of being in office when conditions grew worse. Traditional liberalism, in any case, had no answer to these problems. It was this ideological disarray, and not just the structural weakness of parties, that contributed to the disaggregation in the Democratic party and its inability to hold together and govern effectively.

During the 1970s, the Republicans, meanwhile, were unable to clearly articulate an alternative public philosophy, or at any rate were unable to convince Americans of the viability of their programs. The Watergate affair also damaged any hope of a powerful Republican resurgence. Thus while one party was down, the other was not up. The political situation was characterized by the ideological disarray of the majority part and the seeming weakness of the minority party. American politics was in a strange interlude.

Some electoral analysts, among them Walter Dean Burnham, concluded that the existence of this interlude was proof of the complete decline of

American parties.[16] The cause of the interlude, in this view, lay in the weakness of the political parties. Political conditions of the 1970s may have contributed to the disarray of the period, but the main reason why American politics could not recover from this malaise rested with the incapacity of weak parties to shoulder the burden of a realignment.

This conclusion may have been based on an inappropriate and even a faulty reading of American history. Some analysts seemed to regard the interlude of the 1970s as a unique phenomenon in our history and therefore proof of the fact that parties had lost their capacity to serve as vehicles for realignment. In the past, these analysts implied, one party would always immediately take advantage of a vacuum and solidify its position through a realignment.

Even if this reading of history is accurate, it would not prove the point about total party incapacity today. Merely because events happened a certain way in four instances in the past would not constitute clear evidence that they must occur in exactly the same way in the present. All historical analogies should leave room for special and contingent factors, such as, for example, the effect of an unforeseen crisis like Watergate. More important, however, is the fact that America has had interludes in the past similar to that of the 1970s. Prior to the realigning election of 1896, for example, there had been a rather long period during which the majority party (the Republicans) lost a clear sense of purpose and began to decline. The Democrats, however, were unable to capitalize on the situation.

We have, then, no clear grounds for concluding that the decline of parties has proceeded to the point where realignments are impossible. Although parties have become much weaker, the chief cause for the interlude of the 1970s may have had more to do with the political context—that is, with the absence of any common purpose within the majority party—than with structural weakness of the parties. Nevertheless, it is likely that the structural weakness of parties will have a profound impact on the character of any future realignment. Although the parties as associations with a common purpose may still be capable of initiating a realignment, their weakness as institutions may make it difficult or impossible for a new majority party to maintain sufficient energy and consistency to sustain a majority and carry out its policies for an entire era.

Thesis #3: The strength of the parties today is also likely to be exaggerated. Political factors are contributing temporarily to the strength of the Republican party.

The discussion of this thesis is the obverse of the second thesis. In 1980, the Republican party emerged as a genuine association of individuals committed to a basic public philosophy. Despite all the structural factors that make for weak parties in America, the strength of this common commitment has served to forge a unity among Republicans and has transformed the party into a formidable policymaking instrument. Indeed, if the Republican party controlled the House of Representatives today, one would probably have seen decisive, coordinated action of the kind that occurred after the elections of 1932 and 1964; and even with the House in Democratic hands the president has demonstrated enough support in the nation to pressure many Democrats, especially from the South, to back important aspects of his program. Weak party structures paradoxically can now work to the President's advantage, enabling him to secure needed support from the opposition party.

It should not be supposed, of couse, that the Republican party today is completely unified in every respect. American parties seldom, if ever, achieve a total unity. There are today three basic domains of Republican policy: (1) The economic program consisting of a plan to reduce the growth of the domestic public sector by program cuts and stimulate private incentives through cuts in the marginal tax rate; (2) the foreign-policy program, consisting of a plan to increase significantly America's military strength and to rekindle the suspicions of Americans toward communism and the Soviet Union; and (3) the "social" policy program, consisting of the opposition to the Equal Rights Amendment and pledges to end abortion and stimulate private and religious schools as alternatives to public education.

Republicans are united on the first part of their economic problem, which calls for cuts in the size of the domestic budget, but there is much disagreement on "supply side" theories that would cut taxes and leave budget deficits for at least the next four years. Republicans are also basically united on a foreign policy program, although its tenets are so general that much room is left for disagreement on particular measures. On the social issue, however, there is at most nominal agreement. Most Republicans take a more "conservative" posture than Democrats on these issues and agree that no further steps should be taken to increase freedom of expression or to provide more rights for the accused. Yet the party is clearly divided between moderates, and elements of the "New Right" and "Moral Majority." The former are content to maintain the status quo on social issues, while the latter are pressing for quick action against abortion and would even like to see reintroduction of prayers in the schools.

These disagreements among Republicans are significant. But until the most controversial aspects of the social issues come up for the consideration, Republicans should be able to maintain a broadly unified front. Their differences among each other are less significant than their common opposition to liberal programs; and as long as Kennedy-type liberalism remains a possible alternative, Republicans will have the incentive to settle their differences through bargain and compromise. Thus at the present moment, the centripetal forces tending to unite the Republican party are stronger than the centrifugal forces leading to disintegration.

For Republicans, however, the challenge is not merely whether they can remain united, but also whether they can win the support of a majority of the electorate. For an entire generation, public opinion polls have shown the Republican Party to be the minority party in regard to partisan preference, and even the election of 1980 did not change this result (see table 12–1). Yet there are strong reasons for supposing that these figures do not accurately describe the actual condition of the American electorate. Party identification is no longer as accurate a predictor of actual voting behavior as it once was, and many who still claim a Democratic preference actually vote Republican fairly regularly. Moreover, the growth of independents may also indicate a loosening of the grip of Democrats on their following and the beginning of a trend towards the Republican party. Indeed, because partisan preference polls have never been taken before during a realigning period, social scientists have no way of knowing how partisan preferences would actually change in the initial stages of a realignment. A reasonable hypothesis, however, is that a change in voting behavior would precede the formal declaration of a change in party preference. Analysis of the election results and a common sense weighing of ideological and electoral trends may therefore constitute a better method of assessing the possibilities of realignment than a narrow, but detailed analysis of partisan preference polls.

As a phenomenon of mass politics on America, a realignment can be defined as a fundamental shift in public opinion on the level of the prevailing public philosophy about the role of government in society or the ends of the regime. Thus the change that occurred in the 1930s, from support of the limited or negative state to support of the positive or welfare state, represented a re-alignment. Realignments are usually, though not always, associated with major changes in the partisan orientation of the voters, since political parties generally serve as the vehicles for either initiating or ratifying the proposed change in public philosophy. The party that manages successfully to identify itself with the dominant new public philosophy becomes the majority party

Table 12.1

Party Identification in America, 1960–1980 (in Percentages)

	1960	1964	1968	1972	1976	1980
Democrats	47	53	46	42	48	32
Independents	23	22	27	31	29	41
Republicans	30	25	27	27	23	25

SOURCE: 1960–1976, Gallup Polls; 1980 (postelection), ABC-*Washington Post,* Sunday, March 1, 1981.

the ensuing era. The minority party, of course, will win some elections in the interim, but its victories are always attributable to special, short-term factors, such as nominating an extremely popular candidate (for instance Dwight D. Eisenhower), or by capitalizing on the temporary failures of the majority party (as the Republicans did in the cases of the Korean and Vietnam wars).

Realignments, however, are more than changes in public opinion or partisan voting patterns. They are also one of the mechanisms of American politics— and perhaps the chief mechanism—that supply the energy and political power to accomplish fundamental changes in policy. They constitute, so to speak, America's "mini-revolutions." By establishing the basic political configuration for an entire era, realignments enable a transformative leader, like President Lincoln or President Roosevelt, to influence the political context in the nation long after they have left office. No president having in mind a dramatic shift in the nation's politics can hope to accomplish all his goals in the course of one or even two terms. To fix indelibly his imprint on American public life, a president must find a way to retain influence even after he has left office. Realignment offers the means. It allows a president to articulate a new majority public philosophy that sets the terms of the debate for future policymaking; and it bequeaths to the president's successors the political support—in the form of a majority-party status—that can accomplish the long process of grinding out the many laws that transform a set of ideas into a working framework of public policy.

If the condition of American politics is analyzed according to this definition of realignments it would appear that America is in the midst of a realignment, but without any assurance that it will reach a conclusion. Realignments involve a change in public opinion from one public philosophy to another, and today the American public has gone through only half of that process. The American people have rejected, at least for the time being, the old liberal public philosophy of an expanding welfare state, but the American people have not yet adopted the new public philosophy of Ronald Reagan's conservatism. The accomplishment of the Republican campaign of 1980 was impressive, but limited: it did not convert the American people to conservatism, but it did convince a majority of the voters, in circumstances short of an outright crisis, that conservatism was credible enought to deserve a *chance* to work its proposed solutions.

Predicting realignments from election results alone is impossible, because realignments in the final analysis are forged not in elections but in the process of governing after elections. The conditions for a realignment are clearly present: President Reagan has now set forth a relatively coherent domestic program that contrasts starkly with the direction of politics in the period of Democratic dominance and that embodies a new public philosophy respecting the role of government in American society. But the realignment the president seeks will only stand a chance of being completed if his economic program by 1984 shows tangible signs of success as measured by the rate of inflation and the growth of the economy. And even then, to insure that the new public philosophy can be sustained over an entire era and supported by a firm majority, future Republican presidents will need the backing of a stronger party structure.

The Republican party today is held together by the euphoria of its recent victory and its momentary enthusiasm and commitment to a broad political program. It is sailing on a summer sea. But when the flush of victory and newly won power begin to fade, and when more difficult times arrive, as they inevitably will, the unity of the Republican party may quickly dissipate. The Republican party is not nearly so strong as it appears as of 1981.

Thesis #4: The situation today presents a new opportunity for genuine party revitalization through structural changes.

Party leaders and legislators concerned with the institutional strength of America's political parties find themselves today in a markedly different situation than before the 1980 election. It is not just that the 1980 election demonstrated that large partisan changes in Congress are still possible. Nor is it simply that many political analysts since the middle of the 1970s have begun to warn that weak political parties are dangerous to the American political system and leave it in a condition in which effective governing is more difficult than usual. Rather, the change has been more profound.

From 1968 to 1980, a doctrine known as reform dominated Americans' views about the nature of their political institutions. The reform doctrine sought to establish the principles of democracy and openness as the standards by which to judge an institution's performance and legitimacy. Reformers attacked those aspects of an institution that involved group accommodations in traditional representative settings, and they argued that the public interest could only be ascertained in institutions that were democratic in their pro- cedures and fully open to public observation.

The reform movement first came to prominence at the strife-torn convention in Chicago in 1968. Disgruntled antiwar activists and advocates of the so- called "New Politics" launched an attack not only on the procedures of presidential nominations, but on many of the processes of American repre- sentative institutions as well. The movement, which quickly added many in leadership positions as it gathered momentum, set in motion a whole series of initiatives that sought to transform the character of the political system. The movement had its greatest impact at the point of its origin. The nominating system was changed from a predominately representative process, in which the delegates and party leaders had the greatest power in choosing the nominees, to a system based on the principle of direct democracy, in which voters in primaries determined the outcome. The reform impulse spread out from the parties to other areas—to Congress, where power in the House was dispersed from committee chairmen to the large number of subcommittees and where procedures in both the House and the Senate were opened to unprecedented public scrutiny; to the election process, where campaign finance legislation limited the publicized campaign contributions and provided for public funding for presidential campaigns; and finally to the entire lawmaking process itself, where an unsuccessful effort was made to pass an amendment establishing a mechanism for a national referendum.

Today, this strength of the reform movement has ebbed. Its governing precepts, if not discredited, no longer hold sway as unassailable doctrine. In area after area, people have begun to question its legacies and to propose changes. It would be too strong to say that a doctrine of antireform has replaced that of reform, but it is at least clear that proposals calling for corrections of reforms can now be seriously presented and discussed without the fear of being dismissed out of hand. Indeed, since the election of 1980, many political leaders have begun to stand up and advocate far-reaching proposals that would have been considered unthinkable—or at any rate unmentionable—a short time ago. Thus the previous chairman of the Democratic party and President Carter's National Commission on the "Agenda for the Eighties" both advocated extensive "corrections" of the reforms that would return the function of party nominations back to representative conventions comprised of a significant number of party officials, unbound in their choice to any national candidate.[17] The opportunity for rebuilding parties is now at hand.

Conclusion

One of the arguments developed in this essay might lead one to conclude that the entire question of party strength is irrelevant. In distinguishing among the causes of party strength, it was indicated that one cause—the political context—influences the short-term strength of political parties irrespective of party structure. In those unusual instances in which individuals form a genuine association of common purpose, adhere to a coherent public philosophy, and win a firm majority, a strong party structure may be unnecessary for a party to act effectively. Such is probably the case today with the Republican party. Contrariwise, in instances in which a party is composed of individuals who share no common public philosophy and who have lost a sense of common purpose, a strong party structure may be of little help. Such was the case for the Democratic party in the 1970s, and a strong party structure would probably not have saved the party completely from its dissensions and its need to redefine its purpose.

These two instances, however, represent the extremes of the political situation. Most of the time, political activity takes place in circumstances between these extremes. It is then that the institutional structures of parties can make the critical marginal difference between a political system in which a modicum of effective coordination can be squeezed from a narrow consensus and a political system in which disaggregation and volatility are the order of the day.

It would seem, then, that legislators and party officials have every good reason in theory to attempt to strengthen America's political parties. But is there anything they can do in practice to reverse the decline of parties? Various arguments have been cited in this essay that hold that legal rules have no independent effect on party strength and that the institutional status of parties is determined by environmental factors beyond human control. It is indeed strange to hear that determinist argument from many who in other instances proclaim so loudly the power and efficacy of planned human intervention to change institutions and social conditions. It may be no accident, however, that some who make this determinist argument, like Arthur Schlesinger, Jr., also happen to be supporters of the recent reforms and staunch opponents of any efforts to strengthen parties. The rhetorical effect of their argument serves their political interests: since action is futile, there is no reason to act.

The determinist argument might be correct. But there is no way of proving or disproving it short of putting it to the test. Advocates of stronger parties accordingly owe it to themselves to make the effort at change. If they succeed in accomplishing what is said to be impossible, it would certainly not be the first time that deterministic hypotheses have fallen to the stubborn challenge of human will.

Notes
Contributors

Notes

Chapter 1
The Presidential Nominating Process

1. Saul Pett, "Ex-Candidates Fault Presidential Race," *New York Times,* August 31, 1980.

2. Pett, "Ex-Candidates Fault Presidential Race."

3. *Congressional Quarterly Weekly Report* (August 16, 1980): 2351.

4. *Congressional Quarterly Weekly Report* (August 16, 1980): 2351.

5. See the discussion by Paul T. David in chapter 4, "The National Conventions of 1980," in this volume.

6. *Congressional Quarterly Weekly Report* (August 16, 1980): 2353.

7. *Congressional Quarterly Weekly Report* (August 16, 1980): 2353.

8. *Congressional Quarterly Weekly Report* (August 16, 1980): 2353.

9. *Congressional Quarterly Weekly Report* (July 19, 1980): 1990.

10. *Congressional Quarterly Weekly Report* (October 27, 1979): 1982.

11. *Congressional Quarterly Weekly Report* (July 19, 1980): 1982.

12. *Congressional Quarterly Weekly Report* (July 19, 1980): 1983.

13. See Paul T. David's chapter 4, "The National Conventions of 1980," for a further

discussion of the events of the national convention.

14. For a discussion of these developments see: William Crotty, *Decision for the Democrats* (Baltimore: The Johns Hopkins Press, 1978); and W. Crotty, ed., *Paths to Political Reform* (Lexington, Ma.: Lexington Books/D. C. Heath, 1980), pp. 207–38.

15. See chapter 8 by Robert D. McClure, "Media Influence and Presidential Politics," in this volume.

16. See Pett, "Ex-Candidates Fault Presidential Race."

17. *Congressional Quarterly Weekly Report* (December 8, 1979): 2775.

18. *Congressional Quarterly Weekly Report* (December 8, 1979): 2775.

19. *Congressional Quarterly Weekly Report* (December 8, 1979): 2775.

20. Adam Clymer, "Hostage Issue", *New York Times,* September 25, 1980.

21. David E. Rosenbaum, "Easing of School Desegregation Steps in Chicago Stirs Up Dispute," *New York Times,* September 26, 1980.

22. Jack Nelson, "Carter Aides Told They Can Politick," *Chicago Sun-Times,* September 8, 1980. See also: Dudley Clendinen, "Campaign Report," *New York Times,* October 27, 1980.

23. Professor Kenneth Janda of Northwestern

University analyzed the 1976 Carter role and Carter's projected 1980 role based on the assumption that the voting pattern would be essentially the same but that the incumbency factor would work to Carter's disadvantage (depressing his vote by 2 percent). On this basis, Janda predicted a sweep for Reagan (34 states, 355 electoral votes)—while the polls showed a close race. The Janda assumptions were closer to the final outcome, suggesting that at this point the incumbency factor did work against the president. Kenneth Janda, "Predicting the 1980 Election Outcome," (Northwestern University Mimeo, 1980). For other views of the outcome at the time, see Hendrick Smith, "Poll Shows President Has Pulled to Even with Reagan," *New York Times*, October 23, 1980; and F. Richard Ciccone, "War Fears Kill Reagan Lead; 2 Candidates Even, Poll Says," *Chicago Tribune*, October 23, 1980. See also chapter 5 by David H. Everson, "The Presidential Campaign," and chapter 9 by Paul T. David, "The Election of 1980 and Its Consequences" in this volume.

24. See, for example, Richard Coakley, "Carter Beats Hasty Retreat on Reagan 'Racism' Issue," *Chicago Tribune*, September 19, 1980.

25. This development is contrary to studies of presidential nominations that focus principally on the period before the 1970's. See William R. Keech and Donald R. Matthews, *The Party's Choice* (Washington: The Brookings Institution, 1976).

26. E. J. Dionne, Jr., "Polls in New Hampshire Support View of a Volatile Voters' Mood," *New York Times*, March 2, 1980.

27. For an analysis of these trends, see Crotty, ed., *Paths to Political Reform*, pp. 35–66.

28. Everett Carll Ladd, "A Better Way to Pick our Presidents," *Fortune*, (May 5, 1980): 132ff.

29. Report of the President's Commission for a National Adenda for the Eighties, *A National Agenda for the Eighties* (New York: New American Library, 1981), p. 107.

Chapter 2
The 1980 Democratic Primary in Illinois

1. The importance of the Illinois Primary is covered well in David H. Everson and Joan A. Parker, "Illinois 1980 Presidential Primary," *Illinois Issues* 6, no. 8 (August 1980): 8–12.

2. John Kessel, *Presidential Campaign Politics* (Homewood, Ill.: The Dorsey Press, 1980), chs. 1–2.

3. *The Gallup Opinion Index* Report no. 172 (November 1979): 11.

4. *The Gallup Opinion Index* Report no. 171 (October 1979): 7–16.

5. ABC-Louis Harris poll taken September 11, 1979; *The Gallup Opinion Index*, Report no. 182 (October-November 1980): 13.

6. CBS Poll as reported in *New York Times*, October 19, 1979.

7. *Chicago Tribune*, November 18, 1979.

8. *The Gallup Opinion Index* Report no. 182 (October-November, 1980): 13.

9. *Time Magazine* poll as reported in *Arkansas Gazette*, December 24, 1979, p. 4A.

10. ABC News-Louis Harris poll as reported in *Arkansas Gazette*, December 25, 1979.

11. The "major goals of most delegates" as described in Nelson W. Polsby and Aaron Wildavsky, *Presidential Elections* (New York: Scribner's Sons 3d ed., 1971), pp. 121–122; for the classic study in this field see: Paul T. David, Ralph M. Goldman and Richard C. Bain, *The Politics of National Party Conventions* (Washington, D.C.: The Brookings Institute, 1960).

12. Source: Newsletter for congressional district coordinators circulated by the Carter-Mondale campaign and listing specific names and addresses of these.

13. The author was the director of five interns who worked (for college course credit) in the Carter-Mondale campaigns in the 24th, 20th, 21st, and 22nd Congressional Districts during the primary and general election. Material reported in this section is partially based on the term papers written by these students. The students were Bill Tapella, Bill Ward, Scott Gager, Matthew Purvis, and Sturgis Chadwick.

14. Carter finally ended "the Rose Garden strategy" on April 30, 1980. "Carter To End Self-Imposed Ban on Presidential Travel," *Chicago Tribune*, May 1, 1980.

15. This thesis is well captured in James David Barber (ed.), *Race for the Presidency* (Englewood Cliffs: New Jersey: 1978); see

especially the chapters by F. Christopher Arterton and Donald Matthews.

16. On the Democratic side the perceived domination of the primary by Mayor Daley probably decreased the interest and investment in the Illinois primary by both media and national candidates in 1968 and 1972.

17. *Chicago Sun-Times,* February 3, 1980.

18. *Chicago Tribute,* March 18, 1980.

Chapter 3
The 1980 Republican Presidential Primary in Illinois

1. Jules Witcover, *Marathon* (New York: Viking, 1977), p. 326.

2. Arthur Twining Hadley, *The Invisible Primary* (Englewood Cliffs, N.J.: Prentice-Hall, 1976).

3. *Chicago Tribune,* December 13, 1979.

4. *Illinois Issues,* (March 1980).

5. *New York Times,* March 18, 1980.

6. Hadley, p. 2.

7. *Time* (March 24, 1980).

8. *Illinois Issues,* (August 1980).

9. March 19, 1980.

10. March 31, 1980.

11. March 19, 1980.

12. Interview, August 17, 1981.

13. *Chicago Sun-Times,* July 16, 1980.

14. *Chicago Sun-Times,* April 16, 1980.

Chapter 4
The National Conventions of 1980

1. A Note on Sources: The television reporting of both conventions was monitored by the author, keeping a log of timing and events, and changing channels at each commercial interruption. Staff members at both Democratic and Republican National Committees were interviewed before the conventions, and the final session of the Democratic Platform Committee was observed. Where necessary, basic documentation was obtained from the official final calls for the conventions and from the official reports of the convention committees. Other sources included *Congressional Quarterly Weekly Report,* the *New York Times, Newsweek, Time,* and *U.S. News and World Report.*

2. *Congressional Quarterly Weekly Report* (January 27, 1980): 173.

3. *Congressional Quarterly Weekly Report* (April 21 and June 30, 1979): 763 and 1300.

4. Paul T. David, Ralph M. Goldman, and Richard C. Bain, *The Politics of National Party Conventions* (Washington, D.C.: The Brookings Institution, unab. ed., 1960), pp. 494–501.

5. *The Report of the Rules Committee to the 1980 Democratic National Convention,* p. 7.

6. *Congressional Quarterly Weekly Report* (July 12, 1980): 1940.

7. *Congressional Quarterly Weekly Report* (August 16, 1980): 2437.

8. *Congressional Quarterly Weekly Report* (August 16, 1980): 2351.

9. *Rules Report,* pp. 20–21.

10. *Congressional Quarterly Weekly Report* (July 19, 1980): 2012.

11. Gerald M. Pomper with Susan S. Lederman, *Elections in America* (New York: Longman, 2d ed., 1980), ch. 8, esp. table 8.1; Paul T. David, "Party Platforms as National Plans," *Public Administration Review* (May/June, 1971), pp. 303–15.

12. *Congressional Quarterly Weekly Report,* (February 9 and June 28, 1980): 356, 1799–1800.

13. *New York Times,* July 9, 1980.

14. *Republican Platform of 1980,* p. 10.

15. *Republican Platform of 1980,* p. 13; *Congressional Quarterly Weekly Report* (July 12, 1980): 1924.

16. *Congressional Quarterly Weekly Report* (July 12, 1980): 1924.

17. Adam Clymer in *New York Times,* July 16, 1980.

18. *Republican Platform of 1980,* pp. 4–5.

19. *Congressional Quarterly Weekly Report* (June 28, 1980): 1796.

20. *Congressional Quarterly Weekly Report* (June 28, 1980): 1796.

21. *Congressional Quarterly Weekly Report* (June 28, 1980): 1796–98.

22. *Congressional Quarterly Weekly Report* (June 28, 1980): 1797.

23. *Congressional Quarterly Weekly Report* (June 28, 1980): 1798.

24. *Congressional Quarterly Weekly Report* (June 28, 1980): 1798.

25. *Congressional Quarterly Weekly Report* (August 16, 1980): 2354.

26. *The Report of the Platform Committee to the 1980 Democratic National Convention,* p. 120.

27. *Congressional Quarterly Weekly Report* (August 16, 1980): 2354.

28. *Democratic Platform Committee Report,* p. 120.

29. *Congressional Quarterly Weekly Report* (August 16, 1980): 2351–52.

30. *Congressional Quarterly Weekly Report* (July 19, 1980): 1987.

31. *Final Call for the 1980 Democratic National Convention,* pp. 8–9.

Chapter 5
The Presidential Campaign of 1980

1. See Gerald M. Pomper with Susan S. Lederman, *Elections in America* (New York: Longman, 2d ed., 1980, chaps. 7–8.

2. The source of these generalizations is the superb paper by Jeff Fishel, "Presidential Elections and Presidential Agendas," Paper prepared for delivery at the 1980 Meeting of the Western Political Science Association, San Francisco, March, 1980.

3. Norman H. Nie, Sidney Verba, and John R. Petrocik, *The Changing American Voter* (Cambridge, Ma.: Harvard University Press, 1979).

4. See Paul T. David, chapter 4 of this volume, lecture delivered at Sangamon State University, September 15, 1980.

5. These quotations are from the *Congressional Quarterly Weekly Report* (September 13, 1980): 2709.

6. See "Playing Catch-Up Ball," *Newsweek* (November 3, 1980): 33–34.

7. Most notably in the debate. See the text in *Congressional Quarterly Weekly Report* (November 1, 1980): 3289.

8. *New York Times,* October 10, 1980.

9. See Theodore H. White, *The Making of the President 1964* (New York: New American Library, 1965), pp. 443–4.

10. For a representative discussion of this point, see Richard M. Scammon and Ben J. Wattenberg, "Is is the end of an Era?" *Public Opinion* (October/November, 1980): 9.

11. Angus Campbell, Philip E. Converse, Warren E. Miller and Donald E., Stokes, *Elections and the Political Order* (New York: John Wiley and Sons, 1966), pp. 170–1. On the prevalence of valence issues in American political campaigns, see William Schneider, "Styles of Electoral Competition," in Richard Rose, ed., *Electoral Participation* (Beverly Hills: Sage, 1980), pp. 75–100.

12. The *Congressional Quarterly Weekly Report* reported on the "evangelical conservatives." *Congressional Quarterly Weekly Report* (September 6, 1980): 2627–34.

13. *Congressional Quarterly Weekly Report* (September 6, 1980): 2634. For an analysis on Reagan's relationship with the Christian Right, see Howell Raines, "Reagan Backs Evangelicals in their Political Activities," *New York Times,* August 23, 1980.

14. *Congressional Quarterly Weekly Report* (August 30, 1980): 2564.

15. For example, Reagan promised to appoint a woman to the Supreme Court. The scornful Carter response was predictable.

16. *New York Times,* October 1, 1980.

17. *Chicago Tribune,* October 19, 1980.

18. *Congressional Quarterly Weekly Report,* (September 20, 1980): 2767. Also see Thomas J. Moore, " . . . While they offer ideas . . ." *Chicago Sun-Times,* October 19, 1980.

19. *Congressional Quarterly Weekly Report* (September 13, 1980): 2711.

20. *Congressional Quarterly Weekly Report* (September 13, 1980): 2710.

21. October 9, 1980.

22. Adam Clymer, "Presidential Hopefuls Court Electors with Local Themes," *New York Times,* October 6, 1980.

23. Of course, the number of electoral votes is not directly proportional to population since every state is guaranteed three electoral votes (two senators plus one representative) regardless of population.

24. The exception is Maine, which awards two electoral votes to the winner of the state and one each to the winner in each of the state's congressional districts.

25. See Steven J. Brams, *The Presidential Election Game* (New Haven: Yale University Press, 1978), pp. 80–133.

26. This despite the fact that American presidential politics is becoming more nationalized in results. See Gerald M. Pomper *et al.*, *The Election of 1976* (New York: McKay, 1977), pp. 58–60. Despite the validity of Pomper's point, the fact remains that in 1976 the regional divisions of the electoral vote were impressive. In 1980, however, it can be said that Pomper's thesis was supported by the impressive national scope of Reagan's victory.

27. *Newsweek* (October 13, 1980): 38.

28. The *New York Times* reported that "rifts in the South could cause Carter defeat in a close race." *The New York Times*, October 16, 1980. The article indicated that Reagan had "reactivated the old ideological right, the fervent advocates of states' rights, with an intensity that has not been seen since 1964."

29. In 1976, Carter lost Oregon by just 1700 votes. And "Washington has a strong Democratic heritage." See the analyses, "The 1980 Election," *Congressional Quarterly Weekly Report* (October 11, 1980): 13 (Oregon) and 16 (Washington). (Nor were the Carter forces willing to completely give up on California).

30. On Oct. 13, *Newsweek* reported that "Both Carter and Reagan are concentrating on six key states in the nation's industrial crescent." *Newsweek* (October 13, 1980): 38. (The states were: New York, New Jersey, Pennsylvania, Ohio, Michigan, and Illinois.) For another example of similarity of analysis, see *Time* (September 15, 1980): 18–19. (Of course, each side is a little more optimistic about its chances in certain states than is the opponent).

31. See Everett Carl Ladd, Jr., with Charles D. Hadley, *Transformations of the American Party System* (New York: W. W. Norton & Company, 2d ed., 1978).

32. See, for example, "Republicans Make New Efforts to Win Black Voters," *New York Times*, July 7, 1980.

33. *New York Times*, September 2, 1980.

34. See Albert R. Hunt, "Pivotal Jewish Voters are Down on Carter Because of Israel Policy," *Wall Street Journal*, September 22, 1980.

35. *New York Times*, September 5, 1980.

36. See *Congressional Quarterly Weekly Report* (November 1, 1980): 3232.

37. "Carter, Reagan Camps Focusing on Suburbs in the Swing States," *Washington Post*, September 28, 1980.

38. Hedrick Smith, "Anderson Receives Debate Invitation so Carter Declines," *New York Times*, September 10, 1980.

39. *Congressional Quarterly Weekly Report* (September 27, 1980): 2831. It should be noted that President Carter's main insistence was that the *first* encounter be one-on-one. He did not foreclose the possibility of debating Anderson later.

40. *Congressional Quarterly Weekly Report* (September 27, 1980): 2869.

41. *Congressional Quarterly Weekly Report* (September 27, 1980): 2831.

42. Grace-Marie Arnett, "Harris Poll." *Illinois State Journal-Register, September 24, 1980.*

43. *Washington Post*, September 28, 1980.

44. *New York Times*, October 18, 1980.

45. *New York Times*, October 18, 1980.

46. *New York Times*, October 18, 1980.

47. *Congressional Quarterly Weekly Report* (November 1, 1980): 3279.

48. *Congressional Quarterly Weekly Report* (November 1, 1980): 3279.

49. For example, at one point, Carter remarked that his opponent's tax cut proposals were "completely irresponsible and would result in inflationary pressures which would destroy this nation." *Congressional Quarterly Weekly Report* (November 1, 1980): 3281. On the call to the coalition, see p. 3232.

50. It is often assumed that Democratic candidates benefit from higher turnout because of the low turnout propensities of groups normally supportive of the Democratic party. But see Angus Campbell *et al.*, (ed.), *Elections and the Political Order* (New York: Wiley, 1966), pp. 28–30 and James DeNardo, "Turnout and the Vote," *American Political Science Review* 74 (June 1980): 406–420. An important point in both articles is that when partisan defections are high, more turnout can benefit the minority party (the Republicans).

51. Reported in *Congressional Quarterly* (November 1, 1980): 3232. And the *New York Times* reported that "initial polls rated their

performance as close to even or gave a modest edge to Mr. Reagan.'' *New York Times,* October 30, 1980.

52. *Time,* (November 197, 1980): 23.

53. Bloomington *Daily Pantagraph,* November 12, 1980. President Carter's polls also found that Reagan got a boost from the debate. See Martin Schram, ''Poll Takers Find Gains for Reagan,'' The *Washington Post,* November 1, 1980.

54. For example, Reagan's own polls showed him seven points ahead prior to the debate. *Time,* (November 17, 1980): 32.

55. *Time,* (November 17, 1980): 32.

56. This would be consistent with the interpretation of the 1960 debates provided by Harold Mendeljohn and Irving Crespi in *Polls, Television and the New Politics* (Scranton, Pa.: Chandler), pp. 275–6. On the absence of a major impact of the 1976 debates, see Frank B. Feigert and Weldon J. Rowling, ''The Impact of the Televised Debates on the 1976 Election.'' Paper delivered at the Annual Meeting of the Midwest Political Science Association, Chicago, Illinois, April 24–26, 1980.

57. See Daniel A. Mazmanian, *Third Parties in Presidential Elections* (Washington, D.C.: Brookings, 1974), pp. 57–58.

58. *Congressional Quarterly Weekly Report* (September 20, 1980): 2761.

59. *Congressional Quarterly Weekly Report* (September 27, 1980): 2833.

60. *New York Times,* October 16, 1980.

61. See, for example, the *Chicago Tribune,* October 14, 1980.

62. The *New York Times*/CBS News Exit Poll showed that Anderson fared best among ''liberal independents'' (4 percent of the electorate). *New York Times*/CBS News Exit Poll as reported in *New York Times,* November 9, 1980.

63. See John E. Mueller, *War, Presidents and Public Opinion* (New York: John Wiley, 1973), pp. 208–213. Such an effect had clearly aided Carter after the seizing of the hostages.

64. See the discussion in David Broder *et al., The Pursuit of the Presidency 1980* (New York: Berkley Books, 1980), pp. 304-5.

65. *Time* (November 17, 1980): 35.

66. *New York Times,* November 9, 1980.

67. An early formulation can be found in the work of M. Ostrogorski. See Seymour Martin Lipset (ed.), *Democracy and the Organization of Political Parties,* vol. 1 (Garden City, N.Y.: Anchor Books, 1964), pp. XXXIX–XLI.

68. Paul Lazarsfeld, Bernard Berelson, and Hazel Gaudet, *The People's Choice* (New York: Columbia University Press, 1944), p. 100.

69. See *Public Opinion,* (August/September, 1980): 24–25.

70. On the concept of party identification and its significance for voting behavior, see Angus Campbell, Philip E. Converse, Warren E. Miller and Donald E. Stokes, *The American Voter* (New York: John Wiley & Sons, 1960), especially chaps. 6–7.

71. William J. Crotty and Gary C. Jacobson, *American Parties in Decline* (Boston: Little, Brown and Co., 1980).

72. See data provided by Herbert Asher, *Presidential Elections and American Politics* (Homewood, Illinois: Dorsey, 1980), p. 270.

73. These data were calculated from the codebooks for the 1972 and 1976 elections provided by the Center for Political Studies, University of Michigan.

74. Al Manning, ''Gallup,'' *State Journal-Register,* September 19, 1980.

75. David M. Alpern, ''A Poll shows Carter Moving Up,'' *Newsweek,* (November 3, 1980): 30.

76. Gallup Poll figures as reported in the *Congressional Quarterly Weekly Report* (September 20, 1980): 2761.

77. *Newsweek,* (November 3, 1980): 29. However, Reagan led ''42 to 39 percent . . . among those considered most likely to vote.''

78. See ''Variance of Polls and Election Results is Defended,'' *New York Times,* November 6, 1980. (The Harris Poll was closest to the final outcome, flatly predicting a Reagan win).

79. *Washington Post,* October 5, 1980.

80. *Chicago Sun-Times,* October 6, 1980.

81. See Mervin Field, ''Presidential Election Polling: Are the States Righter?'' *Public Opinion* (October/November, 1981): 16-19, 56-58.

82. Jerome R. Watson, ''Blue Collar Workers Deserting Carter in Ohio,'' *Chicago Sun-Times,* October 15, 1980.

83. Reported on October 16, 1980, pp. 1, 9.

84. Jeff Greenfield, "We've been through worse," *Chicago Tribune*.

85. *Congressional Quarterly Weekly Report*, (November 8, 1980): 3297.

86. I ran across numerous issue-oriented stories in newspapers during the campaign. It may be true that "horse race" aspects received more coverage, but the issues were there to be found.

87. "It was only four years ago that commentators were having a field day deploring the tone and substance of the Carter-Ford contest." Greenfield, "We've Been Through Worse."

88. See Steve Neal, "The Fine Art of Mudslinging," *Chicago Tribune*, Oct. 15, 1980.

89. Neal, "The Fine Art of Mud-slinging."

90. See McClure, chapter 8, "Media Influence and the Presidential Election of 1980" in this volume.

Chapter 6
Minorities in the Politics of 1980

1. *The Black Vote*, (Washington, D.C.: Joint Center for Political Studies, August, 1977), p. 5.

2. *Black Politics 1980: A Guide to the Democratic National Convention* (Washington, D.C.: Joint Center for Political Studies, 1980), p. 23.

3. *Black Politics 1980: A Guide to the Democratic National Convention*, p. 29.

4. Earl Raab, "Election '80 Jewish Unease and the Democratic Party," *Moment*, 5, no. 9 (October, 1980): 16.

5. "Carter Wins Black Vote in Early Primaries" (Washington, D.C.: Joint Center for Political Studies, Monday, April 7, 1980), pp. 1–4. (Mimeographed.)

6. "JCPS Analysis Shows Kennedy and Bush Captured Pennsylvania Black Vote," (Washington, D.C.: Joint Center for Political Studies, Friday, May 2, 1980), pp. 1–3. (Mimeographed.)

7. *Black Politics 1980: A Guide to the Democratic National Convention*, p. 29.

8. *The Southern Israelite*, (November 14, 1980): 16.

9. Cynthia Ozick, "Carter and the Jews," *The New Leader* (June 30, 1980). See the entire Special Edition.

10. "Carter Post-Mortem," *New York Times*, November 9, 1980.

11. Earl Raab, "Election '80 Jewish Unease and the Democratic Party," *Moment*, 5, no. 9 (October, 1980): 13.

12. Ozick, p. 6.

13. Ozick, p. 11.

14. Ozick, pp. 16, 20–21.

15. Ozick, p. 6 and *The Southern Israelite* (November 14, 1980): 16.

16. Ozick, p. 6 and *The Southern Israelite* (November 14, 1980): 16.

17. Ozick, p. 6.

18. Ozick, p. 11.

19. *Black Politics 1980: A guide to the Republican National Convention*. (Washington, D.C.: Joint Center for Political Studies, 1980), p. 20.

20. See, for example, Jesse L. Jackson, "An Analysis of Our 1980 Political Options and My Endorsement," (Speech at Operation PUSH, Chicago, Illinois, September 13, 1980). (Mimeographed.)

21. Andrew Young, "Why Carter Should Be Re-Elected," *The Atlanta Constitution*, October 28, 1980.

22. Ira J. Jackson, "The Carter Presidency and Blacks," *Focus on Civil Rights*, pt 2 of a 5-pt series, 1980), p. 10.

23. Carl Rowan, "Why I'm For Carter," *The Atlanta Daily World*, October 19, 1980.

24. "Abernathy, Williams Support Reagan," *The Atlanta Daily World*, October 19, 1980, p. 1.

25. "Lowery Endorses Carter, Claims Reagan Drawing Racist Support," *The Atlanta Constitution*, October 24, 1980.

26. For much of the discussion on issues in the Jewish community as herein cited see Cynthia Ozick. "Carter and the Jews, an American Political Dilemma," *The New Leader*, Special Issue, (June 30, 1980).

27. Ozick, "Carter and the Jews," p. 8.

28. *Miami Herald*, November 1, 1980.

29. *The Southern Israelite*, November 14, 1980, p. 16.

30. Ozick, "Carter and the Jews," p. 10.

31. Ozick, "Carter and the Jews," p. 10.

32. "The Black Vote in Perspective," *Black Politics 1980: A Guide to the Democratic National Convention.* (Washington, D.C.: Joint Center for Political Studies, 1980), p. 76. The statistical data herein cited for blacks is taken from this publication, unless otherwise noted.

33. Ozick, "Carter and the Jews," p. 7.

34. Ozick, "Carter and the Jews," p. 8.

35. "The Latino Population in the U.S." (Statement prepared by The Southwest Voter Education Project, San Antonio, Texas, 1980.) (Mimeographed). The statistical data cited herein for Latinos are taken from this statement, unless otherwise noted.

36. "Latinos Helped Carter in '76 but '80 is a Different Story," *Miami Herald,* November 1, 1980.

37. *Miami Herald,* November 5, 1980.

38. "Collapse of the Democrats' Old Coalition," *New York Times,* November 5, 1980.

39. "Voting Hits High Record in Election, Reports NAACP," *The Atlanta Daily World,* November 16, 1980. There is disagreement, however, between the NAACP and the Joint Center for Political Studies which claims only a 40 percent turnout. See "Ticker Tape, U.S.A.," *Jet Magazine* (December 11, 1980): 13.

40. "Displeasure with Carter Turned Many to Reagan," *New York Times,* November 9, 1980.

41. "Displeasure with Carter." *New York Times,* November 9, 1980.

42. "Much of Reagan Vote was Anti-Carter, Poll Shows," *The Atlanta Journal/The Atlanta Constitution,* November 9, 1980.

43. *Miami Herald,* November 1, 1980.

44. "Will South Florida Retire Carter," *Miami Herald,* November 2, 1980.

45. "New Poll Shows More Jews Voted for Carter Than For Reagan," *Jewish Telegraphic Agency Daily News Bulletin,* November 7, 1980.

46. "Election," *Los Angeles Times,* November 5, 1980.

47. "New Poll Shows More Jews Voted for Carter," *Jewish Telegraphic Agency,* November 7, 1980.

48. "Young, Bell, Analyze Defeat, Disagree." *The Atlanta Constitution,* November 6, 1980.

49. "Carter," *The Atlanta Journal/The Atlanta Constitution,* November 9, 1980.

50. "Carter," *Los Angeles Times,* November 5, 1980.

Chapter 7
Financing the Campaigns and Parties of 1980

1. See Adam Clymer, "Inflation and a Limit on Contributions Strain Presidential Hopefuls' Budgets," *The New York Times,* February 4, 1980; see also "Inflation Runs Wild on Campaign Trail," *U.S. News & World Report* (March 31, 1980): 33–34; and Maxwell Glen, "It's More Expensive to Run for President as Inflation Takes to the Campaign Trail," *National Journal* (February 23, 1980): 311–313.

2. See T. R. Reid, "The Artful Dodge," *The Washington Post,* July 21, 1980.

3. See "Kennedy's 'Convention Sweepstakes' Contest Ruled Not Violating Matching Funds Rules," *Campaign Practices Reports,* (August 4, 1980).

4. Eleanor Randolph, "Kennedy Cuts Payroll 50%, Will Focus on Illinois, New York," *The Los Angeles Times,* March 1, 1980.

5. "Key Kennedy Aides Resigning as Funds Run Short," *The Los Angeles Times,* March 14, 1980.

6. "Key Kennedy Aides Resigning as Funds Run Short," *The Los Angeles Times,* March 14, 1980.

7. "Reagan to Reduce Costs with Layoffs, Use of Volunteers," *The Los Angeles Times,* March 14, 1980.

8. "Reagan Cancels Plane to Save Money, Stumps by Bus," *The Los Angeles Times,* March 8, 1980.

9. Jeff Prugh, "New Reagan Aide Fights Money Crunch," *The Los Angeles Times,* March 9, 1980.

10. Rhodes Cook, "Fund Raising Doubles Since Four Years Ago," *Congressional Quarterly Weekly Report* (February 23, 1980): 570.

11. Rhodes Cook, "Straw Presidential Polls Gain Early Notice," *Congressional Quarterly Weekly Report* (November 3, 1979): 2473.

12. Cook, p. 2473.

13. Cook, p. 2473.

14. "Independent Expenditures Suddenly Become Hottest Item in Campaign Financing," *Campaign Practices Reports* (July 7, 1980): 8.

15. FEC news release, May 10, 1979.

16. Cited in Richard O'Reilly, "Millions Spent to Get Data for Strategy," *The Los Angeles Times,* March 23, 1980.

17. Richard Bergholz, "Reagan and GOP Losers Band Together to Pay Off Campaign Debts for 'Unity'," *The Los Angeles Times,* March 29, 1980.

18. Bergholz, "Reagan and GOP Losers."

19. Bergholz, "Reagan and GOP Losers."

20. Richard Bergholz, "GOP Chairman Brock Wins Reagan Confidence Vote," *The Los Angeles Times,* June 14, 1980.

21. "GOP Gets Its Candidates to Join in Unique TV Fund Raiser," *Campaign Practices Reports,* July 17, 1980. p. 6.

22. "GOP Gets Its Candidates to Join," p. 6.

23. "Baker Pays Off Campaign Debt of $1.3 Million," *The Los Angeles Times,* July 16, 1980.

24. "Connally Plan to Sell Art Works is Limited to $1,000 by FEC," *Campaign Practices Reports,* (May 26, 1980), 708.

25. "Connally Artists Return to Drawing Boards," *Political Finance/Lobby Reporter,* (May 28, 1980): 4.

26. See Martin Tolchin, "Kemp's Friends Push Him as Vice-Presidential Choice," *The New York Times,* July 12, 1980; see also, Frank Lunn, "Kemp Counting Gains of Detroit, Isn't Ruling Out Key State Races," *The New York Times,* July 19, 1980; and Larry Light, "Senator Jesse Helms," *Congressional Quarterly Weekly Report* (July 19, 1980): 2001.

27. Robert Shogan, "Democratic Group to Work to Nominate Someone Other Than Carter, Kennedy," *The Los Angeles Times,* July 3, 1980.

28. The $60.2 million figure includes the following items: spending by the candidates' committees—$43.6 million; spending by the national party committees—$4.2 million ($2.8 million by the Democratic National Committee; $1.4 million by the Republican National Committee); independent expenditures and communication costs—$1.4 million ($1.2 million in behalf of Carter; $200,000 in behalf of Ford; these expenditures could not be separated for the primary or general election). Also included is an estimated $11 million spent by labor unions on activities in behalf of the Carter-Mondale ticket. Not included are amounts spent by state, county, congressional district and city committees in support of their presidential tickets. There is little evidence that many such party committees actually took advantage of the provision of the federal election law that allowed them to spend money for specified purposes on the presidential campaigns, and no compilation of such spending was made by the FEC. For further information see Herbert E. Alexander, *Financing the 1976 Election* (Washington, D.C.: Congressional Quarterly Press, 1979), pp. 165–201.

29. For further information see Alexander, pp. 165–201.

30. All such expenditures made by or in behalf of a vice-presidential candidate are considered to be made in behalf of the presidential candidate.

31. See William J. Lanouette, "For the Presidential Candidates, $34 Million Is Not a Dime Too Much," *National Journal* (October 4, 1980): 1654.

32. See "Carter's Campaign Cost-Cutting," *Newsweek* (September 8, 1980); "Funds for Later," *The Los Angeles Times,* September 9, 1980.

33. See Jack Nelson, "Carter Writing Off Most of the Western States," *The Los Angeles Times,* October 2, 1980.

34. Rhodes Cook, "Money Woes Limit Anderson, Third Party Presidential Bids," *Congressional Quarterly Weekly Report* (August 16, 1980): 2375.

35. Cook, p. 2375.

36. Richard J. Cattani, "Anderson Campaign—Why He (Probably) Won't Pull Out

as Carter Hopes," *The Christian Science Monitor,* West ed., October 7, 1980.

37. Ed Magnuson, "Taking Those Spot Shots," *Time* (September 29, 1980): 18.

38. William Endicott, "Anderson Hopeful Despite His Big Problem," *The Los Angeles Times,* September 3, 1980.

39. Rhodes Cook, "Money Woes Limit Anderson, Third Party Presidential Bids," *Congressional Quarterly Weekly Report* (August 16, 1980): 2378.

40. Cook, p. 2378.

41. Kenneth Reich, "Libertarians Get Boost From TV Ads," *The Los Angeles Times,* September 29, 1980.

42. Reich, "Libertarians Get Boost."

43. Reich, "Libertarians Get Boost."

44. Roger Smith, "Commoner Campaigns Amid the Smog," *The Los Angeles Times,* October 2, 1980.

45. Timothy B. Clark, "The RNC Prospers, the DNC Struggles As They Face the 1980 Elections," *National Journal* (September 27, 1980): 1618.

46. Rhodes Cook, "National Committee Given Major Role in Fall Campaign," *Congressional Quarterly Weekly Report* (July 19, 1980): 2011.

47. Clark, p. 1618.

48. Clark, p. 1618.

49. Cook, "National Committee Given Major Role in Fall Campaign," p. 2011.

50. See Clark, p. 1620; see also, Michael J. Malbin, "The Republican Revival," *Fortune* (August 25, 1980): 87–88.

51. Clark, p. 1620.

Chapter 8
Media Influence in Presidential Politics

1. Richard Jensen, "Armies, Admen and Crusaders," *Public Opinion* (October/November, 1980): 46.

2. C. Richard Hofstetter, *Bias in the News* (Columbus, Ohio: Ohio State University Press, 1976).

3. Hofstetter, Chaps. 3, 4 and Edwin Diamond, *The Tin Kazoo,* (Cambridge: The MIT Press, 1975), Ch. 11.

4. See Walter Lippmann, *Public Opinion,* (New York: The Macmillan Company, 1961).

5. Thomas E. Patterson and Robert D. McClure, *The Unseeing Eye,* (New York: G. P. Putnam's Sons, 1976).

6. Thomas E. Patterson, *The Mass Media Election,* (New York: Praeger, 1980), p. 28.

7. Michael Robinson with Nancy Conover and Margaret Sheehan, "The Media at Mid-Year," *Public Opinion* (June/July 1980): 43. Although this study includes only CBS, past research has documented that all three networks have very similar content and emphasis. Indeed the similarity extends to major newspapers and magazines as well.

8. Michael Robinson and Margaret Sheehan, "How the Networks Learned to Love the Issues," *Washington Journalism Review* (December 1980): 16.

9. Robinson and Sheehan, p. 16.

10. Robinson and Sheehan, p. 16.

11. Robinson and Sheehan, p. 16.

12. "In These Times," October 22-28, 1980, p. 7.

13. Jensen, p. 46.

14. All my personal experience as a newspaper reporter in the early 1960s as well as my experience as a congressional aide tell me this is so. See also Patterson and McClure, Chap. 1, and Patterson, pp. 22–25.

15. Patterson, p. 29.

16. Patterson, p. 105.

17. Patterson and McClure, p. 80.

18. Thomas Patterson, Social Science Research Council, *Items,* June, 1980, pp. 25–30.

19. A media candidate is a political figure whose following is the result primarily of media attention. This is not the case with Reagan. Reagan's base of power for his assault on the presidency was rooted in his successful two terms as governor of the nation's largest state and in a decade of effort to build a traditional grassroots organization on the right of the Republican party. Thus Reagan is more akin to FDR as a candidate than to any of the true media-political figures of the modern era, George McGovern, Jimmy Carter, and John Anderson. The effect of Ronald Reagan's careful constituency

building is evident in a number of pieces of data collected during the election. A CBS News/New York *Times* exit poll of 12,782 voters reported that Reagan supporters by a ratio 5:2 cast their ballots because they were enthused about him rather than negative about the other candidates. The same ratio for Carter was 3:2 and for Anderson it was 2:3. In Anderson's case nearly 50 percent of his support was motivated by dislike for the other two. An NBC News/Associated Press poll, October 22–24, 1980, pointed up the vigor of the Reagan organization. While 29 percent of the likely voters had been contacted by a Reagan worker, just 16 percent had heard from the Carter camp and 17 percent from the Anderson camp. Reagan's speeches and record had created a solid positive following which was activated effectively by strong grassroots organization.

20. *Public Opinion* (April/May, 1980): 38–39. It's important to note, however, that when independents were ignored and only Republicans were queried, Ronald Reagan never trailed George Bush.

21. In 1976, Jimmy Carter was able to do what George Bush could not because his main challenger, Sen. Henry Jackson, did not have the solid constituency Reagan had.

22. William Crotty, "The Presidential Nominating Process in 1980," paper delivered at Sangamon State University Lecture Series on the 1980 Election, Springfield, Illinois, September 24, 1980, p. 6.

23. Patterson, *The Mass Media Election*, Ch. 13.

24. See V. O. Key, *The Responsible Electorate*, (Campbridge: Belnap Press, 1966) and Anthony Downs, *An Economic Theory of Democracy*, (New York: Harper & Row, 1957).

25. See *New York Times*, November 16, 1980; *Public Opinion* (December/January 1981): 2–12, 63–64, and *Public Opinion* (February/March, 1981): 43–49.

26. Jensen, pp. 44–46.

27. This is not to deny that persons and personalities always have played a major force in politics and in symbolizing political ideas. From the battles of Hamilton and Jefferson to those of Haig and Bush, personal clashes

have been a part of our politics. The media, however, tends to make personal clashes *all* there is to our politics.

28. The proliferation of primaries also has helped the personalization of politics. Elections fought within parties narrow issue differences and force more attention on the candidates.

29. Patterson, Social Science Research Council, *Items*, p. 27.

30. Robinson and Sheehan, p. 44.

31. Michael Grossman and Martha Kumar, *Portraying the President*, (Baltimore: Johns Hopkins, 1980).

32. Robinson and Sheehan, pp. 43–44.

33. Robinson and Sheehan, p. 45.

34. Patterson and McClure, Chaps. 5–7.

35. Richard Wirthlin, Vincent Breglio and Richard Beal, "Campaign Chronicle," *Public Opinion* (February/March 1981): 48.

36. Patterson, *The Mass Media Election*, pp. 163–65.

37. The first debate audience was estimated at only 50 million viewers. This compares with the 70 million viewers estimated to have seen the first Nixon-Kennedy debate in 1960 and the more than 100 million who saw the first Carter-Ford debate. See Austin Ranney (ed.), *The Past and Future of Presidential Debates* (Washington, D.C.: American Enterprise Institute, 1979).

38. The *New York Times*, September 23, 1980.

39. In 1976 the Nielsen Organization reported 53.5 percent of the total television audience viewed the first debate. The figure in 1980 was 58.9 percent.

40. The *New York Times*, October 30, 1980.

41. Indeed Carter lamented this tendency in a postelection interview in *U.S. News and World Report*, (November 17, 1980). When asked about the proposal for a six-year presidential term, Carter replied:

Yes, if I could just in a stroke of a pen change the Constitution, I would personally prefer a single six-year term. I think the adverse consequences of potential lame-duck presidents toward the end is relatively minor compared to the removal of the stigma or insinuation that everything is done for political reasons. I hadn't been in this office a year before almost every decision I made was tainted with the allegation—at least by some—that an element of sincerity or objectivity was missing and was replaced by a grasping for political advantage. . . . stature of the presidency.

Chapter 9
The Election of 1980 and Its Consequences

1. *Congressional Quarterly Weekly Report* 38 (November 8, 1980): 3297; *Federal Election Commission Record* 7 (February 1981): 2.

2. *Public Opinion* 4 (February/March 1981): 50–51.

3. *Congressional Quarterly Weekly Report* 38 (November 8): 3297.

4. *Congressional Quarterly Weekly Report* 38 (November 1): 3242.

5. *Congressional Quarterly Weekly Report* 38 (November 8): 3300.

6. *Congressional Quarterly Weekly Report* 38 (November 8): 3300.

7. *Congressional Quarterly Weekly Report* 38 (November 8): 3317.

8. *Congressional Quarterly Weekly Report* 38 (November 15): 3362.

9. *Congressional Quarterly Weekly Report* 38 (November 8): 3317.

10. *Congressional Quarterly Weekly Report* 38 (November 15): 3363.

11. *Congressional Quarterly Weekly Report* 39 (January 31): 223.

12. E. C. Ladd, Jr., with C. D. Hadley, *Transformations of the American Party System* (New York: W. W. Norton, 2d ed., 1978).

13. *Public Opinion* 3 (December/January 1981): 44, citing CBS/*New York Times* poll on election day.

14. *Public Opinion,* 3 (December/January 1981): 30, citing CBS/*New York Times* survey, October 16–20, 1980.

15. *Public Opinion* 3 (December/January 1981): 30.

16. *Public Opinion* 3 (December/January 1981): 30.

17. *Public Opinion* 3 (December/January 1981): 30.

18. *Public Opinion* 3 (December/January 1981): 28, citing NBC/Associated Press survey of October 22–24, 1980.

19. *Public Opinion* 3 (December/January 1981): 28, citing CBS/*New York Times* survey of October 30–November 1, 1980.

20. *Public Opinion* 3 (December/January 1981): 27, citing NBC/Associated Press surveys, latest September 22–24, 1980.

21. *Public Opinion* 3 (December/January 1981): 28, citing survey by the Gallup Organization for *Newsweek*, October 17–20, 1980.

22. *Public Opinion* 3 (December/January 1981): 27, citing NBC/Associated Press surveys, latest September 22–24, 1980.

23. *Public Opinion* 3 (December/January 1981): 27, latest survey October 22–24, 1980.

24. *Public Opinion* 3 (December/January 1981): 30, citing ABC/Louis Harris survey of October 22–26, 1980.

25. *Newsweek* (November 3, 1980): 27.

26. All from *Public Opinion* 3 (December/January 1981): 19, 32–33.

27. *Time* (November 17, 1980): 31.

28. *Public Opinion* 3 (December/January 1981): 34, citing CBS/New York Times survey of October 30—November 1, 1980.

29. *Time* (November 17, 1980): 35.

30. *Time* (November 17, 1980): 32.

31. "Where the Polls Went Wrong," *Time* (December 1, 1980): 21–22.

32. "Where the Polls Went Wrong," *Time.*

33. *Time* (October 13, 1980): 28–35.

34. *Congressional Quarterly Weekly Report* 38 (November 15, 1980): 3372–73.

35. *Congressional Quarterly Weekly Report,* 38 (November 15, 1980): 3372–73.

36. Adam Clymer, "Displeasure with Carter Turned Many to Reagan," *New York Times,* November 9, 1980.

37. In data for 1976 and 1980, the Gallup Poll found a decrease in the number of conservatives from 33 percent to 31, while the National Opinion Research Center found an increase from 31 percent to 34. Both 1980 figures were above the 28 percent of the voters leaving the polls in 1980 who considered themselves conservatives; see table 9.2. *Public Opinion* 4 (February/March 1981): 20.

Chapter 10
Illinois and the Presidential Election of 1980

1. Hedrick Smith, "Carter is Gaining as Reagan Falters in Close Illinois Contest, Poll Shows," *New York Times,* October 14, 1980; Francis X. Clines, "Cemetery is a Tableau for 'Boss' Politics in Chicago," *New York Times,* November 5, 1980.

2. Peter W. Colby, David H. Everson, and Paul Michael Green (major contributors), *Illinois Elections: Parties, Patterns, Reapportionment, Consolidation* (Springfield, Illinois: Illinois Issues, 1979).

3. Kevin L. McKeough and John Steinke, "Partisanship and Independence in Chicago's Suburbs," paper presented at the "Crossroads '80" Conference at Sangamon State University, Springfield, Illinois, October 4, 1980; but for the views that formed the basis of Carter's strategy, see: Lawrence N. Hansen, "Mayor Daley and the Suburbs," *Illinois Issues,* (January and February 1978): 14–17, 12–14; Edgar G. Crane, ed., *Illinois* (Dubuque, Iowa: Kendall-Hunt, 1980) pp. 186–91.

4. Peter W. Colby and Paul Michael Green, "Downstate Holds the Key to Victory," *Illinois Issues,* (February, 1978).

5. *Southern Illinoisian,* November 5, 1980.

6. *Champaign-Urbana News Gazette,* November 5, 1980.

7. *Rockford Register Star,* November 5, 1980.

8. Peter W. Colby and Paul M. Green, "Voting Patterns in the 96 Downstate Counties," *Illinois Issues* (August 1978): 8–14.

9. *Quincy Herald-Whig,* November 5, 1980.

10. Norman Nie et al., *The Changing American Voter* (Cambridge: Harvard University Press, 1976).

11. Gerald C. Wright, Jr., *Electoral Choice in America* (Chapel Hill: University of North Carolina Press, 1974), pp. 67–68, 104–11, 155–6.

12. Edgar G. Crane, ed., *Illinois: Political Processes and Governmental Performance* (Dubuque, Iowa: Kendall-Hunt, 1980), pp. 156–66.

13. Hedrick Smith, "Carter is Gaining as Reagan Falters in Close Illinois Contest, Poll Shows," *New York Times,* October 14, 1980.

14. Steven R. Weisman and Terence Smith, "Carter Post-Mortem," *New York Times,* November 9, 1980.

15. Interview with Richard Wirthlin, Ronald Reagan's pollster, by Walter Cronkite, CBS News Election Night Coverage, November 4, 1980.

16. "Perception of Presidential Candidates," *New York Times,* October 31, 1980.

17. Gerald M. Pomper et al., *The Election of 1976* (New York: McKay, 1977), p. 63.

18. Adam Clymer, "Poll Shows Iran and Economy Hurt Carter Among Late-Shifting Voters," *New York Times,* November 16, 1980.

19. Adam Clymer, "Displeasure With Carter Turned Many to Reagan," *New York Times,* November 9, 1980.

20. Clymer, "Displeasure with Carter Turned Many to Reagan."

21. Clymer, "Displeasure with Carter Turned Many to Reagan."

22. Peter W. Colby and Paul M. Green, "Vote Power," *Illinois Issues* (November 1978): 16.

23. Adam Clymer, "Collapse of an Old Coalition," *New York Times,* November 5, 1980.

24. Richard M. Scammon and Ben J. Wattenberg, "Jimmy Carter's Problem" *Public Opinion,* (March/April 1978): 3–8.

25. Alan D. Monroe, "Cultural Influences on Voting in Illinois," paper presented at the "Crossroads '80" Conference at Sangamon State University, Springfield, Illinois, October 4, 1980, pp. 31–34.

Chapter 11
The Transition: From Nomination to Inauguration

1. Of the other transition types, since 1900 we have had four deaths in office, one resignation, and two by election of a new president from the same party as his predecessor. The latter circumstance has not occurred since 1928, which tells us something

about the dynamics of the party system in modern times.

2. For a historical survey of transitions, with emphasis on the period from 1912 through 1953, see Laurin L. Henry, *Presidential Transitions* (Washington, D.C.: The Brookings Institution, 1960).

3. Richard E., Neustadt, *Presidential Power* (New York: John Wiley & Sons, 1980), especially Chap. 11, "The Hazards of Transition."

4. Henry, *Presidential Transitions*. For the Eisenhower-Kennedy transition, see Paul T. David, et al., *The Presidential Election and Transition, 1960–61* (Washington, D.C.: The Brookings Institution, 1961), Chaps. 8, 9. For a briefer view of the Johnson-Nixon transition, see Laurin L. Henry, "Presidential Transitions," *Public Administration Review* 19, no. 5 (September-October 1969): 471–81. The Ford-Carter experience has not been thoroughly analyzed, but Bruce Adams and Kathryn Kavanagh-Baran, *Promise and Performance* (Lexington, Ma.: Lexington Books, 1979) discusses the Carter staffing from a reformist viewpoint.

5. Presidential Transition Act of 1963 (P.L. 88–277, 1964, 78 Stat. 153, as amended by P.L. 94–499, October 14, 1976, 90 Stat. 2380), *U.S. Code*, Title 3, Sec. 102, pp. 252–53.

6. *New York Times*, September 27, 1980.

7. Adams and Kavanagh, Chap. 2, "Carter's Talent Search"; Neustadt, Chap. 11.

8. Dick Kirschten, "The Reagan Team Comes to Washington," *National Journal* (November 15, 1980); *Wall Street Journal*, October 24, 1980.

9. Kirschten, "The Reagan Team Comes to Washington."

10. Interview with Robert E. Freer in Washington, D.C., on August 26, 1980 and follow-up interview February 6, 1981. Freer had been an assistant to Weinberger in his first Washington appointment as chairman of the Federal Trade Commission. Freer was now counsel in Washington for the Kimberly-Clark corporation.

11. The Heritage Foundation's product was eventually published and available in Washington bookshops and newsstands under the title *Mandate for Leadership*.

12. As an example of his reach into nonpartisan groups having no particular connection with Reagan, Meese displayed interest in a study of the presidency being made by the National Academy of Public Administration and discussed with that organization a plan for providing expert briefings on the responsibilities of political executives to appointees of a new administration.

13. *Washington Post*, November 5, 1980.

14. Interview with Harrison Wellford in Washington, D.C., on January 9, 1981; Dom Bonafede, "Leaving Office—The Other Side of the Transition Isn't as Much Fun," *National Journal* (December 20, 1980).

15. *New York Times*, November 7, 1980.

16. *New York Times*, November 13, 1980.

17. Kirschten, "The Reagan Team Comes to Washington," *Washington Post*, November 16, 1980.

18. Harrison Wellford interview. Interview with Loren Smith, cluster director of transition teams in the legal and regulatory area, in Washington, D.C., on February 6, 1981.

19. *New York Times*, December 4, 1980; *Washington Post*, December 11, 1980; Dick Kirschten, "Spinning the Revolving Door," *National Journal*, (December 13, 1980).

20. Loren Smith interview.

21. One of the most complete accounts of the James operation appeared in *Wall Street Journal*, December 11, 1980.

22. *Washington Post*, December 9, 1980; *Richmond Times-Dispatch*, December 16, 1980; interview with Edwin L. Harper, deputy director of the policy division of the transition staff and subsequently Deputy Director of OMB, in Washington, D.C., on January 9, 1981.

23. Evans and Novak column in the *Washington Post*, March 20, 1981. This staff was actually installed in the Executive Office Building for a couple of months after inauguration day until it was dissolved, reportedly at the insistence of Meese.

24. *The Wall Street Journal*, December 11, 1980, contains a good round-up on the growth and financing of the transition organization, with comparisons to Carter.

25. *Washington Post,* November 22, 1980. Both the *Post* and *New York Times* provided almost saturation coverage of Reagan's week in Washington and have been relied on in this account of those events.

26. *Washington Post,* November 15, 1980.

27. *Washington Post,* December 10 and 12, 1980.

28. *Washington Post,* December 12, 1980.

29. Evans and Novak column in *Richmond Times-Dispatch,* January 9, 1981; Caspar Weinberger, "Yes Washington, We Can Have Cabinet Government," *Washington Post,* December 1, 1980.

30. William J. Lanouette, "Reagan Plays Chairman of the Board to Carter's Corporate Comptroller," *National Journal,* (July 19, 1980), Arthur Schlesinger, "Bureaucracy and the Republicans' Businessmen," *Wall Street Journal,* January 7, 1981.

31. Dick Kirschten, "Reagan and the Federal Machine—If it Doesn't Work, Then Fix It," *National Journal,* (January 7, 1981).

32. Richard Beal, Director of Planning and Evaluation, The White House. Presentation to American Society for Public Administration, Detroit, Michigan, April 14, 1981.

33. *Washington Post,* March 1, 1981.

34. *New York Times,* November 24, 1980.

35. *New York Times,* November 18, 1980.

36. *Washington Post,* December 14, 1980.

37. *New York Times,* January 5, 1981.

38. *New York Times,* November 6, 1980.

39. *Washington Post,* December 2, 1980.

40. *Richmond Times-Dispatch,* December 4, 1980.

41. *Washington Post,* December 7, 1980.

42. *New York Times,* December 4, 1980; *Washington Post,* December 10, 1980.

43. *New York Times,* November 19, 1980; *Washington Post,* November 20, 1980.

44. *Washington Post* December 3, 1980.

45. *New York Times,* December 7, 1980.

46. *Washington Post,* November 20, 1980; *New York Times,* December 1, 1981.

47. *Washington Post,* November 14, 1981; *Time,* (November 17, 1980).

48. *Richmond Times-Dispatch,* December 1, 1980.

49. *New York Times,* January 15, 1980; *Washington Post,* January 15, 1981.

50. *Washington Post,* January 16, 1981; *New York Times,* January 16, 1981.

51. *National Journal,* (January 24, 1981); January 13, 1981. *Washington Post,* March 4, 1981.

52. William J. Lanouette, "Reagan's Team Agrees with Carter's—The Government Can't Keep Pace," *National Journal,* (March 7, 1981).

53. *Washington Post,* January 23, 1981.

54. *New York Times,* December 19, 1980.

55. *Washington Post,* January 25, 1981.

56. *New York Times,* January 7, 1981.

57. *Washington Post,* January 9, 1981.

58. *Washington Post,* December 29, 1980.

59. This account of the final negotiations has leaned heavily on the round-up stories, "The Hostages," *Washington Post,* January 22 and 25, 1981.

Chapter 12
American Parties in the Eighties: Declining or Resurging

1. The Gallup Poll, June 13–16, as reported in *Public Opinion Magazine* (December/January 1981): 17. After June, Anderson slipped steadily in the polls and ended up receiving 6.6 percent of the vote against Reagan's 50.8 percent and Carter's 41.0 percent.

2. Austin Ranney, *Curing the Mischiefs of Faction, Party Reform in America* (Berkeley: University of California Press, 1975), p. 22.

3. Jeane Jordan Kirkpatrick, *Dismantling the Parties* (Washington, D.C.: The American Enterprise Institute, 1978), pp. 2, 3, 20.

4. Everett Ladd, *Transformations of the American Party System,* (New York: W. W. Norton, 2d ed., 1978), pp. 329, 331.

5. Arthur Schlesinger, Jr., "The Crisis of the Party System, II" *Wall Street Journal,* May 10, 1978.

6. Alexis de Tocqueville, *Democracy in America,* trans. George Lawrence (New York: Doubleday, 1964), pp. 174–5.

7. James Sundquist, *Dynamics of the Party System* (Washington: Brookings Institution, 1973), pp. 281, 296.

8. The Federalist party, which after 1800 had very limited congressional membership, began to nominate by meetings of party leaders that included participants other than those in Congress. After 1816, the Federalists stopped making nominations for the presidency, and the political system from 1816 to 1828 was controlled by one political party.

9. Some of the reformers wanted to strengthen the party-run delegate selection processes as an alternative to the states' adopting primary laws. Many state legislatures, however, found the new national party rules objectionable and adopted primary laws to avoid the Democratic party's open caucuses.

10. This immediate legal authority is limited by Supreme Court decisions based on the Constitution, but for the most part the Supreme Court in recent years has protected the quasi-private status of the national parties as self-governing associations. See especially, *Cousins v. Wigoda,* 419 U.S. 477 (1975), at 490.

11. Such a law in the United States, however, would almost certainly be declared unconstitutional as a violation of the First Amendment.

12. See, for example, Anthony King, (ed.) *The New American Political System* (Washington, D.C.: The American Enterprise Institute, 1978), pp. 213–48.

13. See James W. Ceaser, *Presidential Selection, Theory and Development* (Princeton, N.J.: Princeton University Press, 1979) for further development of these themes.

14. James Q. Wilson, "American Politics Then and Now" in *Commentary Magazine* (February 1979): 41.

15. Lawrence Dodd and Bruce Oppenheimer, ed., *Congress Reconsidered* (New York: Praeger Publishers, 1977), pp. 241, 242.

16. David Abbot and Edward Rogowsky, *Political Parties* (Chicago: Rand McNally, 1978), p. 370.

17. For John White's comments, taken from his final speech to the Democratic National Committee, see the *Washington Post,* December 10, 1980. The Commission's recommendations are included in the Report of the Panel on the Electoral and Democratic Process, *The Electoral and Democratic Process in the Eighties* (Washington: U.S. Government Printing Office, 1980), pp. 26–30.

Contributors

Herbert E. Alexander, University of Southern California

James W. Ceaser, University of Virginia

Peter W. Colby, State University of New York, Binghampton

William Crotty, Northwestern University

Paul T. David, Emeritus, University of Virginia

David H. Everson, Sangamon State University

Paul M. Green, Governors State University

Laurin L. Henry, Virginia Commonwealth University

John S. Jackson III, Southern Illinois University, Carbondale

Robert D. McClure, Syracuse University

Lois B. Moreland, Spelman College

James D. Nowlan, University of Illinois, Urbana